Joseph F. O'Brien
and
Andris Kurins

BOSS *of* BOSSES

The Fall of the Godfather:

The FBI and Paul Castellano

SIMON & SCHUSTER

New York London Toronto Sydney Tokyo Singapore

SIMON & SCHUSTER
Simon & Schuster Building
Rockefeller Center
1230 Avenue of the Americas
New York, New York 10020

SIMON & SCHUSTER and colophon are registered
trademarks of Simon & Schuster Inc.

Designed by Laurie Jewell
Manufactured in the United States of America

10   9   8   7   6   5   4   3   2   1

Library of Congress Cataloging-in-Publication Data

O'Brien, Joseph F.
    Boss of bosses : the fall of the godfather : the FBI and Paul
Castellano / Joseph F. O'Brien and Andris Kurins.
        p.   cm.
    1. Castellano, Constantino Paul, 1915–1985.   2. Hoodlums—New York
(N.Y.)—Biography.   3. Mafia—New York (N.Y.)—History.   4. United
States. Federal Bureau of Investigation.   5. Organized crime
investigation—New York (N.Y.)—Case studies.   I. Kurins, Andris.
II. Title.
HV6248.C368027   1991
364.1'092—dc20   91-8273
[B]   CIP

ISBN 0-671-70815-5

All photographs have been supplied by either the authors or Gloria Olarte.

ACKNOWLEDGMENTS

This book is based on a long and multifaceted investigation into the life and milieu of Paul Castellano—an investigation that was, by definition, a group effort. Accordingly, many of our fellow Agents and several federal prosecutors have contributed to this volume. Special acknowledgment should go to Federal Prosecutors Douglas Grover and Laura Ward. Other colleagues are named and duly credited in the pages ahead. Some—for reasons of space or protocol—are not. But we would like to thank all who helped and to express our admiration of the professional team that has done so much to defeat the Mafia in America. In this connection, let us make particular mention of the FBI Special Operations Technical Team—the experts with whom we worked on the bugging of the Godfather's house.

We would also like to thank Nick Pileggi, our friend and mentor, for guiding us into the literary world, and Joe Spinelli, for believing in this project when few others did. Other early and constant believers who derserve thanks are Arlene O'Brien, Will O'Brien, Alice Alexander, and Guy Hart.

We are grateful to the FBI, especially the Office of Public Affairs, Legal Counsel Division, and the Organized Crime Section for their fair consideration, moral support, and sound advice. In this connection, we would like to state that while this book is true and factual, we have taken pains to respect Bureau guidelines in terms of not endangering informants or compromising Bureau methods and techniques.

Our appreciation also goes out to Gloria Olarte, whose candor did much to enhance our understanding of the Godfather, and whose trust and good will were invaluable to our efforts at making a full, honest, and authentic presentation of Paul Castellano, the man. Our thanks go as well to the FBI informant who can be identified only as "G"—and about whom we cannot even reveal whether he remains alive or has been killed.

Finally, we owe a debt of gratitude to those who shepherded our story from manuscript to finished book. Michael Korda inspired us with his great enthusiasm. Chuck Adams brought to the project a tremendous amount of expertise, good cheer, and hard work. Sterling Lord and Stuart Krichevsky labored long and deftly to make sure we were made an offer we could not refuse. And Laurence Shames, a writer of remarkable talent, proved to be an invaluable ally in bringing to life our experiences and the incredible people we met. Without him, we wouldn't have had a ghost of a chance.

To my wife Margie,
and my daughters Jill, Julie, and Kelly,
for their unwavering support.

J.O'B.

To my wife Sharon,
and my daughters Lena and Anna.
Thank you all for the patience,
understanding, and sacrifice that made
this book possible.

A.K.

O N DECEMBER 16, 1985, at approximately five forty-five in the evening, Paul Castellano, the most powerful gangster in America—the Mafia's Boss of Bosses—was gunned down on a busy Manhattan street, along with his driver, bodyguard, and underboss, Thomas Bilotti.

The rubout was a classic instance of how the Mob deals with difficult questions of succession, and with qualms about internal security. Castellano had been at the top of the Mafia pyramid for nine years, since the 1976 death of his cousin and brother-in-law, Carlo Gambino. His reign had been a time of prosperity and relative stability for New York racketeers. But now Big Paul was seventy years old, and had diabetes, high blood pressure, and heart trouble. Unprecedented legal pressures were being brought to bear on him. He was a man beset, and he was tired; according to some, his grip on reality was loosening.

Some of his associates hated him, and he knew it. Being hated was not in itself a problem. It went with the job. Being hated without being feared, however, was dangerous, and Castellano was coming to realize that some of his young lieutenants—most especially the cocky and ambitious John Gotti—no longer feared him.

Or rather, they feared not his strength but his possible weakening. At the time of his death, Paul Castellano was on trial for running a stolen car ring and conspiring to commit murder. These charges, while serious enough, said less about the full gamut of Castellano's crimes than about the government's subtle and painstaking strategy of building cases against him piece by piece, one by one. He had already been indicted, arrested, and freed on bail in the famous Commission case, which would come to trial in 1986, and would essentially dismantle the Mob's entire leadership structure. The even more personally damning Castaway case, stemming from the bugging of Castellano's residence, was also being readied. The bottom line was that, win or lose, Big Paul would be in and out of court for years, and this made his underlings very nervous.

Unlike younger Mafiosi, whose mettle was proved and whose careers were sometimes made by an early show of loyalty and defiance that led to a conviction for contempt of court or obstruction of justice, Castellano had nothing to gain from a prison term. At seventy, the idea is not to impress but to survive. Castellano didn't want to be away from his doctors, from his supply of insulin and heart pills. He didn't want to be away from the gaudy comforts of his Staten Island mansion. He didn't want to be away from his mistress, who happened also to be his, and his wife's, Colombian maid.

For all those reasons, it was feared that Big Paul might sing. And to those who might be implicated in what Paul Castellano had to sing about, killing him seemed less trouble than enduring the worry and the sleepless nights that would attend his private confabulations with the authorities.

So the hit was arranged.

It was to be a highly public act—no Hoffa-like disappearing routine—and this, in the language of the Mob, sent a message: The murder was not a rebellion by some splinter faction of the Gambino clan, but a stratagem sanctioned by the five major Cosa Nostra families of New York. As in some primitive ritual, all members of the tribe would acknowledge, accept, and share responsibility for the slaying of the patriarch; they would all, so to speak, eat a piece of Paul.

Telling, too, was the fact that the killing took place uptown. Old-style Godfathers, when their time was up, tended to be eliminated in the linguine joints of Little Italy. They landed facedown in the clam sauce, their blood blended with the red-and-white-checked tablecloths, and the bullet holes in the walls behind them became tourist attractions. But Paul Castellano, who fancied himself a savvy and thoroughly American businessman, and who imagined that he was guiding the Mob into the promised land of legitimate enterprise, was murdered on the tony East Side—to be exact, on Forty-sixth Street, between Second and Third avenues.

His last meal, had he lived to savor it, would have been eaten at Sparks Steak House, and would have consisted of the third cut of a prime rib of beef. Big Paul, a former butcher, claimed that this was absolutely the most succulent slice; it was his custom to examine the meat, raw, at his table before actually ordering. But regulars were expected to be demanding at Sparks. If the hundred-dollar Bordeaux was the slightest bit cloudy, back it went; sometimes even perfect wine was rejected, simply as a ceremony of power. Only three miles north from Angelo's of Mulberry Street, the uptown eatery was galaxies removed from the straw-covered Chianti bottles of Little Italy, from the communal wedges of pungent cheese, the thick espresso cut with anisette.

But despite the thin veneer of sophistication, the Mob was still the Mob, and the assassination of Castellano and Bilotti might as easily have happened in the Chicago of Al Capone.

Three men in trench coats, tipped off to Castellano's expected arrival by a confidant-turned-traitor named Frankie De Cicco, loitered in the urban shadows of the early Christmas-season dusk. Thomas Bilotti turned his boss's black Lincoln onto Forty-sixth Street, and parked it directly in front of a No Parking sign; the car had a Patrolmen's Benevolent Association sticker on the windshield. As the two victims emerged, the assassins approached them, producing semiautomatic weapons from under their coats and loosing a barrage of bullets at close range. Castellano and Bilotti were each shot six times in the head and torso. Nothing if not thorough, one of the killers then crouched over Castellano's body and delivered a coup de grâce through the skull. In no particular hurry, the assassins jogged down Forty-sixth Street to Second Avenue, where a getaway car was waiting. Witnesses of the hits, of whom there were several, remembered no details except for the trench coats, and that the getaway car was a dark color.

Thomas Bilotti, a short, thickly muscled man who in life had been a hothead, a loudmouth, and a show-off, ended up sprawled in the middle of Forty-sixth Street, his arms and legs splayed wide apart in a final insistence on being noticed; around him spread a huge red stain, as though little Tommy's last gesture of machismo was to demonstrate how much blood his squat body had contained.

Paul Castellano, by contrast, had lived a life that was all discretion and self-effacement. He had worked hard at keeping his name out of the papers, and even in death he hid his face from public view. Shot, he fell backward toward the open door of his Lincoln, coming to rest with his head and neck grotesquely propped against the floorboard, his spine cantilevered over the curb, his long legs blocking the sidewalk like those of a sleeping wino. He hardly bled, as though age, sickness, and dread had already drained him dry.

If it is true that the manner of a person's death speaks the last word on his life, then the death of Paul Castellano, Boss of Bosses, made it clear that, for all the man's illusions of legitimacy and suavity, of business savvy and executive prowess, he had in fact remained a thug. Stripped of his power, bereft of his mystique, he ended up as one more gangland corpse, dead in public with his trousers unflatteringly hiked up to reveal a white sliver of calf above the translucent nylon sock.

If Paul Castellano's murderers had needed justification for killing him, they could have made a fairly persuasive case that their leader had doomed himself by a singular act of carelessness, lack of vigilance, or fatal overconfidence: he had somehow, in March 1983, allowed the FBI to bug his house.

Special Agents, with court approval, had foiled Castellano's complex alarm system and eluded the Doberman pinschers that patrolled his grounds. They had entered the Boss's private quarters—the sanctum sanctorum of Mob business—and planted a live microphone that functioned, undetected, for almost four and one-half months. From the point of view of law enforcement, the Castellano bug was one of the most significant and fruitful surveillances in history.

From the Mafia's perspective, it was not only an unforgivable blunder on Castellano's part but a calamity of major proportions—probably the greatest breach of Mob secrecy since a small-time hood named Joe Valachi decided to go public with his life story in the early 1960s. More than thirty Gambino crime family members were recorded discussing their illicit activities. Schemes were hatched, roles were assigned, while the Bureau listened in. Conversations with high-ranking members of other Cosa Nostra families provided fascinating insights into how the Mob's pie is divvied up. The machinery was laid bare.

So fertile were the Castellano tapes that even as the 1990s were beginning, prosecutions stemming from the three thousand pages of transcripts were still under way. In all, more than a hundred indictments resulted from the bugging of Big Paul's Todt Hill residence. It is not an exaggeration to say that the destiny of the entire Gambino crime family was reshaped as a direct result of the surveillance.

Castellano's power and prestige were irreparably compromised by the bug. Not only did its successful placement cause him profound loss of face but the unflinching microphone caught him deriding associates, mocking fellow mobsters, setting factions against each other. As prescribed by law, everyone against whom the tapes were used as evidence had a right to review their contents; hearing themselves victimized by Big Paul's caustic wit, even formerly loyal cohorts turned on him. If ever a man was undone by thinking out loud, that man was Paul Castellano.

We—the authors of this book—are in a unique position to write about the Castellano surveillance, because we conducted it. We went in. We planted the mike. And we listened to the voices.

Special Agent Joseph F. O'Brien is one of two men who first penetrated the Staten Island mansion and made the bugging operation plausible, thus capping a four-year assignment to corner the Mafia chieftain. For this, in 1987, O'Brien was awarded the Attorney General's Distinguished Service Award, the nation's greatest honor for a law enforcement officer.

Special Agent Andris Kurins spent months monitoring the Castellano bug and supervised the painstaking process of transcribing the more than six hundred hours of recordings. In doing so, he became so conversant with the tapes' contents that he has been called to testify at eight different trials in which the material has figured as evidence.

It is our belief that there has never been a book like *Boss of Bosses*—a work that, from the inside and largely through actual dialogue, tells the true story of a Godfather. It is a story that exists on several levels. In part, it is a classic cops-and-robbers yarn, a tale of stakeouts, pay phones, code words, confrontations, and occasional danger. It is, in another sense, a sociological tract, a look at a curious organization which, in some surprising ways, resembles many other businesses—except that this business's product line features extortion, theft, intimidation, and sometimes murder.

But beyond that, this is the very personal story of one man, Paul Castellano. In the course of our investigations, we got to know Big Paul intimately—perhaps too intimately, because it seems to be part of our human makeup that intimacy carries with it sympathy, and we did not want to feel sympathy for our sworn enemy. Castellano was a hood—but he was also a gentleman. He presided over an evil enterprise—yet in his dealings with us he was always gracious, even courtly. Without question, Big Paul was responsible for many deaths, yet there is no evidence that he ever pulled a trigger, and some of his associates despised him for being too eager to make peace and too reluctant to take decisive, violent action. He was a bad man, but not the worst man.

Through the untiring microphone, we learned details of Castellano's private life that we almost wish we didn't know. His affair with his maid, under his own roof, was a squalid and blatant violation of the Mafia code of the sacredness of the home. Mafiosi had mistresses, of course, but they were not domestic servants, they were not Spanish-speaking, and they did not usurp the marital bed. Moreover, Castellano's age and infirmities were rendering him impotent, and as the tapes revealed, he would resort to extreme and bizarre medical procedures to try to recover some semblance, or some parody, of sexual manhood. At moments at least, it was difficult to think of him as the mighty, all-powerful *capo;* he seemed like an old, sick, and ordinary man, trying desperately to hold on to what remained of a flawed and faltering life.

There is an odd and sometimes uncomfortable bond between law enforcement officers and criminals. In a strange way, they need each other, as hunters and hunted need each other to establish their identities. Cops need criminals as a basis for their sense of mission. Criminals need cops to make them feel important and to assure them that they are, in fact, flouting legitimate authority. But in the case of the FBI and the Mafia, there is a more specific bond as well. Both Bureau men and gangsters live by codes that are in certain ways more stringent than those of ordinary citizens. Codes of duty. Codes of loyalty. The fact that those respective codes are in every way opposed does not change the fact that they share certain common emotional and psychological threads. A good FBI man understands the Mafia mind. And it is probably true that a smart Mafioso understands the motivations and the pride of a Special Agent.

We feel we understood Paul Castellano, and it is our hope that this book reflects that understanding. While we bore Big Paul no personal animosity, we realized that we were locked with him in a deadly serious game where only one side could walk away the victor. We had confidence that, sooner or later, we would win. Did Castellano know that he was fated to lose? He never told us, as it would have been a violation of the stubborn dignity he retained to the end.

We are proud of the work we did in investigating the New York La Cosa Nostra, and proud of the effect it had in exposing and disrupting the workings of organized crime in America. But it would be callous and dishonest not to acknowledge that we also feel some dim element of regret that in the process a human being named Paul Castellano was humiliated, discredited in his own circle, and ultimately destroyed.

PART 1

CHAPTER 1

BACK IN 1981, a lot of people wanted to talk to Paul Castellano.

Every street-level wiseguy, from the garment district to the docks to the union halls to the espresso joints of Bensonhurst, would have jumped at the chance to sit down with the Boss and humbly inquire if he had any small favors he wanted done. Law enforcement officers from half a dozen different agencies would have found it very edifying to spend a quiet hour with Big Paul, learning what was on his mind. As for the media, they had long before established the convention of making celebrities out of Mafia bigs; they would have given a lot for an interview or some exclusive camera footage.

Strangely, though, for all the people who wanted to chat with Castellano, no one seemed to adopt the simple expedient of going to the front gate of his house and ringing the doorbell.

There were few things easier than finding Big Paul. Even in 1981, before his serious troubles had begun, he was mostly a stay-at-home, a recluse: the Howard Hughes of Mafiosi. Why go out? Why sit in traffic, why hang around on a torn vinyl chair in the back room of some crappy social club, when everything he needed was contained in his three-and-a-half-million-dollar mansion—nicknamed the White House, which it somewhat resembled—in Staten Island's pricey Todt Hill neighborhood?

At home, Castellano was literally on top of his world; his house occupied the highest point of land in the entire city of New York. He had a bocce court in his backyard. He had a swimming pool, Olympic size. He had ornately carved furniture upholstered in brocade, and huge lamps shaped like Renaissance sculptures and covered in gold leaf. He had a gorgeous view of the bold arc of the Verrazano-Narrows Bridge, looking across the water to profitable Brooklyn. He had a loyal and devoted wife, a frisky and diverting mistress, and an affectionate and charming daughter, all right there in the compound. It was pleasant, it was quiet, and it was safe. Why leave?

Still, though Castellano's whereabouts were hardly a mystery, most people seemed disinclined to drop in uninvited on the *capo di tutti capi*.

One of the few who weren't disinclined was Special Agent Joseph F. O'Brien of the New York office of the FBI, who, in late summer of 1981, had some rather pressing business to discuss. A contract, it seems, had been taken out on the life of one of his colleagues and the lives of the colleague's wife and children.

Such an action was out of bounds even in terms of La Cosa Nostra's own rules. At the famous Apalachin, New York, conference of 1957, the Mob—with Paul Castellano already a ranking member—had decreed that certain activities were forbidden, not on humanitarian grounds but because they were lousy for public relations and would bring too much heat from law enforcement. Why get the cops mad if you could avoid it? Why make stars out of prosecutors? Why get the public clamoring for more funding and more manpower for the feds? Certain pastimes, while pleasurable or profitable or both, were just bad business. Taking revenge on FBI agents was one such activity. Dealing in narcotics was another.

But as in many sorts of American organizations, traditional Mafia standards had been eroding in recent years. Respect for the old rules was fading, internal discipline was getting ever harder to maintain, and no one knew this better than Paul Castellano. More and more of his time and energy seemed to go toward keeping his troops in line.

Rather like their counterparts on Wall Street, younger Mafiosi tended to put personal income ahead of the long-term good of the firm. It nettled them, for example, that they should be barred from dealing in heroin, cocaine, or crack while other, generally less well organized and usually despised ethnic groups made legendary sums from traffic in those substances. Since they didn't like the rule, the younger wiseguys ignored it. In this they were not so different from other generations of Mafia soldiers, who free-lanced in drugs, official prohibitions notwithstanding. But now a sinister new wrinkle had been added: the eighties dealers also tended to be users, especially of cocaine. They had the decidedly mixed blessing of easy access to huge amounts of stuff at wholesale prices. Drug use, in turn, further eroded discipline, self-restraint, and long-term thinking.

Given the increasing anarchy and hopheadedness, some of the younger guys simply could not see the logic of the ban on attacking the FBI. A guy is following you around, bothering you, interfering with your business and your digestion, hurting your profits, trying to put you in jail, and you're not allowed to shoot him or stick him in a bucket of cement? This, to some mobsters, seemed almost like a violation of their civil rights.

With each passing year, there were fewer old-style Dons around to explain, and enforce, the ancient wisdom. Some had died. Some were in prison. One—Joe Bonanno—had forfeited all authority by becoming an author. By the beginning of the 1980s, Paul Castellano had reason to feel he was the only one responsible for carrying on the old traditions. He was virtually the only one left with a long enough memory to recall the thinking behind the Apalachin edicts, and with enough muscle to see that, on his own turf at least, the edicts were obeyed. If a fed was attacked, the buck would not stop until it reached the Staten Island White House. Some trigger-happy punk with a noseful of blow might not take the time to consider this, but Castellano knew it painfully well. And the Bureau knew that Castellano knew it.

Not that the Mob didn't have reason to be upset with the agent whose life had been threatened. His name was Joseph D. Pistone, and he was without doubt the finest undercover man American law enforcement had ever produced. Pistone, under the alias of Donnie Brasco, had infiltrated the Bonanno crime family in 1976. Posing as a jewel thief, he had gotten close to one Lefty "Guns" Ruggiero, who'd vouched for him and gotten him accepted. Every day and night for six years, Pistone gave an Academy Award performance as an ambitious punk totally loyal to the organization. He only came out from "under" when his lieutenant ordered him to kill a rival family member. In the meantime, "Donnie" had gathered a vast amount of information that was later used in the Pizza Connection trial and the Commission case, and that helped put away more than one hundred Mafiosi. For his extraordinary efforts Pistone received the Distinguished Service Award in 1983.

Pistone beat the Mob fair and square, and under the old code of honor, that should have been the end of it. But it wasn't. Lefty Ruggiero, speaking brave words from his prison cell, had vowed to "get that motherfucker Donnie if it's the last thing I do." This, however, was not the main problem; Ruggiero would be away until 1992, and besides, chances were good that as soon as he was released, he'd get whacked—as punishment for his poor judgment in sponsoring Pistone in the first place. No, the real problem was that an open contract offering $500,000 for Pistone's life and/or the lives of his family had been put on the street. Any connected guy could cash in on it.

This could not be abided. The contract had to be canceled, and it could only be canceled from the top. It could only be canceled by the chieftain who was variously known as the Old Man, the Boss, and the Pope. It was time, therefore, to put good manners aside and drop in unannounced on Paul Castellano.

CHAPTER 2

WHO EES EET?"

The coy, Spanish-accented female voice was not what Special Agents Joe O'Brien and Frank Spero had expected to hear from the other end of Big Paul Castellano's intercom. Playful and breezy, the voice threw them off stride for just a moment. They stood between two massive pillars on the portico of the Staten Island White House, shuffling their feet. Then Spero collected himself and put on an authoritative tone. "FBI," he said. "We have official business to discuss with Mr. Castellano."

"I see eef Meester Paul ees home," said the voice.

The intercom went silent, and for what seemed a long time, the two agents lingered on the porch, gazing off at the Verrazano Bridge and the waters of New York Bay, which, on that muggy August morning, glinted a greenish silver. Inside the house two large dogs were barking. Spero and O'Brien didn't speak, for fear that an open intercom line would monitor their conversation; surveillance, after all, worked both ways. They were acutely aware of the two security cameras trained on them, panning slowly back and forth. All these things were parts of the Godfather's personal early-warning system, the machinery for guarding his cherished privacy.

Frank Spero, to pass the time and break the tension, put his hands in his pockets and started to whistle. He had been with the FBI since 1971, and like many law enforcement officers of Italian descent, he seemed to bring a special sense of mission to fighting organized crime. He had studied the Gambino crime family for years, becoming an expert on its complicated workings and far-flung personnel. Spero was also a particularly sturdy individual. He'd attended Wagner College, right there on Staten Island, on a football scholarship. He'd done three years in the Marines. He'd been a probation/parole officer—a job known to entail a considerable, if unofficial, physical component. Now he was with the FBI, and, joined by the six-foot-five Joe O'Brien, established for the Bureau a commanding presence on Paul Castellano's porch.

Still, it was hard for both men not to feel intimidated standing there. The intimidation did not have to do with physical danger, which, at Castellano's home, in broad daylight, was virtually nil. Rather, it had to do with reminders of the sheer scale and wealth of the enterprise of which Big Paul was chief. The broad semicircular driveway, through which passed not only mobsters but a wide array of legitimate businessmen seeking favors or advice, bespoke the extent of Castellano's influence. The fluted white columns that dwarfed the agents provided a reminder of the old characterization of the Mafia as "a second government." The manicured grounds suggested order, confidence, even class. One might as well have been dropping in on the chairman of General Motors.

Except that the chairman of GM, one expects, would probably not greet guests as Castellano did that morning: in a carmine-colored satin bathrobe over ice-blue silk pajamas, and in black velvet slippers, which on smaller feet might have looked effeminate, but on Castellano's seemed imperial. Nor would most legitimate executives choose to conduct their business on the porch. But Castellano, unaccompanied and confident, emerged abruptly from his house, quickly closing the enormous oak front door behind him, as if he didn't want the feds to have even a glimpse of the interior of his residence. Perhaps he had a premonition that FBI men in his house would be the start of his undoing.

"Okay," he began, as abruptly as he'd appeared, "what can I do for you gentlemen?" His tone was neither friendly nor surly, simply businesslike.

As previously agreed, Spero did most of the talking, apprising Castellano of the contract on Joe Pistone, and leaving O'Brien free to study the Pope himself.

Castellano was a big and bulky man, six feet two, not handsome but imposing. Although he was then sixty-six years old, his hair was still thick and mostly dark, shot through here and there with silver threads, carefully combed back and slicked down. His posture was ramrod straight as far as his shoulders, but his massive head hung slightly forward on his heavy neck, creating a somewhat buzzardlike effect. He had a strong Picasso nose that branched off directly from his forehead, and black eyes that seemed vigilant yet tired, with liverish sacs under them. His mouth was broad but thin-lipped, and his expressions—as the agents were to learn—always seemed ambiguous, as though from a lifetime's practice at not revealing too much. When Castellano smiled, the grudging upturn of his lips also suggested something of a grimace, something mocking; on the other hand, when he looked most serious, most grim, the impact was leavened by a certain facetious curl that hinted at bleak amusement. His hands were huge, and although the nails were immaculately manicured, the thick wrists and gnarled fingers betrayed a past of manual labor. In Castellano's former trade of butchery, he'd hoisted a lot of carcasses, plucked out many rough ribbons of sinew, hacked through thousands of ribs.

"And we want to advise you," Frank Spero was summing up to Castellano, keeping the language formal and temperate, "that if any harm comes to Agent Pistone or any member of his family, the full resources of the FBI and the Department of Justice will be brought to bear against you and your associates. Is that clear, Mr. Castellano?"

The Boss stood with his arms crossed, looking out calmly toward the bridge. He didn't seem surprised by the agents' errand, he didn't seem ruffled, and he didn't seem angry. "I understand your concern," he said.

To those whose impression of the way Mafia Dons talk has been forever shaped by the gravelly, mouth-full-of-marbles performance of Marlon Brando in the *Godfather* films, Castellano's voice would have sounded strangely familiar. Not that Big Paul was quite so thick-tongued and portentous. No—in volume and cadence, his speaking voice was standard Brooklyn-American; it could have belonged to a cabdriver, a grocer, or, for that matter, a cop. Yet there was a certain labored breathiness in his tone, a suggestion of forcing the air through a clenched throat and not parting his teeth if he could help it. "I understand," he repeated, "your concern about your friend."

"We'd like more than understanding," Spero pressed. "We'd like some assurances."

This request put Castellano in a difficult position. He didn't want to acknowledge that the contract in fact existed, or that he had known of it before; he certainly would not admit that he had the power to have it squelched. So he just put his enormous hands into the pockets of his red satin robe, and issued forth a smile that would have seemed positively benevolent had not one corner of his mouth pointed stubbornly down. "Gentlemen," he said, "if you know anything at all about me, you know that I would never go along with anything like that."

There was a pause, during which Spero and O'Brien each concluded that they had probably gotten the Boss to go as far as he was going to. They'd contacted him. They'd made their pitch. He'd listened. To expect more than that would have been unrealistic. Mobsters, after all, had a well-earned reputation for speaking in half-thoughts, half-sentences, half-promises. It was a point of pride with them to say as little as possible. It was almost a game: he who made things more explicit was the loser. The Bureau men should be happy with what they'd gotten.

But then, rather to the agents' surprise, Castellano spoke again, picking up exactly where he had left off. "I have too much respect for the FBI for that," he said.

Was he being sincere, or sarcastic? Was he making nice, or goading? From his neutral tone of voice and crooked half-smile, it was impossible to tell.

"Nice of you to say," said O'Brien. It was the first time he had spoken, and he was trying to answer Castellano's ambiguity in kind. It wasn't something he was used to, and he secretly felt he didn't do it very well. The mixed message, like any other art form, took practice to perfect.

"Just do me one favor," Castellano said.

"What would that be, sir?" asked Frank Spero.

"Don't frame me. You have a case to make sometime, make it. But don't play games. Don't make something out of nothing. I've seen that happen, and it stinks."

O'Brien considered protesting this remark, then let the moment pass. It wasn't the time to discuss the question of justice with Paul Castellano. On very rare occasions, it was true, a mobster got nailed big for something small. This compensated in some tiny way for the many times said mobster got away scot-free for crimes that were large—murder, for example. No one ever said the system was perfect, only that, over the long haul, it usually balanced out.

"We won't frame you, Mr. Castellano," said Joe O'Brien. And this time, without any conscious effort on his part, he managed to imbue the words with a full freight of ambiguity, hitting a note of patient menace even while keeping a pleasant smile on his face.

CHAPTER 3

FRAMING CASTELLANO. The very idea was absurd, though it did reflect the bizarre thinking of most top Mafiosi. The big boys seemed to imagine that if the dirty work was delegated sufficiently far down the chain of command, and if the accounting was discreetly done, then they were not really committing crimes at all.

It wasn't just that they had their cadres of smirking lawyers, who for fat fees would contrive elaborate and shameless dances through the loopholes of the law. It was that the Dons seemed truly able to convince themselves that once they had advanced beyond a certain level in the hierarchy, they ceased being criminals and became august administrators, elder statesmen who enjoyed something like a Mob version of diplomatic immunity. They fancied themselves beyond legitimate prosecution, and even, by some weird standard, beyond reproach.

By 1981, a fair amount was known—though not yet in the airtight form needed to prosecute—about the illegal activities presided over by Castellano, this man who was worried about being unfairly accused. He oversaw, for starters, such traditional mob rackets as loan-sharking and the numbers game. His minions did a nice business in video and print pornography and peep shows. He had people hijacking trucks, and people stealing cars. He bribed cops and tampered with juries. He controlled unions in the meat business and bragged of being the de facto boss of at least one chain of supermarkets. He dispensed no-show jobs in the garment district, through an "industry association" that manufacturers felt well advised to join and bankroll. In the building trades, Castellano's influence was reflected in New York's having the highest construction costs in the country; cement, especially, came with a hefty surcharge. Restaurants and hotels were avid to rent their linens from companies under the Castellano umbrella, and to have their trash carted away by private sanitation companies that had long been a profit center for the Mob.

As with other sorts of businesses, however, transactions within the Castellano empire did not always go smoothly. Negotiations could sometimes become heated. People sometimes quibbled over price, sometimes even threatened to patronize the competition. When that happened, it was sometimes necessary to smash windows, call strikes, burn down premises, break knees, strangle people, or cut them into small pieces and take them away in garbage trucks. But these unpleasantnesses were carried out at a sufficient remove from the Staten Island White House so that Paul Castellano could muster up quite a head of righteous indignation when he griped about the possibility of being framed.

In fact, Big Paul had led a charmed life, as far as avoiding prosecution was concerned. In a career that spanned more than fifty years of virtually nonstop criminal activity, he was jailed only twice, for a grand total of ten months.

He was born Constantino Paul Castellano, in Brooklyn, on June 26, 1915. His parents—father: Giuseppe; mother: Concetta, maiden name: Casatu—had emigrated from Sicily. Castellano senior was a butcher and a very small-time racketeer. He controlled—at least on Seventeenth Avenue in Bensonhurst—the gambling operation known as the La Rosa Wheel, a lottery whose winning number was drawn in Italy. In itself, La Rosa was fairly innocent; it was as much a cultural tie to the old country as a serious gambling enterprise, and if the poorest of the immigrants seemed to squander the most on tickets, well, that was human nature. Still, La Rosa bore the hallmarks of the Mob's insidious methods: exploitation of the recently arrived Italian community provided working capital for rackets that would then move beyond the ghetto, becoming increasingly violent, immoral, and destructive as they did so.

Paul was the youngest of three children, and the only son. Not academically inclined, he dropped out of school in the eighth grade and started selling lottery tickets for his father, at the same time learning the trade of meat cutting. From an early age, however, he seems to have preferred making his living on the wrong side of the law. Butchers, he'd noticed, went around in bloodstained smocks and boots speckled with gore, while gangsters wore blue suits and supple loafers. Butchers walked to work, carrying thermoses of soup; gangsters drove Packards and Stutzes and went to fancy restaurants, where they were served thick steaks and treated with respect. For young Castellano the choice was clear. By the age of nineteen, lanky and slightly hollow-cheeked, he was already wearing wide lapels and raffish ties held snugly in place by collar pins that pushed the single Windsor knots upward toward his chin.

We know this because it is how Paul Castellano is pictured in his very first mug shot, taken in 1934. In that year, the teenage hustler was arrested for an armed robbery that was stupidly conceived and abominably executed. It gave not the slightest hint of the talent for planning and for stealth that Castellano would later evince.

On July 2, young Paul and two Brooklyn friends left for Connecticut, in Paul's car—from the fact that he had his own vehicle in that Depression year, we may reasonably infer that he was already involved in the rackets more deeply than just as an errand boy for his father. Ostensibly, the purpose of the journey was to visit relatives over the Fourth of July weekend, but by the time the trio reached Hartford, they had decided—spontaneously, it seems—to stick up a clothing store. No one knows why they bothered with this imbecilic caper. Maybe they'd counted up their money and realized they were short of cash. Maybe they just got bored.

They entered the premises of one Nicholas Leone, at 515 Zion Street. Castellano had a gun—which, unfortunately, several witnesses saw him removing from the glove compartment of his car. The Brooklyn threesome pushed Leone into the men's room and relieved him of his wallet, which contained fifty-one dollars. In their haste, however, the apprentice gangsters neglected to lock Leone's front door, and two customers wandered in while the holdup was in progress. Inconveniently, these bystanders now had to be held at gunpoint while the three rifled the cash drawer, which turned out to be empty. So the thieves kicked over a rack of suits, and departed with a take of seventeen dollars each—but not before a passerby had copied down the license plate number of Castellano's car. Back in Brooklyn, having dropped off his friends, he was promptly arrested. The .32-caliber Colt pistol was still in his glove compartment.

It is not known whether Paul Castellano was already at this time an initiated member of La Cosa Nostra, but he had clearly absorbed the principle of never ratting on one's friends. Asked to identify his accomplices, he concocted the ludicrous story that they were hitchhikers, he'd never seen them before, and they'd just decided to collaborate on a heist. Castellano took the rap alone, and this was not only good for his health but a wise career move as well. It helped establish his reputation as a stand-up guy, a guy who took the old traditions seriously. He pleaded guilty in Connecticut Superior Court to a charge of committing robbery with violence, and was sentenced to one year in the Hartford County Jail.

He was released on December 24, just in time for Christmas. He returned to Bensonhurst as a beloved son and a neighborhood hero, after having been in jail a grand total of three months and four days.

CHAPTER 4

AFTER THE HARTFORD FIASCO, Castellano enjoyed almost twenty-three years of virtual invisibility, at least as far as law enforcement was concerned.

He set himself up in the meat business, and did surprisingly well, considering that he had no executive experience and no working capital that he could have come by legally. But producers apparently had no qualms about entrusting him with large consignments, and major supermarkets seemed eager to buy from him. By the early 1950s, he was running a substantial wholesale operation known as Blue Ribbon Meats.

In the eyes of the outside world, Mr. Paul Castellano was at that point nothing more and nothing less than a hardworking businessman, a determined fellow who, like so many other second-generation Americans in those years of broadening opportunity, had overcome the disadvantages of early poverty and limited education to become a solid citizen. He drove a Buick Roadmaster convertible whose wide white sidewalls gleamed against the Brooklyn curbs. He dressed well and with discretion, favoring dark fedoras with painstakingly pinched-in crowns, and cashmere overcoats of ample cut. His youthful lankiness had filled out, though he was still slim, and he carried himself with authority and elegance. He didn't look sinister; he didn't look sleazy. You would not have pegged him as a gangster.

Yet through the thirties and forties, Castellano had been doing a canny job of consolidating his position within the Brooklyn Mob. His silence and his brief jail term had served him well. The extended families of his teenage accomplices owed him debts of gratitude. His elders had not failed to be impressed by young Paul's fortitude and uncomplaining acceptance of his unshared bad fortune. He had proved himself to be the stuff of which good soldiers were made.

Furthermore, in keeping with time-honored practice, Castellano had cemented his crime family loyalties through marriage. In 1937, he wed his childhood sweetheart, Nina Manno—who happened also to be a sister-in-law of Carlo Gambino, who happened, in turn, already to be a cousin to Castellano, related on his father's side. Gambino, additionally, was married to Castellano's sister Katherine. And in case all this does not sound complicated enough, Carlo Gambino's mother and father had been first cousins to begin with. Thus, the traditional Mob had protected its kinship ties, though at the cost of inbreeding side effects like heart disease, mental illness, and a high incidence of low IQs.

In any case, if Paul's web of relationships was complicated, its implication was clear: he was no mere street-corner wiseguy destined for an inglorious career of small-time hustles and shakedowns; he was on the fast track. No one can predict the line of succession in Mafia families, since orderly transitions are the exception, murder and usurpation the rule. In retrospect, however, it is clear that Castellano was ideally placed to inherit the mantle of family leadership that would pass from Lucky Luciano, to Albert Anastasia ("Lord High Executioner of Murder, Incorporated"), to Gambino, to himself.

Cousin Carlo was the key. As his fortunes advanced, so did Paul's. Yet, as it happened, Castellano's special closeness to his elder relative would result in his second arrest and second stint in prison. This misfortune had to do with the notorious Apalachin meeting, held at the upstate New York home of midlevel mobster Joseph Barbara, on November 14, 1957.

Apalachin was a watershed event both for the Mob itself and for law enforcement in its efforts to get to know the Mob's personnel and *modus operandi*. The story of Apalachin has been recounted several times, but it is worth telling again, since it is hardly an exaggeration to say that Apalachin was the dividing line between the "old" Mafia of Al Capone and Salvatore Maranzano and the "new" Mafia that would eventually be headed by Paul Castellano. Involved in the event was not only a changing of the guard but, more subtle, a shift in approach, in self-perception. The Mob, while retaining its essential thuggishness, was taking on a veneer of sophistication. Apalachin was evidence of this process, notwithstanding the fact that, as with many pivotal events in La Cosa Nostra history, the meeting ended in a total and utter debacle.

In 1957, the Mob was in thorough disarray, rife with internal conflicts. Vying for supremacy were Frank Costello—a suave man known for his uncanny way with politicians, and for being ahead of his time in using Mob money to gain a foothold in legitimate enterprises, where said money might be laundered—and Vito Genovese—much more the old-time mobster, better-connected in Italy, and master of the traditional numbers and shylocking rackets.

While Costello's methods would largely shape the modern Mafia in general and Paul Castellano's leadership style in particular, the personal victory would go to the more decisive and brutal Genovese. On May 2, 1957, on Genovese's orders, an assassination attempt was made on Costello. Hit man Vincente "the Chin" Gigante accosted the rival Boss in the lobby of his Central Park West apartment building—no Bensonhurst or Mulberry Street digs for Frank Costello—fired at close range . . . and merely grazed Costello's skull. The victim strolled into Roosevelt Hospital for a bandage.

The Costello rubout having been botched, Genovese now had to fear his enemy's revenge—and most especially, an alliance between Costello and the famously sanguinary Albert Anastasia, whose troops had been responsible for an estimated eight hundred murders. So Genovese, with the agreement of Carlo Gambino—then the number-two man in Anastasia's family—decided on a preemptive strike. On October 25, while Albert A. was luxuriating under a pile of beard-softening hot towels in the barbershop of New York's Park-Sheraton Hotel, two gunmen strolled in and riddled him with bullets.

Would Frank Costello now avenge his chum and try to regain his prestige? Would Joe Bonanno seize this moment to expand his own considerable hegemony? No one knew, and the most pressing reason for the Apalachin meeting was to try to avoid any further top-echelon bloodletting.

But making peace among the Bosses was, in the broader scheme of things, the least important agenda item to be treated at Joe Barbara's big barbecue. Also to be dealt with was a recruiting scandal that embarrassingly belied the much-touted "code of honor," posed a grievous threat to internal security, and demonstrated to what degree the Mafia had absorbed America's commercial culture—a culture that regarded anything as a potential commodity.

Back in 1930, when the contending factions in what is known as the Castellamarese War needed all the warm bodies they could find, La Cosa Nostra membership standards were precipitously relaxed. Basically, anyone of unmixed Italian background who was known by at least one La Cosa Nostra member and who was willing to have a few ceremonial drops of blood drawn from his arm could get in. As soon as the street fighting subsided, however, the folly of this policy became obvious. Kinship ties had been undermined. The threat of blabbermouths or even informers was radically increased. And there were simply too many greedy hands reaching for the profits from Mob rackets. So the membership rolls, for roughly two decades, were officially closed (although certain well-connected youths still managed to get inducted).

Active recruitment did not begin again until 1954, when it was becoming clear that there was a shortage of street-level soldiers, and the Mafia was in danger of being outmuscled by other ethnic organizations. One of the most enthusiastic recruiters was an Anastasia lieutenant named Frank "Don Cheech" Scalice, and by 1957 the reason for his enthusiasm had become known: he was *selling* Mob memberships—as if La Cosa Nostra were a prestigious country club—for prices up to fifty thousand dollars, which he pocketed.

Was nothing sacred? Such venality would have been unthinkable in the old days, when Mob membership was regarded as a high honor, something to be earned by brave and manly deeds—murders, generally—not purchased like a Cadillac. Moreover, why would someone pay fifty grand to get into the Mob, unless he wanted to *brag* about being in the Mob? For his greed and his recklessness in compromising Mafia secrecy, Don Cheech, while squeezing tomatoes at a Bronx fruit market, was shot four times in the neck and head.

Scalice's elimination, however, did not solve the problem of what to do about the "members" who had bought their way in; this question was to be addressed at Joe Barbara's big barbecue.

Finally, Apalachin was aimed at devising a strategy for dealing with the Bureau of Narcotics—in those years, the Mob's most aggressive law enforcement foe. By the fifties, the narcs already had a network of informers in place; further, since jail sentences for drug offenses were getting stiffer, there was ever more temptation for those charged to turn state's evidence. Meanwhile, shipments of heroin were being seized, and other underworld groups were contending for pieces of the action.

Additionally—and most significant, as far as Paul Castellano's inheritance is concerned—the Mob was just beginning to think in terms of public relations. Officially, of course, La Cosa Nostra did not exist. As of 1957, no one had ever publicly admitted membership, and while the term "Mafia" occasionally found its way into print, it was used imprecisely and generically to indicate almost any group of criminals acting in real or apparent concert.

Still, the leaders of the New York Mob—whose names routinely made the papers and were mentioned increasingly often in that exotic new medium, television news—were beginning to understand that they had an "image." Different criminal activities affected that image in different ways. Efficient intra-Mob rubouts, for instance, sent the message that the Mob was a tightly run ship that enforced an iron discipline within its own ranks but did not harass outsiders. This was good; this suggested toughness with responsibility, brutality within fitting limits.

But other activities—selling heroin, for example—created an image that was far less flattering, a cowardly image of preying on the weak, reducing kids to shivering, vomiting addicts, peddling random death. It threatened the long-standing myth of the Mob as a provider of goods and services—bootleg liquor, crap games—

that the average joe wanted and the killjoy government proscribed.

The tarnishing of the Mob's romantic outlaw image had economic implications which, by 1957, were becoming somewhat dire. It made other Mob rackets more expensive to operate, as cops who might take a small payoff, say, to leave a numbers runner unmolested felt more serious scruples at accommodating drug dealers. Nonviolent rackets that had been tolerated for years—things as innocent as jukeboxes or pinball machines—were coming under pressure because of their indirect connection to the junk trade. And so the final bit of business to be conducted at Apalachin was the adoption of a ban on dealing in narcotics—a ban that was never very effective, and was, in the eyes of some, really a move to concentrate drug profits in the hands of the Bosses by closing the business to the soldiers in the street.

For Paul Castellano, Apalachin was to be a glorious moment, his official introduction to the rarefied heights of the Mob Olympus. Only the cream had been invited to Joe Barbara's—just over a hundred of the leading mobsters from all around the country. Yet even within this select group, Paul Castellano seemed to hold a special place. At forty-two, he was one of the youngest men there, a rising star in what was still, as it had traditionally been, a gerontocracy. If Apalachin may be thought of as something of a Mafia Hall of Fame, then Paul Castellano was Mickey Mantle to such Babe Ruths as Stefano Maggadino of Buffalo, Louis Trafficante of Florida and Havana, and such legendary New York Dons as Joe Profaci and Joe Bonanno.

Moreover, Castellano was present as the confidant and protégé of a man whose own career was at that moment steeply in the ascendant. Carlo Gambino, as reward for his collusion in the erasure of Anastasia, was to become head of the slain leader's family, the largest in New York. Gambino's clout was now second only to that of Genovese himself—and Genovese, though no one knew it at the time, would shortly be going to prison on a narcotics charge; he would be locked up until he died in 1969.

As is well known, however, the Apalachin meeting ended almost before it started. A New York State trooper, Sergeant Edgar D. Croswell, noticed a large number of enormous cars converging on Barbara's home, and Barbara was known to have underworld connections. He was, in fact, the target of occasional surveillances. So Croswell put out a call for reinforcements—and, in that remote area, was able to muster exactly two more cars and three additional troopers. He set up a roadblock on the one route leading away from Barbara's estate. A Mob lookout spotted the police activity, and the big bad Mafiosi panicked.

Some bolted in their limousines, unaware that the troopers had already established a roadblock and were eagerly awaiting the mobsters' arrival. Not that the troopers were authorized to make arrests or anything so portentous as that; all they could do—though this was a great deal, considering the Mob's insistence that it did not exist—was take down names, addresses, and license plate numbers.

Other "men of honor," meanwhile, left their cars behind and lit out cross-country, as if escaping from a chain gang. They bushwhacked through the forest that surrounded Barbara's property. Highly unaccomplished woodsmen, the city dwellers tended to hike around in circles, their pricey suits tattered by brambles, their faces scratched by overhanging boughs. As they rambled along they threw away guns and wads of excess cash, the possession of which would be awkward to explain. Months later, people were still finding decomposing hundred-dollar bills.

An estimated fifty mobsters escaped detection at Apalachin; sixty-three did not. One of the latter was Paul Castellano, who was apprehended at the side of a country road flanked by maple trees. His navy-blue topcoat had suffered a long rent along the flank. His silver silk tie was pulled down near the middle of his chest, its knot askew. His slipperlike black loafers were caked with mud. His hair, ordinarily immaculate, was badly mussed, hanging down in sweaty bundles over his reddened forehead. He was shaken, although apparently not so much by the prospect of confronting the authorities as by the experience of being left out in the woods alone, far away from the familiar streets of Brooklyn.

In 1959, Castellano was called to testify before a grand jury in New York City about his participation at the Apalachin meeting.

On that occasion, his self-possession, which had abandoned him in the face of sinister Nature, held up faultlessly. He was back in his element, among the cracked sidewalks, the numbers runners, the coal dust, and the noise, and he played the old game of terse defiance. He told the grand jury that he had gone to visit Joe Barbara to talk with him about a shared heart condition.

"How old were you at the time, Mr. Castellano?" asked the prosecutor.

"Forty-two," he said.

"Did you *have* a heart condition at age forty-two, Mr. Castellano?"

"I didn't know if I did or I didn't. But I got pains sometimes. In my chest. So I wanted to talk with Joe, 'cause he'd recently had a heart attack."

That much was true. Joe Barbara's health problems were given as the reason for the Apalachin conclave by many mobsters, who claimed they were visiting "to cheer Joe up." Heart troubles, moreover, have figured prominently over the years in Mafia dodges. People get heart trouble when they're subpoenaed, when they're indicted. They get bad heart trouble when they're convicted, and have been known to be carried out of courtrooms on a stretcher; lawyers and cardiologists jockey for position closest to the victim. And it isn't really surprising that Mafiosi have problems with their tickers. They eat a lot of red meat. Miles of sausage. Tons of veal. They salt everything. And there's all that intermarriage. Then, too, there's the pressure of the job.

"Mr. Castellano," continued the prosecutor, "isn't it an odd coincidence that you should be seeking Mr. Barbara's medical advice just at the time that so many of his other friends and associates were visiting his home?"

"Yeah," said Castellano, with a hint of surprise in his voice. "Now that you mention it, I guess it is."

For his refusal to cooperate, Castellano was found guilty of contempt and sentenced to five years in prison; he boasted privately that he would gladly serve this term.

Only seven months into his incarceration, however, he was released. According to the law as it existed in 1957 (before the 1970 RICO [Racketeer-Influenced and Corrupt Organizations

Act] statute broadened federal powers in attacking racketeering enterprises), the Apalachin meeting, in and of itself, could not be regarded as constituting a criminal conspiracy. Convictions resulting from the conclave and its aftermath were therefore overturned.

So Paul Castellano returned to Brooklyn, a bigger and more proven man than he had been before. Once again he'd earned favors and cemented loyalties, and he'd done so without suffering a beating or wasting too much time in jail. Once again he'd shown his mettle, and once again the display had cost him almost nothing. As the 1960s were beginning, Paul Castellano was already nearing the top of his profession, and the ride that was taking him there had been very nearly a free one.

CHAPTER 5

TWO DECADES LATER, as the 1980s were beginning, Castellano's free ride was still in progress, and at the Brooklyn-Queens Resident Agency of the FBI, on Queens Boulevard in Rego Park, certain people were beginning to feel it had gone on far too long.

The fact was, though, that up to that time Castellano had never been specifically targeted. It had not been traditional Bureau strategy to go for the top of the Mob pyramid; in the pre-RICO days, the big boys had simply seemed too well insulated from direct prosecution. As a result, cases were made against street guys, in the hope that they would turn informant and hand over their *capo*s, who in turn might save themselves by squealing on the *consigliere,* and so on up the line. Mob profits, after all, worked on a "trickle-up" principle. Why shouldn't Mob accountability work the same way? In certain instances, in certain families, this approach had gotten good results. In the Gambino clan, it had yielded almost nothing. Therefore, the Gambino clan, largely undisrupted, was becoming better-organized and more dominant all the time.

What made this situation increasingly frustrating was that the 1970s had been, in general, a time of unprecedented progress in the fight against organized crime. Armed with the new racketeering statutes and the use of court-authorized Title III surveillances, FBI teams, working with various local, state, and federal strike forces, had managed to seriously jam up the works of virtually all of the twenty-six La Cosa Nostra families in America. Two of those families—in Dallas, and in Madison, Wisconsin—were believed to have become altogether inactive.

All over the country, not just soldiers, not just captains, but heads of LCN families were being arrested, convicted, and sent away for substantial prison terms. As far as knocking the Mafia off stride went, these top-level convictions had a felicitous multiplier effect, since the fall of a top man often led to a power struggle in which one or more pretenders to the throne were either rubbed out or otherwise rendered ineffective.

In New York, with its five Mob clans, every Boss except Castellano had experienced serious legal headaches through the seventies. Carmine Tramunti, head of the Lucchese family, got five years on federal perjury charges. Carmine Persico, head of the Colombo clan, was doing fourteen years for hijacking; Joe Colombo himself, in a coma since his 1971 shooting at a rally of the Italian-American Civil Rights League, was under indictment for controlling a large gambling empire. Paul Sciacca, head of the Bonanno family, was arrested for the sale of heroin; Philip Rastelli, who assumed his mantle later in the decade, was convicted of antitrust violations and extortion, and put away for eleven years. Frank "Funzie" Tieri, head of the Genovese family, would have the dubious distinction of being the first New York Boss prosecuted under RICO; he was convicted of running a racketeering enterprise whose methods included murder and extortion.

Castellano, at the head of the Gambino family, was the only New York Boss to have stymied law enforcement. True, he had been indicted once during the decade—in 1975, on charges of racketeering conspiracy. By the time the trial rolled around, however, the government's star witness, a man named Arthur Berardelli, decided not to testify. As an FBI informant would later confirm, Castellano had contacted Berardelli and made him the proverbial offer he could not refuse. If Berardelli clammed up, he would be paid many thousands of dollars and would also be granted "absolution" for his earlier folly in cooperating with the government. Absolution, in this case, meant that he would not be murdered, and one did not have to be a genius to understand that the converse of Castellano's proposition also held true. So Berardelli stayed resolutely closemouthed at the trial and earned himself a five-year sentence for criminal contempt, while Castellano walked, a slightly crooked half-smile of vindication on his face.

What was becoming increasingly clear, then, was that Paul

Castellano not only was the biggest fish in the Mafia pond but also was developing into the savviest. Contrary to intra-Mob complaints that would later be made against him, he was not bashful about deploying muscle—not at all. But intimidation alone, he realized, was a stance and not a policy. Policy had more sides to it: persuasion, weighing risks and benefits, knowing how to wait. These skills Castellano possessed to an impressive degree. Of all recent Mob Bosses, he had the most self-discipline, the most restraint. He kept his ego out of his businesses. He did not make the kind of mistakes—mistakes that generally sprang from character flaws rather than mere tactical misjudgments—that precipitously brought down other Dons.

The more impressive Big Paul's track record became, the more he began to haunt the imaginations of certain Special Agents. He was growing into a figure worthy of obsession. His self-effacing style and the sparseness of information about him only added to the mystique. FBI agents sometimes fell into long, absent stares at photographs of Castellano, as if the frozen images might hold some clue about how to get to him. In some recent pictures the Godfather wore slightly tinted aviator-style glasses; they seemed incongruous, as if picked out for him by a daughter, or perhaps by a young girlfriend who wanted to keep the old boy up-to-date. But Castellano was vain, and wary of anything that might hint at waning powers; he wasn't photographed with glasses on if he could help it. Then again, he wasn't photographed at all if he could help it.

"He is the best-insulated son of a bitch I've ever seen in my life."

The speaker was Bruce Mouw, supervisor of the Gambino squad of the Brooklyn-Queens FBI office, who in 1980 was beginning to make Paul Castellano the focus of his energies. Mouw was a thoughtful, soft-spoken, and systematic man. An Annapolis graduate, he had done submarine service as an electrical engineer. He was accustomed to scientific logic and the enforced, exaggerated tidiness of life on a ship; he was a perfectionist. But pursuing organized crime figures was not exactly a logical enterprise, and its

43

methods were seldom tidy; perfection was a concept that did not usually apply in this line of work. So Mouw sometimes got annoyed. When he did, he would bite on the stem of his pipe, and wince. The wince, while it lasted only an instant, pulled down one of Bruce Mouw's eyes and created a vivid impression of a sensitive soul in torment.

"Son of a bitch," he repeated. "Dozens of bank accounts, here and abroad. Shell corporations, with officers I don't know from Adam, and interlocking boards. Lines of influence that wind through the unions like a cab through rush hour. Ties to Seventh Avenue. Ties to wholesale meat. The entertainment business. Garbage. You have to be a goddamn MBA just to find your way through it."

"Not bad for a guy who never finished eighth grade," said Special Agent Andris Kurins.

"Not bad," said Mouw bitterly, "for a guy with a knack for hiring high-paid suits who are sleazy enough to work for him." For Bruce Mouw, as for many FBI men, the Mob's lawyers and advisers were as reprehensible as the gangsters themselves—maybe more so. Out and out criminals, after all, usually got that way because of a real or imagined shortage of alternatives. But the mouthpieces and accountants had generally been privileged to begin with. They had options. Why did they do what they did?

Mouw pointed at Castellano's file. It was fat as the phone book and about as enlightening. "We have to cut through all this bullshit."

"We've been trying," said Agent Joe O'Brien. "But things just seem to go so far. Up to the captain level, usually. Then nothing."

O'Brien looked out the dirty sixth-floor window, across Queens Boulevard. It was seven o'clock on a Friday evening, most working citizens were starting their weekends, and the diffuse glow of neon was mingling with the sooty dusk to turn the air outside a color that produced bad moods.

"We've got to flush him," Bruce Mouw said.

"Tough to do," said Andy Kurins. "He's not the type to panic. He doesn't even like to leave his house."

"But people talk to him," insisted Mouw.

"All the time," agreed O'Brien, who was already familiar with Castellano's horseshoe driveway and its considerable traffic of Mercedeses, Cadillacs, and Jags.

"Well," said Andy Kurins, giving Mouw's desk a halfhearted kick that resounded dully through the otherwise quiet office, "here's what I propose. Let's start talking to the people who talk to him. As many of them as we can find. Let's just go up to them, very friendly, and talk to them."

"About what?" asked Mouw. "They won't talk to agents."

"How sure of that are we?" Kurins pressed. "I mean, they're not *supposed* to talk to agents, sure. But look, they'll be surprised that we're even trying to talk to them. They'll be curious about what we want."

"Besides," O'Brien picked up, "what's the downside?" Like Andy Kurins, he was a veteran of the Bureau's Foreign Counter-Intelligence division. He'd tracked spies up and down the glittering avenues that fanned out from the UN. In that line of work, actually talking to a suspect was considered an enormous luxury. One needed State Department clearance to do it, as an untoward approach to a touchy diplomat—even, or especially, if the smug bastard *was* a spy—could trigger an international incident. That was one big advantage in dealing with Mafiosi—they didn't have an ambassador to go crying to. "I don't see that there's anything to lose."

Mouw chewed his pipe and made little popping sounds with his lips. Just *talking* to guys—it didn't fit in with his ideas about orderliness and strategic rigor. Then again, he didn't seem to have a better idea for shaking the Gambino family tree. "But what do we say to them?"

"Anything!" Andy Kurins said. "Say 'Happy Birthday.' Say 'How've you been doing at the track lately?' It doesn't really matter. Let's just make it known that we're talking to people, and let them think about who's saying what to who. Let 'em all go back to Castellano and dutifully report that they've been talked to."

"Here's what we want," said Joe O'Brien. "We want Paul— six, eight, ten times a day—to shrug his shoulders and say, 'Don't worry, they don't know nothing. They're just dumb cops, snooping around.' We want him to say it so often, to so many different people, that after a while he's not so sure. That's something I've learned about Mob guys—they're so used to lying that the more they hear themselves saying something, the more they start to wonder if it could possibly be the truth."

CHAPTER 6

THUS WAS LAUNCHED the aspect of the Castellano investigation that would feature what Agents Kurins and O'Brien thought of as the "RH factor."

"RH" stood, phonetically, for "Wreak Havoc," which was the effect they hoped their contact with street-level mobsters would have on the smooth running of the Gambino organization and on the magisterial calm of Paul Castellano. Apalachin had proved that even a small dose of police presence could go a long way in disrupting Mob serenity—though of course, a lot had changed since then.

For one thing, the *Godfather* movies had put a sentimental gloss on what it meant to be a gangster; they had also given thugs a whole range of ready-made things to say when they wanted to sound tough, sincere, righteous, or even wise. The scripts—which a fair number of wiseguys seemed to have memorized—made them less disinclined to talk. It is a general truth that, outside their own circle, many wiseguys are painfully insecure and very shy. They've never really grown up; they've never, literally or figuratively, left the neighborhood. They are acutely aware of their lack of education and afraid of sounding stupid. Being able to say something that Al Pacino or Robert De Niro already said helps them get started in a conversation. It tells them how they're supposed to act and what, if anything, they're supposed to feel.

Another thing that had made mobsters less bashful was television news, which romanticized Mob life by presenting it selectively. The cameras rolled only on those occasions when something actually happened—and something happening is very much the exception in the life of a street-level thug.

Fact is, most of the time the routine of a mobster is numbingly dull. You wake up around noon, and meet Vinnie and Frank for an espresso. Vinnie and Frank have to meet Tony and Pete, so you drive all the way to Staten Island and have another cup of coffee. Tony and Pete don't show. So you drag yourself all the way to Queens to see another guy about a couple truckloads of stolen microwaves. But before you can agree on a price, you've got to make some phone calls. You can only use a pay phone, so first you've got to find one that works, and then you can hardly hear what the person on the other end is saying, because some jerk's car alarm is going off. By this time it's dark. You go home to wash your armpits and change your shirt. You talk about what to have for dinner and where you want to have it. But if it turns out that someone you don't want to see is also eating there, you have to go someplace else. By now you've got a stomachache from all the espresso and cigarettes and no food. . . .

It really isn't very exciting; certainly it's not the perpetual orgy of murders, drug scores, and court appearances that television news might lead one to expect. Still, the distortions of the media have had one odd benefit for law enforcement: they seem to have enhanced the self-esteem of wiseguys, which has made them more eager to stand up and be counted—and prosecuted.

In any event, for all the things that had changed since Apalachin, a surprising number of things still had *not* changed. Amazingly, it was not until 1986, during (unsuccessful) defense arguments in the famous Mafia Commission trial, that the existence of the Cosa Nostra was ever acknowledged publicly. Until then, the sacred vow of *omertà* still demanded utter silence as to membership in "this thing of ours." Talking to cops, therefore, was distinctly bad for one's health. The slightest slip, even some remark that might possibly be misconstrued as suggesting the Mafia's existence, could be regarded as a violation of *omertà*, which was punishable by death; even being *seen* with a cop could be fatal, since edgy colleagues had been known to jump to the wrong conclusion and take stern action that could not then be reversed. Better just to hide when the law was around.

It was also true, since human nature doesn't change, that the Mafia in 1980 was made up largely of people who were just as congenitally suspicious as the Mafiosi of 1957. Some of these people had serious personality disorders and would almost certainly be diagnosed as clinically paranoid. But even the ones who were not so far out there on the fringe had more than adequate reason to be jumpy. The cops wanted them. Asian, black, and Puerto Rican competitors would have been pleased to have them off the street. Members of rival La Cosa Nostra clans might turn on them in a minute, and falling out of favor even with their own best friends could prove nasty. So these people were not easy with the idea of being casually approached for a friendly conversation.

The idea now was to make them a notch more uneasy than usual.

Beginning in the spring of 1980, a certain stationery store on Queens Boulevard enjoyed a hefty increase in its sales of Hallmark greeting cards. This surge in business came about because Joe O'Brien, as one small part of the RH stratagem, had taken it upon himself to become a one-way pen pal with nearly fifty known members of the Gambino organization.

Working from computerized FBI records, O'Brien compiled a calendar that noted the birthdays of gang members, from Paul Castellano himself down to the most junior gutter thug. Everybody got a greeting, and along with the Hallmark doggerel, O'Brien sent a quiet message of his own: one of his FBI business cards, impressively emblazoned with the Bureau's seal and containing, of course, the number of O'Brien's office phone, just in case any of the fellows wanted to chat. It seemed they did not—although one Gambino *capo* later acknowledged that O'Brien was the only person other than his wife to remember his birthday. O'Brien also sent Christmas cards and Easter cards. He even sent cards on Saint Patrick's Day.

But it was the special occasion cards that O'Brien took the most pleasure in sending. What a thoughtful way to remind people that one cared enough to pay close attention to their careers! If a Gambino soldier suffered a broken hand, say, in the act of expediting a loan repayment, he was sure to receive a get-well card from the FBI. If said soldier, for his pains, was elevated to the rank of *capo,* Joe O'Brien would send a missive that said, "Congratulations on Your Promotion."

Given all the cards that needed sending, O'Brien could not use equal care in the selection of each one. So he took time and trouble in proportion to how close the recipient of the greeting was to Paul Castellano. Street-level guys got generic cards, a quarter apiece. But Tommy Bilotti, Big Paul's favorite, got fancier goods. When he was made a *capo,* he received a musical congratulation card that played "Happy Days Are Here Again." As a symbol of the increased earnings Bilotti would now enjoy, O'Brien enclosed two crisp one-dollar bills.

As for the cards sent to Castellano himself, they were chosen with a degree of care appropriate to purchasing a gift for the Boss. The one O'Brien remembered most fondly pictured an enormous basket of colored eggs, set in front of a mansion that somewhat resembled the Staten Island White House. The inscription said, "Happy Easter to a Special Godfather."

It was well that O'Brien took pains with the cards he sent to Castellano because, as sources would reveal and Big Paul himself would later confirm, the Boss most assuredly took notice of them.

The first time an O'Brien birthday card was laid before him, it was some moments before Castellano realized it was from the FBI. He was, after all, a popular man, and one whose favor was constantly being courted. He got lots of birthday cards, many from people he barely knew or couldn't remember meeting. Sitting at his dining room table, wearing the carmine satin robe in which he spent a large portion of nearly every day, he went through them in leisurely fashion, carefully slicing open the envelopes with a sterling silver paper knife.

"You see, Gloria," he said in the rather cloying, wheedling tone he used only when speaking to his maid/mistress. "You see how many people write to Mr. Paul?"

Gloria Olarte had become part of the Castellano household on September 9, 1979, and her employer's paramour not long after. She stood in seeming obsequiousness, and cooed supportively as her aging lover indulged his need to boast. Later, when she had displaced the dignified and grandmotherly Nina Castellano as the lady of the house, Gloria would flaunt her power, bullying guests, imposing herself into conversations as no traditional Mafia wife would ever do, even daring to taunt Big Paul himself. But for now a charade of propriety was still under way. The maid stood while the master sat. She spoke only when spoken to. And she was faultlessly attentive to the task of flattering her employer's vanity.

"Yes, Meester Paul," she said. "Berry many. Gloria never get so many mails in all her life."

Castellano flashed her a smile that, in spite of its intent, had elements of a snarl. Then he sliced open the envelope from Joe O'Brien. He read the card, then held it at arm's length, squinting slightly to try and make out the unfamiliar signature. The FBI business card fell onto the mahogany table, and Castellano picked it up.

"Asshole," he muttered.

Far from being offended by the use of vulgar language, Gloria Olarte found dirty words a droll and colorful aspect of her adopted tongue. She was always pleased to expand that dimension of her own vocabulary. "Meester Paul gets mails from assholes?" she asked.

"Lots of assholes," said Castellano, dropping O'Brien's birthday greeting into the trash. As for the business card, he tore it into little pieces and swept it from the table as though it were something unclean.

The same fate befell O'Brien's second missive, and the third. By the fourth contact, however, Castellano had decided to keep Joe O'Brien's business card on file. It never hurt, he reasoned, to know who you were dealing with. Besides, it was not totally outside the realm of possibility that somehow, sometime, the two of them might have something to talk about.

CHAPTER 7

T WENTY BUCKS *just to go inside?*

Andy Kurins had worked at the FBI's New York office for almost four years, and knew the night streets of Manhattan as well as any agent. Still, some things he never quite got used to—things like being squeezed for twenty dollars by a snooty doorman for the privilege of stepping into a disco.

But the heart of the RH strategy was making Gambino family members nervous in their own habitats, and so it happened that at roughly ten P.M. on a Thursday in November 1980, Kurins paid his money and slipped past the discreetly threatening bouncer into the Upper East Side nightspot called Regine's. His target: a Gambino soldier named Tommy Agro, known to be a regular there, and allegedly the point man for the unholy alliance that was believed to exist between the ultrachic nightspot and the Mob.

Nightclubs and the Mafia seemed made for each other. The clubs, for their orderly running, needed freedom from labor hassles, snag-free supplies of linen, garbage collection in the wee hours of the morning. They needed plenty of liquor, and as it happened, one Monique Agro, wife of Tommy, was the salesperson who "earned" a commission on every drop imbibed at Regine's. Additionally, nightspots required efficient mechanisms for dealing with unruly guests, without the mood-dampening side effects of calling in the cops. For that matter, visible Mob presence gave a club a certain cachet, as many solid citizens seemed to get a perverse thrill out of hanging out in the same room as a bunch of gangsters.

All these services the Mafia would gladly provide, and if they came at a substantial premium over the legitimate cost, no problem: successful nightclubs spun off vast amounts of cash, and since the Mob would be paid off in dollars that were never going to be reported anyway, the IRS was in effect subsidizing the relationship. Difficulties occurred only if the club ceased to be trendy, and stopped taking in enough dollars to cover its commitments. The Mafia was always creditor number one. It never took a cut in pay, and believed in renegotiations only if they increased its control over the floundering establishment. Giving the Bosses an equity stake in the enterprise was one possible way of keeping things friendly. Failing that, fires sometimes happened. Garbage sometimes got delivered rather than picked up. "Customers" occasionally fell into altercations with the staff, smashing crockery and furniture, setting a tone that discouraged repeat business.

At Regine's in 1980, however, a crimp in the cash flow was the last thing on anybody's mind. The club was the haunt of the Beautiful People—artists, models, fey Europeans, Arab sheikhs, debutantes intent on being bad—who flocked here to toot cocaine in the bathrooms and dance the night away. In their wake came the Wall Street types, desperate to turn their money into hipness, and the out-of-town executives, who might shyly stake out a square foot or two at the edge of the dance floor and perhaps indulge themselves in the services of an ultra-high-priced hooker. With the noise, the twinkling lights, the clash of perfumes and cigarette smoke, Regine's was New York decadence personified.

An FBI guy, Andy Kurins admitted to himself, felt a little ill at ease there. His suit did not have a designer label. He did not have a large number of acquaintances to wave at and blow kisses to. He didn't dance. So he went to the bar, nursed a drink, and waited for Tommy Agro.

Agro had been a "made guy" in the Gambino family since 1975 or 1976, and while he would never be more than a street-level soldier, certain privileged relationships allowed for an unusual amount of communication between him and Paul Castellano. Agro had been sponsored for Mob membership by Joe N. Gallo, the family's *consigliere*. He was in the crew of *capo* Joseph Armone, one of Big Paul's most trusted associates. Moreover, in 1980, Tommy A. was in a bit of trouble—and soldiers in trouble were always closely watched by their Bosses. It was important to see how they handled the pressure. If they

showed signs of possibly cracking, possibly confessing to something they oughtn't, it might be necessary to take preemptive
steps. Agro was facing extortion charges in Nassau County, on
Long Island. He was also under investigation for alleged involvement in the fixing of horse races at Belmont and Aqueduct. It
was well to keep an eye on him, to know who he was talking to.

At twenty minutes after eleven, Andy Kurins was staring at
his untouched second drink and enduring nasty glances from the
bartender, who clearly hoped to get more volume from that stool.
Regine's was packed by now, and people were standing three-deep
at the bar, clamoring for their overpriced Campari and sodas.
Those who wanted tables were told they would have a long wait.

Suddenly there was a commotion at the door. The maître d'
flitted over, practically flapping his arms in his eagerness to please.
He was flanked by two of the brawnier waiters, who in turn were
flanked by two of the leggier cocktail waitresses. Together, this
flock of employees formed a flying wedge that sliced right through
the cluster of customers who had been suffering in silence, politely
waiting their turn to be seated. When the ripples that ran through
the crowd had subsided, the welcoming committee ushered in a
smiling, pudgy little man. He was immaculately dressed in a
midnight-blue mohair suit. He was manicured. His face shone like
a polished apple. Most resplendent of all, his jet-black toupee was
so sleek it reflected the flashing disco lights, creating the bizarre
effect of sparks coming out of the dapper little fellow's head.

This was Tommy Agro.

Amid great ceremony, he was shown to a table right next to
the dance floor. Men kept running up to shake his hand. Women
kissed his polished cheeks. Seated now, he began distributing bills
to everyone in his procession. The gesture was discreet enough to
be perfectly obvious to anyone looking in Tommy A.'s direction.

For a while Agent Kurins held his ground at the bar, studying
Agro, waiting to see if anyone joined him. No one did—though
people kept stopping by to pay him court. Agro's unfailing genial-
ity contrasted rather dramatically with what Kurins knew of his
on-the-job behavior. Tommy A. was an enforcer. Barely five feet
five, he was a classic bully who seemed to take genuine pleasure in

beating people up. Since he was sickly as well as small, he always needed a couple of helpers to hold his victim down so he could administer his punishment in safety—a condition that seemed to diminish his satisfaction not at all. According to one Agro victim, a favorite method of Tommy's was to approach quite slowly with a flashing knife, giving his pinioned subject ample time to wet his pants before the slashing began. On other occasions, however, Agro's attacks were far more spontaneous—and though no one could have predicted it at the time, one such attack would later play a pivotal part in the chain of events that led eventually to the bugging of the Staten Island White House and Paul Castellano's demise.

Shortly before midnight, Agent Kurins approached Tommy Agro's table. As he did so, Agro rose, headed straight toward the FBI man—then veered abruptly off to the right, slipping neatly through a knot of dancing bodies. Kurins's first thought was that Agro had spotted him and bolted, and for a moment he contemplated the undignified prospect of chasing his quarry across the dance floor.

But in fact Tommy A. was only visiting the men's room, and when he returned, Andy Kurins was still standing, a little awkwardly, midway between the bar and the arc of ringside tables. The sound system was blasting out the Rolling Stones' "Sympathy for the Devil." Agro almost walked right into him.

"Tommy."

By reflex, Agro flashed the same smile he offered everybody else, and held out his pudgy hand to shake. But the hand that Kurins extended contained his FBI credentials, and when Agro saw them, his smile quickly disappeared. He probably thought he was about to be arrested.

"Hey, come on," he said, a note of entreaty in his voice. "No scenes. Not here." Like most Mafiosi, Agro's sense of himself as a big man was quite fragile. It would not hold up to public embarrassment.

"No scenes," Kurins promised. "I just want to talk."

Agro paused, then seemed to decide that the safest course was graciousness. "Will you join me at my table, Agent . . ."

"Kurins. Andy's fine."

Agro led the way, and by the time they'd reached the table, two waiters had outraced them and were holding back the chairs.

"Drink, Andy?"

"Sure."

"Have you eaten? How about some dinner?"

"No thanks, Tommy."

For himself Agro ordered only seltzer. "Can't have alcohol," he said apologetically. "They've got me on this new medication. Lithium. I'm a manic-depressive. Sometimes I think I'm fucking Superman and sometimes I can't get out of bed. It's wild."

"Sorry to hear it," said Kurins.

"Well," said Agro, and left it at that. He drummed his fingers lightly on the table and looked around the room, trying to gauge the reaction to his visitor's presence. He lit a cigarette. "So whaddya want to talk about?"

"How about Aqueduct and Belmont?" suggested Andy Kurins.

"What about 'em?"

"A lot of favorites have been getting scratched lately, and a lot of long shots are sneaking into the money. Some people think it isn't a coincidence."

"Yeah?" said Agro. "Me, I don't know too much about the horses."

"You don't play?"

"Well, sure, I plunk down a couple bucks at OTB now and then . . ."

"You've been seen at the track quite often, Tommy."

Agro drew deeply on his cigarette and coughed into his fist. "I don't think so, Andy," he said. "How could I be? I got a day job. I'm a working stiff. I'm a—"

"Tobacco salesman," said Andy Kurins.

"Oh," said Agro. "You know that."

"I've spoken to your employer, Tommy Deluca. He says you're a great salesman."

"I hold my own," said Agro modestly.

"But he couldn't tell me what accounts you have. He also told me not to bother waiting for you, because you hardly ever come to the office, and not to bother leaving a message, because he had no idea when you'd be checking in."

"It's a road job," said Tommy Agro with a shrug. He stabbed at his wedge of lime with a cocktail straw. "I load up the car with cigarettes, and away I go."

"So let's talk about Paul Castellano."

If the abrupt change of subject rattled Tommy Agro, he didn't let it show. He drained his seltzer, sucking it noisily through the straw, then said, "Who?"

"A fellow I think you know. He lives in a big house on Staten Island."

"Well, I live in a little house in Queens. So how the fuck should I know this guy?"

"I think you have friends in common," said Andy Kurins. "Joey Gallo. Joe Armone. They're all in the Gambino family, and so are you."

"Andy, the only family I'm in is the one that's waiting for me at home." He stubbed out his cigarette and lit another. He glanced around the room, bestowing his genial smile on anyone who might happen to be looking.

The waitress came over and asked Mr. A. if he would like another round. He patted the back of her leg, and she asked him if he had any news about her audition. He told her he hadn't had much time to see his people in the theater district, but he hadn't forgotten, he'd get to it.

"Another, Andy?"

"No thanks."

"Just a seltzer, honey."

"I'm surprised you don't know Paul Castellano," Agent Kurins resumed, speaking over the din of the sound system. "He knows you."

"I doubt that," said Agro, but a look of uncertainty flitted across his polished face. He reached up as if to adjust his toupee, then thought better of it and dropped his hands to the table.

"He's concerned about you," said Kurins. "The strain you're under. The problems you're having. He'd even be concerned, I'll bet, that you're sitting here chatting with me."

All at once, Tommy Agro seemed to reach the end of his composure. His face went slack; he lost the polished apple look. His forehead became so furrowed that his rug shifted. With jerky movements, he reached into various jacket pockets and started producing bottles of prescription pills. Four, five, six different bottles. Suddenly oblivious to his image, he slammed them down on the table in front of him. "Andy, man, shit," he said. "I don't need this aggravation. I'm a sick man. Look at all this fucking shit I gotta take.

"This is the lithium," he went on, picking up a bottle that had fallen on its side and rolled across the table. "This is so I don't go fucking nuts and start handing out hundred-dollar bills outside the Midtown Tunnel. This one here is for my lungs. They fill up with water every time I lay down, and when I try to breathe, it's like I'm fucking drowning. These two are for my goddamn heart. The docs showed me a graph of it—it looked like the fucking stock market. This one's for—"

"Easy, Tommy." Kurins reached across the table and put his hand on Agro's wrist. "You didn't want any scenes, remember?"

"Easy my ass," said Agro, but he quieted down and, almost sheepishly, started putting the medicines back in his pockets. Fortunately for him, odd behavior was the expected mode at places like Regine's. No one much noticed a sudden outburst or a display of pharmaceuticals; besides, for all the waving and the blown kisses, no one much cared about what anyone else was going through.

"I'm leaving now," Kurins said. "Thanks for the drink."

He headed for the door, looking back just once at Tommy Agro's table. Mr. A. seemed to have recovered his self-possession very fast. The waitress had brought him his seltzer, and he had his hand on her thigh.

Outside in the brisk November air, Andy Kurins suddenly felt tipsy. The drinks, the noise, the cigarette smoke, the adrenaline from confronting Agro, all seemed to hit him in delayed reaction. Absently, he stepped off the sidewalk—and was nearly run down by a huge green private sanitation truck going the wrong way down a one-way street. It happened so fast he didn't get to read the name inscribed on the truck's broad flank. Just out of curiosity, he would have liked to know if it belonged to one of the companies controlled by Paul Castellano, the Boss of Bosses.

CHAPTER 8

IN TAKING to the streets to establish contact with members of the Castellano gang, Agents Kurins and O'Brien were in fact implementing a strategy that the FBI had conceived almost twenty years before, but had never really applied. Already in 1960, it was recognized that one of law enforcement's major problems in combating organized crime was the lack of a reliable intelligence base. *Omertà* was a powerful defense as long as its fabric remained unbroken; and, before Valachi, it *was* unbroken. All that agents and prosecutors ever got from mobsters was a wearying litany of *I don't know, Never heard of him,* and *I respectfully refuse to answer on grounds that it may incriminate me.*

Add to this infuriating reticence J. Edgar Hoover's often-criticized and generally misunderstood tardiness in acknowledging the existence and magnitude of organized crime, and you had a situation in which the Mafia remained shadowy and maybe mythic, and in which law enforcement action was stymied by lack of information. In retrospect, it is clear that Hoover was not in fact naive in his assessment of organized crime and its effects; but he had limited forces to deploy, and through the fifties, FBI priority number one was the investigation of Communists in and around the government. If, at this remove of time, that priority seems to have been misguided, it can only be said that the Bureau, like all government agencies, reflects the mood and concerns of the body politic. To put it another way, the FBI does not really decide who is on the Most Wanted list; the public does.

In any case, the program of getting agents onto the streets to chat with Mafiosi had never really gotten off the ground. Several things militated against it. For one thing, agents were encouraged to work in pairs, and as difficult as it was to get a mobster to talk with one cop, it was virtually impossible to get him to say anything at all in the presence of two. For all their lack of education, made guys tend to be pretty savvy about those aspects of the law that apply to them. They understand what is meant by the term "corroboration"; they know that saying or doing something in front of two witnesses is roughly ten times as dangerous as saying or doing it in front of one.

As for sending agents out alone, that, too, presented problems. Confronting a Mob guy one-on-one is not usually dangerous. But stress should be put on "usually." In the typical case, Mob violence is not spontaneous but planned, and not carried out by a single man but by a team that keeps the odds firmly in the Mafia's favor. Still, Mafiosi are known for their hot tempers and their fits of blind rage; things happened. Back in 1963, for instance, an agent had been stomped and beaten for taking pictures at a funeral.

Even leaving aside the possible danger, the fact is that trying to chat up crime family members tends to be a very frustrating enterprise. You spend half a day trying to track someone down. You finally find him, and he stands there shuffling his feet and cracking his knuckles. You ask him a question, and he does one of four things: he dodges it, he lies, he suggests you speak to his lawyer, or he tells you to go fuck yourself. This, in turn, annoys you, which makes it harder to keep things civil. What's the use? Virtually any FBI agent would jump at the chance to go out and arrest a Mafia soldier. But just to pay a social call? The prospect was unappealing.

If agents were disinclined to approach Mob members, Mob members, in turn, had grown unaccustomed to being approached; and Joe O'Brien realized early on that this could be turned to advantage. He decided to avoid guile and stealth, and to make his contacts as straightforward, blunt, and obvious as possible. In what was the exact opposite of an undercover operation, he didn't want to deceive Gambino family members but rather to flabbergast them with his candor and his blatancy.

Consider the case of "Big George" Remini, small-time loan shark and numbers man, and also proprietor of the Top Tomato fruit and vegetable stand on Staten Island. Joe O'Brien dropped in at his premises one sunny afternoon, and set about inspecting artichokes and appraising honeydews until he felt he could approach Big George directly. O'Brien had a camera with him, as one of his tasks was to update the Bureau's photo files.

"G'bye, dear," Remini was saying to a little old lady whose shopping cart was loaded down with broccoli rab and bulbs of fennel. The greengrocer was a hulking man, not fat but jowly, almost handsome in a sloppy kind of way. "Come back soon."

The way clear, O'Brien moved toward Remini. The agent was clutching an eggplant. "How much?"

"Gotta weigh it," Remini said, but when he plucked the vegetable out of O'Brien's hand, he saw the FBI credentials cradled in his palm. Instantly, the grocer's ruddy, unshaven face blanched like a cauliflower, and he took a half-step backward, shielding himself behind a crate of iced spinach. "I ain't done nothin'," he said.

"Didn't say you did," responded O'Brien genially. "I just stopped by to say hello and take your picture."

Remini, apparently for the first time, noticed the camera. At the same moment, a look of recollection crossed his face. "You the guy who's been sending holiday cards?"

O'Brien just smiled and nodded.

"Well, I don't like having my picture took," said Remini, his tone turning feisty. He seemed to realize now that he wasn't in any immediate danger, and he apparently felt he needed to put on a show of bravado, to compensate for his all-too-obvious show of fear. "I don't have to let you photograph me."

"Sorry, George, but the Eastern District of New York Organized Crime Strike Force says you do. Of course, if you'd like to go to court and argue that . . ."

"I don't wanna go to court."

"I didn't think so. I mean, you've got your business to run, and all." O'Brien gestured expansively over the cukes, the cabbages, the pomegranates. Then he started fiddling with the camera, putting on an exaggerated show of clumsiness.

Remini gave a bitter and derisive little laugh. "FBI," he said, shaking his head. "You know, on TV you guys always come across so slick, so *Mission Impossible.* Like with infrared cameras that take pictures in pitch-dark. And here you come in like some tourist taking snapshots. What is this, amateur hour?"

"Amateur hour," O'Brien parroted, without taking offense. "That's a good one, George." He kept fiddling with the camera.

"You want my picture, why don't you at least be cagey about it? Why don't you hide out on a street corner with a camera that points one way and shoots the other?"

O'Brien fumbled with his lens cap, wrestled with his focus ring. "You know why?" he said. "Because you have to be a good photographer to work that way, and, truth is, I'm the pits. Stand a little over this way, George. Away from the celery.

"A good surveillance photographer is an artist," the agent chattered on. "Me, I always seem to get the guy standing in the shadows. Or I get the back of his head. Why, just the other day, I was trying to get a picture of Paul Castellano . . ."

O'Brien dropped the camera to his side, the photo of George Remini still untaken.

"I was standing at the foot of his driveway. You know where I mean."

Remini tried to keep his features utterly still, and said nothing. Absently, he reached out a hand and fondled a peach.

"Anyway," O'Brien continued, "he comes to the door, in his p.j.'s as usual. He's letting the Dobermans out for a run around the yard. So, real cagey like you say, I snap the picture. He doesn't even know I'm there. He looks out toward the Verrazano, takes a deep breath, and goes back in. I go to the lab, real proud of myself. The picture comes back—he's in the shadow of one of the columns. I mean, if you didn't already know what Paul Castellano looked like, the picture wouldn't tell you. Fortunately, you already know, so you could tell. But most people couldn't."

"What makes you think I know anyone named Paul Castellano?" George Remini said, his fingertips making dents in the peach.

"Did I say that?" responded O'Brien. "I only said you knew what he looked like. You know, from the papers. But now that you mention it, I'll bet you do know Paul Castellano."

"You bet, you lose," said Remini. "I don't."

"Okay, my mistake. So let's get back to our portrait."

He raised the camera, and George Remini, perhaps unconsciously, took a moment to preen. No one likes to look disheveled in a photograph, and mobsters are no exception. Remini tucked his rumpled white T-shirt more securely into his jeans. He ran a hand through the lank black hair that fell forward over his brow. He even put on a smile, which only made his unshaven face look a notch jowlier and rather haggard. O'Brien snapped away.

"There, George," he said in a conciliatory tone, "that wasn't so bad, was it?"

Remini just shrugged, and O'Brien picked up a greengage plum. "Put this on the scale for me, would you?"

"Take it," said Big George. "On the house."

"Delicious," said O'Brien, biting into it.

Remini's chin jutted forward in a gesture of professional pride. "You bet it's delicious. We only sell the freshest here."

"Well," O'Brien went on, wiping his mouth with the back of his hand, "that's why I thought you might have an in with Paul Castellano. From what I hear, if you're a friend of Paul's, your trucks always get loaded first."

"Is that what you hear?" said Remini. "Well, here's how it really works. Paul Castellano or no Paul Castellano, if you want your trucks loaded first, you get your ass out of bed at three A.M. to be at the market by four. You push harder than the Koreans and you scream louder than the Puerto Ricans. And that's how you get fresh goods."

CHAPTER 9

LUCK OF THE DRAW," said Andy Kurins in blithe response to the question of why some guys got to do their research surrounded by beautiful women in famous nightclubs, while others interviewed unshaven deadbeats amid baskets full of onions. "Besides," he said to Joe O'Brien, "look at the good part. Working Staten Island keeps you close to your buddy Paul."

And it was true that ongoing surveillance of the Staten Island White House remained an FBI priority. As 1981 progressed, the traffic in and out of Castellano's horseshoe driveway seemed to be increasing, while Big Paul himself seemed to go out less and less. There were, as would become clear in retrospect, several reasons for his staying so close to home.

By 1981, Paul Castellano had presided over the Gambino crime family for half a decade of general peace and prosperity. Ever surer of his position as unchallenged head of the organization, he felt he could afford to withdraw more and more from contact with his lower-level troops. This decision no doubt made the day-to-day life of the Godfather less cluttered and less stressful, spared him a lot of boring conversations and cases of heartburn, but it was almost certainly a serious tactical mistake. He was ceasing to be a hands-on Boss; he was divorcing himself from the smells and rumblings of the street. His self-chosen distance enabled ambitious young lieutenants such as John Gotti to develop powerful bands of soldiers whose first loyalty was to *them*, rather than to some aloof leadership that seemed a thousand miles away—as remote as top management in a Fortune 500 company.

This aloofness, in turn, suggests another factor in Castellano's increasing remove from the nitty-gritty of Mob business—one that, over time, would take on elements of a dangerous delusion: he seemed to imagine that he had somehow "graduated" from gang-sterhood, and was now, by the sheer volume of his enterprise, part of the legitimate capitalist establishment. This illusion of legitimacy—propped up, of course, by bribes to cops and judges and by dubious dealings with politicians of various stripes—seemed to give Big Paul a blasé confidence about how and where he did his business. Everybody knew that Lee Iacocca worked out of Chrysler headquarters; what was the harm in letting people figure out that Paul Castellano, wealthy executive, with holdings in construction, food, clothing, sanitation, etc., etc., etc., often did business at his luxurious and expansive residence?

Then, too, there was another reason, totally removed from professional considerations, that made Paul Castellano stay at home. That reason was Gloria Olarte, with whom Big Paul was becoming increasingly obsessed. He doted on her. Almost like an adolescent, he schemed for rare moments of privacy when he might watch her swim nude in the Olympic-size pool; he loved to dry her off inside his carmine satin robe. Like adolescents, too, the pair indulged in long sessions of kissing and petting, stroking and teas-ing, without ever having actual intercourse. The reason for the abstinence was not moral but medical, involving a problem for which Paul Castellano would later subject himself to a radical solution. Ardor and frustration, desire and constraint—the heady combination brought forth in the Godfather a satyrish streak he seemed powerless to hide.

As time went by, all pretense, all nods to convention, went by the boards in Castellano's dealings with his maid. The lovers made moony eyes and lascivious gestures at each other in the presence of the stoic but increasingly disgusted Nina Castellano. Senior mem-bers of the Gambino organization passed each other worried and incredulous glances as they saw their leader—the Pope, the Boss of all Bosses—behaving like a lovesick teenager. They cringed when he praised "little Gloria," when he spoke to her in that coddling voice that seemed more fit for addressing a child or a kitten. Why did he indulge this crude, sharp-tongued, unglamorous woman, this foreigner with her accent and her appalling table manners? How could he be so frankly slighting toward patient Nina, *appro-*

priate Nina, the partner of his triumphs and travails, the mother of his children?

They disapproved; they all disapproved. But Paul Castellano either was too distracted to notice or simply didn't care. He was having a wonderful time. Gloria was keeping him young, in spirit if not in body. He had worked his whole life to be in a position where he felt in charge, secure, free to do exactly as he pleased. He was there now, and by God, he intended to enjoy it. He was the Boss. If he wanted to combine his personal playground with Gambino family headquarters, that was up to him.

It was his house, after all, his fortress, as safe a place as any and a lot more comfortable than most.

CHAPTER 10

OPERATION MEATHEAD, Joe O'Brien had dubbed it.

It may not have been the most elegantly named investigation in the annals of the FBI, but at least it was descriptive. The Meathead in question was none other than Paul Castellano—though the name was not intended as any sort of slight to the Boss's mental capacities. Rather, it referred to Castellano's ongoing interest in what had been his very first business.

The former butcher seemed to take a special satisfaction from questionable dealings in meat. Perhaps because of his lack of education, he cherished the technical knowledge he had in such matters as the boxing of carcasses and the rendering of fat. He could quarter a lamb with the best of them. He knew all there was to know about tallow.

He knew, as well, the whole range of tricks by which Mob-controlled companies increased profits by passing on to the consumer meat that was tainted, outdated, uninspected, or of dubious provenance. He was familiar, for example, with the process known as "bleaching," in which spoiled meat is drained of its foul-smelling juices, then soaked overnight in a white preservative powder known in the trade as "dynamite," which makes it look red and appetizing again. He understood the value of formaldehyde in masking the stench of decay. He was conversant with the use of counterfeit Department of Agriculture stamps to put a fraudulent grade or expiration date on a carcass. He knew that "beef" did not always come from cows and that "pork" had not necessarily been the property of a pig. To be fair, he probably never knowingly poisoned any of his customers, and bellyaches and bouts of diarrhea are, after all, a part of life.

The wholesale food industry, of course, had been a Mob

profit center in New York long before Paul Castellano came along. Way back in the 1930s, the *New York Times* complained in an editorial that "if there is any downward scale of ignominy in the [racketeering] profession, the man who preys on the city's food supply must stand near the very bottom of it." Historically, however, the Gambino family had not been strong in the protein business. Other LCN groups had staked out the territory first. The Genovese family, with its notorious power over the Fulton Fish Market, had a lock on seafood. As for beef and poultry, the powers had traditionally been the Lucchese and Bonanno clans. It was a Bonanno associate, Charles Anselmo, who gave the famous answer to the question of whether one of his shipments consisted of horsemeat: "Well, some of it moos, and some of it don't moo."

It took Paul Castellano to make the Gambino family a meat business power, and Operation Meathead, conceived as one of several strands of inquiry into Big Paul's activities, was designed to see if he himself had left any tracks while riding roughshod through the industry.

Several things about the Gambino family's presence in the meat business seemed to bear Castellano's personal stamp. For one thing, that the Gambinos were able to muscle in without igniting a turf war with the Lucchese and Bonanno clans was an indication of the tact and quiet strength with which Castellano operated; no one but the top man could have made that move. Moreover, the patience and finesse with which he built his operation were impressive. In all, Castellano's meat business gambit might serve as a compact case study on how to use shady practices to establish a quasi-monopoly position.

The consumer meat business stands on three legs—distribution, retailing, and labor—and Big Paul wielded considerable influence in all three. Back in 1970, he set up two of his sons, Joe and Paul junior, in a Brooklyn-based wholesale operation called Dial Meat Purveyors, Inc.—usually referred to as Dial Poultry. Dial distributed to over three hundred retail butchers, and enjoyed a good deal of clout in determining which brands were promoted and which left to wither on the shelves.

The big volume, however, was not in butcher shops but in supermarkets, and so Castellano quietly set about cementing his relationships with the chains. A man named Pasquale Conte, who sat on the board of directors of the Key Food Cooperative and owned several of the stores himself, became a Gambino family *capo.* Ira Waldbaum, head of the chain that bears his family name, somehow ended up in Castellano's pocket. A rather spineless man, the multimillionaire Waldbaum would later try to justify playing ball with the Mafia by whining to a presidential commission: "Don't forget I have a wife and children."

Labor was the third leg of the meat business tripod, and here, too, Castellano was well connected. He was old friends with Irving Stern, a man who seemed to have no trouble retaining his international vice presidency of the United Food and Commercial Workers Union, in spite of having been imprisoned for tax evasion involving payoffs from supermarket executives and wholesale meat distributors. So what if Irving took money from the people who were his ostensible negotiating adversaries? He talked tough, he was good with the media, and his constituency loved him.

Considered alone, each aspect of Castellano's meat industry presence was significant but not remarkable. Together, however, they were exceedingly powerful, achieving the kind of synergy that legitimate conglomerateurs are so fond of blathering on about, and so seldom achieve. If a retail butcher objected to Dial's prices, he might find himself short of product on the eve of a major holiday, while a Key Food or Waldbaum's gladly took the extra stock. If a given manufacturer preferred not doing business with Dial, that manufacturer might find his goods getting short shrift in the ads and displays of New York's major supermarkets. If certain supermarkets didn't want to go along with Dial's recommendations on such matters, they might find themselves having sudden difficulties with the butchers' union. Pickets might appear; meat might rot in the back rooms. It was easier, all in all, just to go along with the Mafia way of doing business—especially since the added costs of these monopolistic practices were ultimately borne by the consumer, and New York consumers were so accustomed to being abused in various and sundry ways that they seldom even thought to complain. New Yorkers accepted sleaze as part of their diet.

But sleaze is one thing, outright illegality another, and the bedeviling task faced by the FBI in 1981 was to mold these patterns of abuse into prosecutable cases. Dial Poultry, it seemed, stopped just short of extortion in persuading its business partners to play along. When favors were bartered, rather than cash exchanged, it was all but impossible to establish the existence of bribes and kickbacks. Most discouraging of all, it was very difficult to get business people to testify about their own dealings with the Mob, even when they themselves had done nothing unlawful. No doubt people were afraid, and not without cause: stores had been burned; supermarket executives had been murdered.

But it was not only fear that made supposedly responsible businesspeople keep silent. There was a high degree of amorality and cynicism in the industry, an attitude of *What the heck, we're making money.* Why go out on a limb to change things, just because they happened to be corrupt? Then, too, many solid citizens seemed nagged by a kind of formless guilt. Okay, maybe they hadn't broken any laws, but was there anyone in the meat business who was really virgin pure? Anyone who hadn't done certain things, made certain deals, which in a certain light might look a little bit like collusion?

A central goal of Operation Meathead, then, was to bring forward people who'd had dealings with Paul Castellano or his minions—whether as victims, partners, or a little of each.

Joe O'Brien was targeting one man in particular. He was a man who had taken a small family business and built it into a world-famous enterprise, making himself one of America's wealthiest men in the process. He was known, in his public image at least, to be fiercely independent. Yet it was also known that he had a history of entanglements with Dial Poultry and the Castellano family. There were conflicting rumors of approaches and rebuffs, murmurs of favors asked and favors owed. If this man could be persuaded to go public with his story, he could probably draw more attention than anyone else to Mafia influence over the American food supply. He was something of a celebrity, known to tens of millions of people, partly because of his aggressiveness as an advertiser and partly because of his uncanny resemblance, in voice and visage, to his product.

His name was Frank Perdue.

CHAPTER 11

JOE O'BRIEN had a pretty good idea of what would happen if he tried to visit Frank Perdue at his corporate headquarters in Salisbury, Maryland. He'd be greeted by a receptionist with perfect fingernails, who would refer him to a public relations officer with a yellow tie. The public relations guy might or might not actually introduce him to Mr. Perdue for purposes of the official handshake, but would make it clear, in either case, that the people he really needed to talk to were the lawyers. The lawyers, in turn, would be perfectly polite, highly respectful, and wouldn't help at all. They'd weigh O'Brien down with documents revealing nothing. They would know nothing at all of any dealings with a man named Paul Castellano, Sr., although they might make bold to volunteer that Paul Castellano, *Jr.*, was the proprietor of a Brooklyn distribution company with which they sometimes did business. Could they possibly be related? In short, the whole thing would be just the sort of button-down charade for which O'Brien had no patience.

No, he wanted to get to Perdue solo, talk with him one-on-one. But how?

As is well known, Frank Perdue is a man who loves to sell chickens. He sells big chickens and little chickens. He sells them whole, he sells them cut up. In 1981, he was trying out the idea of selling them cooked in his very own restaurants. And in the city of New York, with its thousands of street corners and hundreds of thousands of retail spaces, the very first Perdue Chicken Restaurant turned out to be located at 95-25 Queens Boulevard, in Rego Park, on the ground floor of the building that housed the Brooklyn-Queens Resident Agency of the FBI. The entrance was roughly sixty feet, almost straight down, from Joe O'Brien's desk.

One blisteringly hot summer day, O'Brien was returning from

lunch at his favorite pizzeria when he saw Perdue himself standing in the street in front of the restaurant, hailing a taxi. He was wearing a neatly cut gray suit, and looked perfectly unrumpled in spite of the wilting humidity. The agent reached the chicken magnate just as a cab was screeching to a halt on the softening asphalt in front of him.

"Mr. Perdue."

The poultry king flashed his well-known, almost lipless smile as though expecting to be asked for his autograph.

"Joe O'Brien. FBI. I've wanted to talk to you for quite some time."

Perdue, a tall, slender man with a balding head and somewhat gawky neck, had opened the taxi door and was just about to climb in. "Oh? FBI? Well, I've got an appointment in Manhattan," he said. "But we can chat for a minute if you like."

"I think it'll take longer than that," said O'Brien. He reached gently but decisively for the car door, and closed it. The cab drove away.

Perdue watched in disbelief as it vanished into the traffic and heat mirages of Queens Boulevard. "It took me fifteen minutes to get that cab," he squawked. "What is this all about? How long have you been following me?"

"I haven't been." O'Brien pointed up at the dirty sixth-floor windows. "That's the FBI office. I work there."

"Jesus," said Perdue. Then, as if to recapture his poise, he fell into character as the world's greatest chicken salesman. "Do you fellows eat my birds?"

"I see some of the guys in there sometimes. Some get takeout and eat at their desks. The grease comes through the bags."

"What about you?" Perdue asked.

"Me? No," said O'Brien.

"What?" said Perdue. "It's so convenient, and you don't go? Don't tell me you eat hamburgers for lunch. With all that cholesterol."

"Truth is," O'Brien replied, "I don't like chicken."

"Don't like chicken?" said Perdue, his voice rising to that high tenor cackle so familiar from his commercials.

"It leaves a fowl taste in my mouth," said Joe O'Brien.

Perdue didn't laugh. He was very serious when it came to poultry. Poultry, after all, had reportedly made him the sixtieth-richest man in America, with a personal fortune of roughly a hundred million dollars. Besides, Perdue was only half paying attention to his chat with Joe O'Brien while he scanned Queens Boulevard for another taxi. "Well, whaddya want to talk about?" he said.

"Dial Poultry, for starters," said O'Brien. "Your dealings with Paul Castellano, Sr. Your presence, in 1976, at the Westchester Premiere Theater, when Frank Sinatra was photographed with his arms around some of the leading Mob figures in America. Then maybe the labor problems you've been having."

"Labor problems," muttered Perdue, skipping over the rest. "Character assassination is what I call it. The union is on a smear campaign against me."

A cab appeared through the wavering summer air, and Perdue flagged it down. "Listen," he said, "I'm late. I get to New York very often. You want to talk, we'll talk another time."

He climbed into the taxi, and O'Brien gave him a business card. "You'll call?"

"Go have a chicken on me," said Frank Perdue. "Just tell my manager I sent you in."

But O'Brien didn't claim his chicken, and Frank Perdue didn't call.

After a month had passed, the agent did go into the chicken restaurant, but only to get the name of Perdue's personal secretary down in Maryland. He contacted her, and learned that her boss had in fact been in New York within the past several weeks. He learned, too, that the visiting businessman usually stayed at the posh Hotel Pierre, located at the corner of Fifth Avenue and Sixty-first Street.

Now, the heads of security at major hotels are often former law enforcement officers. They are almost always happy to help out the FBI, and even happier to get involved in something a little more interesting than the usual run of pickpockets in the lobby and emerald earrings lost in the ballroom. As a group, they enjoy intrigue, are enthusiastic about code words, and like nothing better than doing surveillance on their guests. So the security officer at the Pierre was glad to confirm that Frank Perdue did in fact take a suite there on the average of once a month, generally with a companion much younger than himself and of the opposite gender. He agreed to notify O'Brien next time the businessman came to town.

A couple of weeks later, on August 28, 1981, the FBI received a cryptic phone message from a man who identified himself only as Pierre. The message said, "The chicken is in his nest." A phone number followed.

Perdue sounded slightly winded when Joe O'Brien called. "How'd you get through?" the poultry king demanded.

"Just dialed," said O'Brien breezily. "I thought you were going to call me."

"It slipped my mind," Perdue said. "Besides, I really can't imagine it's that important."

"It is to us."

"All right, O'Brien," said Perdue. "I'll be the good citizen and all of that. But if I sit down and get the damn interview over with, will you please stop hounding me?"

"Probably. Not definitely."

"All right. Meet me here at one o'clock. I take it you know where I am?"

"Yup," said O'Brien. "Exactly."

Traveling from Queens to Manhattan over the Queensboro Bridge is always an adventure, and Joe O'Brien did not want to be late. By 12:35 he had installed himself across Fifth Avenue from the Pierre's entrance and was ordering lunch in the form of a Sabrett's hot dog with onions, mustard, and relish, to be washed down with a can of Coke.

At 12:40 he was halfway through his meal, when his attention was captured by a striking young redhead exiting the hotel, being shown to a taxi by a doorman. Tall and slinky, the redhead moved slowly, apparently accustomed to drawing glances. Only as she was climbing into the car did O'Brien realize she was not alone. A slender and somewhat birdlike man was following half a step behind her. It was Frank Perdue. He was flying the coop, running out on his appointment.

The chicken magnate was ducking toward the car door when Joe O'Brien bolted across the four lanes of traffic on Fifth Avenue. He had half a hot dog in one hand, a can of soda in the other, and he underestimated the speed of an oncoming taxi that was running a red light.

The cab hit him.

The front fender caught O'Brien just above the left knee, and the impact threw him upward onto the hood. He rolled backward, up against the windshield, where he splayed out for an instant like a giant bug encountered on the highway. Then, as the taxi screamed to a stop, he rolled back down the hood, flattened the Dodge ornament with his ribs, somersaulted backward, and somehow landed on his feet. If he was hurt, he didn't know it.

Traffic had frozen. Pedestrians had stopped in their tracks, transfixed by that blend of horror and morbid fascination known to city dwellers everywhere. Horns blared, and the terrified driver ran toward O'Brien, screaming in either Greek, Russian, or Persian, no one could be sure.

But the agent headed straight toward Frank Perdue, who had been as immobilized as everyone else by the scene in the street. Ordinarily soft-spoken, discreet, and dignified in the performance of his duties, O'Brien was feeling feistier than usual. There's something about getting hit by a car that gets a guy pumped up. "Where the hell do you think you're going, Perdue?" he shouted.

The chicken king looked around nervously, blinking his pale eyes. He was a media figure, after all, a celebrity. He didn't need loud scenes on Fifth Avenue with a young redhead in the car. "Something's come up," he said softly. "I have an important engagement."

"You have an engagement," O'Brien insisted, planting his hip firmly against the taxi door, "but it's with me. It's for one o'clock, but we may as well start now."

Perdue sighed, clucked, and looked down at his shoes. "You have mustard on your suit," he said. "And relish."

O'Brien checked himself out, and sure enough, he had a lightning bolt of French's across his jacket and a telltale track of pickle juice on his trousers. He realized, too, quite suddenly, that he was still clutching half a hot dog, though the can of soda was gone. But he stayed silent and held his ground. The doorman was hovering; Perdue's driver was getting impatient; the cabbie who'd hit O'Brien had gotten back in his car and driven off.

"All right," Perdue said at last. "We'll talk." Then, to the redhead, "Get out."

She slithered across the backseat of the taxi and expertly swiveled her knees toward the door. She turned an accusing pout on Joe O'Brien, making it clear that her fun was being spoiled and it was all his fault. Perdue handed her some money. "Here," he said. "Go shopping."

Then he turned back to O'Brien and made a gesture of disgust toward the half-eaten frankfurter. "Would you mind not bringing that into the hotel, at least?"

O'Brien, who was no longer hungry anyway, looked around but couldn't find a trash can.

"Give it to the doorman," said Perdue.

Since the chicken magnate was a regular guest, the liveried fellow had no choice but to accept the offending object with a smile.

"Jesus, O'Brien," said Perdue as he led the way into the hushed, cool lobby, "do you have any idea what's *in* those things?"

CHAPTER 12

T HEY'RE ALL CROOKS, Andy, all crooks. Every last god-damn one of them. All they want is your money."

The speaker was Joseph N. Gallo, a mobster for over forty years, the last dozen of those spent as *consigliere* of the Gambino family. The position of *consigliere,* or counselor, was the third-highest in the Cosa Nostra hierarchy, and it suited Gallo perfectly. He was a natural diplomat. He understood what drove people, and he had great instinct for knowing when to talk tough and when to smooth things over. He was a suave, generally calm, and effective liar. In this he was far different from most mobsters, who lied with no particular goal in view but simply because it was second nature to them to steer clear of the truth. Gallo lied purposefully and with wisdom—and also with a certain diabolical charm.

In his role as *consigliere* he had several duties to perform. When intrafamily squabbles arose over the divvying up of turf, it was up to the counselor to present the various viewpoints to the Boss, or to mediate between the *capos* if a sit-down was necessary. If a soldier was in trouble with the law, his *capo* needed to discuss with the *consigliere* whether the man's steadfastness could be trusted, whether he should be allowed to flee, or whether it would be more prudent to have him whacked. In quarrels among the crime families, it was the respective counselors' duty to defuse tensions that could lead to all-out gangland war.

The *consigliere,* strictly speaking, had no power of his own and derived his clout solely from the Boss. Still, a trusted and experienced man like Gallo had broad discretion in the way he implemented edicts from above. Typically, Paul Castellano would issue some brief and gruff directive on a matter that was, to him, of very minor interest: *Agro's taking too much. Tell him to take less.* Gallo would then have to decide what sort of spin to put on the order. Threaten Agro? Have Agro's rug mussed up? Talk to Agro like a kindly uncle, and counsel patience? Give Agro a piece of someone else's racket to make up for lost income? If Castellano decided the substance of family decisions, a crucial role in setting their tone resided with Joe Gallo.

"Fucking lawyers," Gallo was saying. "All crooks. The way they change sides back and forth makes me wanna puke. When I meet some high-minded prosecutor or some smug-ass government attorney, you know the first thing I do? I very politely ask for their card. You know why? Because I know that, someday, sometime, they're gonna say, 'Enough of this shit,' working for the feds for lousy pay, making cases that half the time are garbage, and they're gonna go into private practice defending us. Then they're gonna get fucking rich.

"We've both seen it happen, right, Andy? Tom Puccio. Joel Cohen. One day they're wearing white hats and cheap suits, next day they're wearing black hats and custom-mades. And what about that little cocksucker Roy Cohn? One night he's out hob-nobbing with high society, the next day he's making Tommy Gambino pay through the nose for defending some bullshit case. That's what they do, Andy. They pay their dues working for the government, then they squeeze our balls because of all the con-nections they've developed. They make thousands just talking on the phone from Southampton. Is this bullshit, or what?"

Joe Gallo, because of his unrestricted access to the Staten Island White House, had seemed a natural target for the FBI's Wreak Havoc strategy. *Capo*s needed special dispensation to be allowed a sit-down with Paul Castellano, but Gallo was like the Secretary of State. All he had to do was drop a quarter in a pay phone and say, "Paul, I think we oughtta talk."

Andy Kurins coming around, asking questions, dropping names, was supposed to make Gallo nervous, which was supposed to make Big Paul edgy, which was supposed to lead to a prose-cutable misjudgment. But sitting in the chatty presence of Joe Gallo, Kurins had reason to doubt that the strategy was working.

If Gallo was the slightest bit nonplussed, he didn't let it show. In fact, the more the old boy gabbed, the more relaxed he seemed to get.

The *consigliere* was holding forth at his unofficial headquarters—Sperrazza's Luncheonette, on the southeast corner of Broadway Avenue and Crescent Street, in Astoria, Queens. Sixty-nine years old in 1981, Gallo did his business the old-fashioned way. Given his long tenure with the Mob and the plateau to which he had risen, he was almost certainly a millionaire, yet he continued to live in a modest apartment on decidedly unfashionable Crescent Street. He owned absolutely nothing in his own name and did not even have a checking account. He always carried a fat wad of fifty- and one-hundred-dollar bills but tried not to show the cash if he could help it. Money, he seemed to feel, became dangerous as soon as it was visible.

If Mob colleagues wanted to chat with the Gambino *consigliere*, they knew to call him "at the candy store"—that is, on one of Sperrazza's three pay phones. (For years, Gallo was convinced his home phone was tapped, which in fact it never was.) As for face-to-face meetings with Gambino members, including John Gotti, Joe Armone, Tommy Agro, and many others, these were held, over coffee, either in one of Sperrazza's green vinyl booths or at one of half a dozen other diners within a radius of eight blocks or so.

Gallo was not a fancy sort of guy. He didn't crave the glitz of Manhattan or even the relative flash of Mafia Brooklyn. He was content to preside quietly and even meekly over his own little fiefdom in Queens, and when he wanted a new girlfriend, he was content to pick from among the neighborhood's manicurists and beauticians. Many other mobsters, at the first sign of graying hair, reached for the bottle of Grecian Formula; Gallo was content to let his hair turn a grandfatherly white. Nor—except when he had to leave Astoria for major LCN powwows—did he like to dress up. He spent his days in loose-fitting shirts that he didn't bother tucking into his pants. He strolled the neighborhood, rather incongruously, in Nike running shoes, and used his black Cadillac (registered to one Peter Porcelli of Staten Island) only rarely. He played OTB, ate pills for his angina, and talked to neighborhood people on the sidewalk. While his circumscribed and circumspect life might have struck other mobsters as so dull that it resembled the dreary days of citizens, Gallo's self-effacing style had served him well: remarkably, he was never convicted of a crime until 1987.

"Same bullshit with these supposedly legitimate business-men," the *consigliere* resumed, barely taking time to sip now and then at his cooling espresso. "The government seems to have this cockamamy idea that there's this thing called the Mafia, and the Mafia goes around corrupting perfectly honest and upstanding people. Gimme a break! Andy, you're in the human nature busi-ness, right? It's human nature that you can't corrupt someone who doesn't want to be corrupted. And someone who wants to be corrupted is *already* corrupt. You follow that? So who is kidding who with this bullshit about these nice-guy businessmen getting muscled in on?

"Let me tell you something, Andy. If there was a Mafia, which there isn't, here's how it would work. It wouldn't have to go after legitimate businesses. Guys who ran so-called legitimate businesses would come to it. And you know why? Because they'd want to screw somebody, some competitor, the working stiffs, maybe even a partner, and they wouldn't have the balls to do it themselves. Morality has nothing to do with it. It's about lack of balls. So they'd come to the Mafia, pay the Mafia, fucking *beg* the Mafia, to do the screwing that they wouldn't do themselves, to give them an edge. Then, later, if things went sour, they'd turn around and cry the blues. *What could I do?* they'd say. *The Mafia had me by the short hairs.*

"Fucking hypocrites, Andy. We're surrounded by fucking hypocrites. I am. You are. We all are.

"Lemme ask you something. How many people do you know who really live by what they say they believe in?"

Agent Kurins shifted slightly in the vinyl booth and took a sip of his coffee. But before he could answer, the *consigliere* was off again. Kurins had hung around Astoria for months before Gallo would say a single word to him; all he got was dirty looks and the

81

occasional derisive laugh. But once the old fox had broken down and started chatting, it was hard to get him to stop.

"I see what you're thinking," Gallo said. "I have this knack that we call the art of reading faces. You're thinking, *Me. I, Andy, live by what I believe in.*

"And you know what? I think that's so. I believe you, Andy. And I respect that. I respect it in a cop. I respect it in any man.

"But you know what, Andy? I have to tell you that whatever passes between us is going to be bullshit. Come here and see me all you like, talk about whatever's on your mind, it's all going to be bullshit. Not because I'm lying to you, because I'm not.

"It's going to be bullshit because I have this certain sense of how things are, this code if you want to use that word, and you believe my code is bullshit. You also have your sense of how things are, this high-minded crap about the law and the good of society, and I happen to believe that that is bullshit.

"Maybe you're right to think that my way is bullshit, and maybe I'm right to think that your way is bullshit.

"But lemme ask you this, Andy. What if we're both right? What then, Andy?"

CHAPTER 13

AFTER THE HEAT, grit, noise, and hostility of Fifth Avenue in the middle of a summer business day, the cool and spacious lobby of the Hotel Pierre seemed a haven of tranquillity. The lighting was soft; feet scudded effortlessly over polished marble floors. Everyone smiled graciously. Here and there wing chairs and settees, discreetly spaced, were arranged in cozy conversational groupings.

Since Joe O'Brien was in the company of the well-known and esteemed Mr. Perdue, no one looked askance at his stained jacket and ruined trousers. *This is really what money buys you in New York,* the agent thought as he followed the poultry magnate to a pair of chairs. *A little peace and quiet. Some relief from the irritation. A break from the bad manners.*

But for all the serene elegance of the setting, Frank Perdue was in a lousy humor. "Okay," he said, looking at his watch. "Here we are. Let's please try to do this quickly."

"Fine," said O'Brien, crossing his legs to hide as much of the relish stain as possible. "Let's start with the first time you met Paul Castellano, Sr."

"What makes you think I've met him?"

"Haven't you?"

"Well, yes, as a matter of fact I have. In public. Broad daylight. At a food trade show in the early seventies. He was with his son, Paul junior, and they said they'd like to distribute chickens for me in New York."

"And what did you say?" asked O'Brien.

"I told them I appreciated their interest, but I didn't have enough product to go around. Everyone wanted my birds, and I just couldn't produce enough."

"How did they take the refusal?"

"I don't think they were happy," said Perdue. "But they were gentlemen about it."

"Did you know at the time about the Castellanos' Mob connections?"

"I'd heard some things. But that's nothing new. We hear a lot of things, some of them just malicious gossip. Look, everyone knows the industry is filthy. Payoffs. Pressures. I was in the luxurious position of having so much demand that I could pick and choose who I did business with. If I had the slightest qualm, I could say no."

"But you *did* start doing business with Dial."

Perdue shifted in his seat and grabbed a few pecans from a bowl on the table next to him. "That was 'seventy-six. My production was up. In the meantime, I did some checking around. Other reputable people were selling to them. Joe and Paul junior seemed like honest, hardworking guys. They paid their bills."

"It didn't have anything to do with the problems you were having getting your chickens promoted in the Waldbaum's and Key Food chains?"

"Look," said Perdue. "Business is business. If you're asking me, was there coercion, were there threats, the answer is absolutely not."

"Okay," O'Brien said, "let's move on to the second time you met Paul Castellano, Sr."

Perdue blinked his pale eyes and turned his head on his stalk of a neck. "You're going to have to tell *me* about that one," he said.

"Westchester Premiere Theater," said O'Brien. "Nineteen seventy-six. At a performance by Frank Sinatra and Dean Martin."

Perdue knitted his brows. "No. I didn't meet him there. I was there as the guest of Paul junior."

"You were the guest of the son, and you didn't so much as say hello to the father?"

"That's right. It's a big place."

"Or to the father's friends? Carlo Gambino? Jimmy "the Weasel" Fratianno? Salvatore Spatola? Gregory DePalma?"

"That's right."

"How about Frank? Did he introduce you to Sinatra?"

"Yes."

"Does Sinatra like chicken?"

"Look, O'Brien, I don't know what Sinatra likes or doesn't like. To tell you the truth, I don't really remember if I was actually introduced to Sinatra or if I just stood there while he held court. Who cares? I don't give a damn about celebrities."

"How about Irving Stern? You give a damn about Irving Stern?"

Perdue winced at the mention of the name. In 1981, the international vice president of the United Food and Commercial Workers Union was making his life miserable. Organizers had been agitating at Perdue's huge nonunion processing plant at Accomac, Virginia. In support of the unionization effort, and in retaliation for Perdue's alleged unfair labor practices, Stern had called for a boycott of his chickens. For two weeks in early 1981, pickets had marched under Joe O'Brien's office window, in front of Frank Perdue's Queens restaurant. Gleefully, the union did all it could to publicize a Justice Department investigation into possible restraint of trade on Perdue's part. Pickets also distributed leaflets listing various violations registered against his company by the Department of Agriculture. The Dial Poultry connection notwithstanding, Key Foods and several other chains were bowing to union pressure by refusing to mention Perdue chickens in their advertising and sale circulars.

"I have no choice but to give a damn about Irving Stern," said Perdue.

"Do you know him personally?"

"I've spoken with him a couple of times."

"What does he want? Has he asked for a payoff?"

"He hasn't asked and I haven't offered. He wants me to hand over my workers."

"And you don't want to?"

It was not a question that needed answering, and Frank Perdue just stared at Joe O'Brien.

"Have you spoken to Paul Castellano about your union difficulties?"

Perdue hesitated, perhaps gauging how much Joe O'Brien already knew and wondering how he knew it. "Yes," he said. "I've called him."

"How'd you get the number?"

"From Paul junior."

"And?"

"And what?"

"What did you ask him? What did he say?"

"I asked if he could help get the union off my back. He said he doubted he could do anything in Virginia. It was pretty far away. In New York, maybe."

"What did you think he could do?"

"I have no idea."

"I think maybe you do."

"I don't."

"Did he want money for this help?"

"No," said Perdue. "Money was never mentioned. I was asking as a favor, and I felt it wasn't out of line to ask, because of the business relationship with Dial."

"So what did Castellano do for you?"

Perdue shrugged. "Some of the problems went away. Some didn't. It's not like Castellano calls you on the phone and says he did A, B, and C for you. If he helped, I don't know about it."

"But, Mr. Perdue," said Joe O'Brien, "what made you think that Paul Castellano might be able to help in the first place?"

For the first time in the conversation, the chicken magnate looked slightly at a loss. Was this some sort of trick question? If not, why ask it, since the answer was so obvious?

"Why," said Perdue, giving forth a somewhat nervous cackle, "because he's the Godfather."

Several days later, on September 2, 1981, Frank Perdue voluntarily appeared at the FBI office on Queens Boulevard, to review, in the presence of a second agent, Joe O'Brien's written report of their conversation at the Hotel Pierre. At this meeting, the businessman confirmed, expanded, and in some cases modified his earlier comments.

He reiterated that he had never made a payoff to get his chickens into New York stores, claiming that his advertising had created great consumer demand which had "pulled" them into the market; they didn't need to be "pushed" into the market. He stressed again that his dealings with Dial Poultry were voluntary and mutually satisfactory. He emphasized that he did not intend to say anything that would jeopardize his relationship with any of his distributors.

On the subject of having contacted Paul Castellano, Sr., in regard to his labor problems, Perdue altered his earlier remarks. Rather than claiming to have spoken to Castellano once, by phone, he now acknowledged having met with him twice, in person. He would not divulge the times or locations of those meetings, beyond saying that they had taken place within the last twelve months.

"I probably shouldn't have told you so much," he said. "I should probably have talked to my attorneys before coming here."

Joe O'Brien advised Perdue that he was free to contact an attorney at any time, and offered him use of the phone. Perdue neither called a lawyer nor moved to terminate the interview.

When the agents pressed for more information about Perdue's meetings with Castellano and his expectations about what the Godfather could do for him, the chicken magnate said, "Look, I'll lie to you if I have to, Joe, to protect my business, but I hope I won't have to."

"There's no reason for you to lie," said O'Brien.

"And if you put me before a jury," Frank Perdue continued, "I'll forget everything."

CHAPTER 14

I JUST LOVE THIS," said Bruce Mouw, biting down on the stem of his pipe and indulging in one of his spiritually pained little winces. "We got geriatric Mafiosi sharing with us their philosophies of life. We got leading businessmen saying they'll cooperate with us, as long as it doesn't jeopardize their Mob connections. And what do we got on Paul Castellano? We got a file that keeps getting fatter, and we got just about nothing we can use."

He dropped Castellano's dossier on his desk. It made a louder slap than it used to make before Operation Meathead and the RH stratagem had been put into effect, but it still lacked the heft that would be required to put Castellano away. The Boss was still secure, still free to loiter in his bathrobe, play bocce in his carefully landscaped backyard, frolic with his maid. The Mercs and the Cadillacs still clustered in his driveway, rackets money still flowed unabated into his meaty hands. For almost two years, Big Paul had been a prime FBI target, and there was no compelling proof that all the Bureau's efforts had as yet cost him so much as a bad night's sleep.

Andy Kurins searched for something to say that might cheer up his supervisor—or, for that matter, himself. "We could go out and arrest fifteen, twenty guys tomorrow."

"Yeah, we could," acknowledged Mouw. "But we don't want the coffee pickers. We want El Exigente."

Desperate men launch desperate schemes, and desperate schemes, to mask their desperation, are often introduced in jest. Joe O'Brien was looking out the dirty sixth-floor windows, through the grime that held the mix of dusk and neon in an ugly sulfurous smear. "Well, hell," he said, "I guess we're just gonna have to bug his house."

Mouw made little popping sounds around his unlit pipe. "Right," he said. "And after that, we'll bug the Kremlin."

But Andy Kurins and Joe O'Brien were holding each other's eyes. They had gotten to know each other pretty well. They were starting to think alike, finish each other's sentences. And they both realized in that moment that they had stumbled upon the way to go.

PART 2

THOUGH IT WOULD have pained him greatly had he realized it, Tommy Agro, in 1981, had done the FBI a tremendous
favor. He did this favor with a baseball bat, beating a former
partner in the loan shark and extortion business so badly that the
victim became disenchanted with Mob life and decided to cooperate with authorities.

The former partner's name was Joseph Iannuzzi, nicknamed
"Joe Dogs" because of his abiding passion for the greyhound races.
Iannuzzi's shylocking and strong-arm activities were centered in
West Palm Beach, Florida. He had been an associate of Agro's for
years, trading Gambino family protection and sometimes capital
for a cut of his action in the Sunshine State. But Iannuzzi had
problems of his own. He gambled. He didn't run his operation as
tightly as New York custom demanded. By early '81, he was no-
tably behind in his interest payments, and Agro decided to pay him
a visit.

Iannuzzi was summoned to a Mob hangout called Don Ritz's
Pizzeria, on Singer Island. He didn't expect the meeting to be
pleasant; discussing money owed never is. But neither did he expect to be jumped from behind by two thugs with lead pipes who
pummeled his back and arms, softening him up for the frontal
attack by the manic Mr. A., with his manicured hands, his expensive toupee, and his Louisville Slugger. Iannuzzi's ribs were broken, his nose smashed, his spleen ruptured. The punishment ceased
only when Ritz's wife wandered in, saw blood flowing out of the
twitching body on the floor, and started screaming.

Some months later, after Iannuzzi had begun wearing a government microphone, Agro, ever the gracious winner, would say
to him: "You're only alive, my friend, because that broad walked

in. You weren't supposed to walk away. I was making an example out of you for any motherfucker who tries to cross me."

Several far-reaching cases were developed with the help of Joseph Iannuzzi, who became the central figure in an FBI investigation code-named Home Run, in honor of Agro's level and authoritative swing. Tommy A. himself, at one of four Home Run trials held in Florida in 1984 and 1985, would be convicted of loan-sharking, extortion, and attempted murder, and sentenced to fifteen years in prison.

But Agro, the brutal little man with his pockets full of prescription bottles, was small potatoes. More significant by far were the complicated strands of connection that ran outward and upward from him, and which would be revealed through Iannuzzi. The Home Run investigation, directly or indirectly, would accomplish several things. It would link Agro to Joe N. Gallo, the suave *consigliere* who had been inaccessible to prosecution for four decades, and would lead to his arrest in 1986. It would uncover the existence of a Mafia mole within the offices of the United States District Court for the Southern District of New York—a woman who tipped off mobsters to sealed indictments so that they might flee. Further, Agro's legal problems, and his lunatic way of dealing with them, would necessitate a sit-down—monitored by the FBI— between underboss Joe Armone and Paul Castellano himself; their discussion of Tommy A. would implicate them both in his crimes.

Even Castellano's death, if one accepts certain premises, was connected to Agro's beating of Iannuzzi. Consider: Castellano was murdered because he was facing a heavy prison term and had compromised Mob security. Both these things resulted from the bugging of his house. The bugging of his house, in turn, could not have been accomplished unless the FBI was already familiar with the interior of the Castellano mansion. And it was a subpoena involving Tommy Agro—that, and some unwitting assistance from Paul's own wife and daughter—that first allowed law enforcement officers to get beyond the Godfather's threshold.

CHAPTER 16

THE OLD, dark green government Plymouth had dented fenders, some rust around the side-view mirrors, and leaked either oil, transmission fluid, or both. Parked in Paul Castellano's horseshoe driveway, it made an inelegant contrast to the immaculately polished luxury sedans usually found there.

"D'ya bring the subpoena?" Joe O'Brien asked his partner for that day, Special Agent Walter Ticano. Ticano, like O'Brien, was a former Foreign Counter-Intelligence man. In making the leap from spies to mobsters, they had traded the ethereal realms of high tech and microfilm for the grittier world of threats and curses. They liked it; it was more human. And, sometimes at least, you could see the results of your labor. Still, certain habits of observation carried over from the FCI days.

"Don't be cute, O'Brien," said Ticano. "You have it in your inside jacket pocket. Left side. Along with a roll of assorted Life Savers and a pack of Dentyne."

The document in question demanded Paul Castellano's presence in Florida, to give a deposition as to his relationship, if any, with one Thomas Agro. It was October 15, 1981, and O'Brien had as yet no reason to believe that Agro's problems would reach far enough up the line of command to seriously affect the Boss. Still, he was most pleased to be serving the subpoena. It would give him another chance to study Castellano. Big Paul knew who Joe O'Brien was by now. He'd been receiving his Hallmark cards. He'd been hearing about the street activities of the Wreak Havoc stratagem. It would be interesting to see how the Boss's composure and good manners were holding up, now that Joe O'Brien had been—to use the playground term—getting in his face.

The two agents climbed the stairs and stood between the

stately pillars of Castellano's portico. They took in the view of the bridge and the surprisingly graceful Brooklyn shoreline. Then O'Brien rang the doorbell, enduring the gaze of the security cameras, waiting for the screening voice of a household servant through the intercom.

But the intercom stayed silent, and after a moment Nina Castellano opened the door herself. "Yes?"

By reflex, Joe O'Brien reached for his FBI credentials, but the wife of the Godfather waved away this formality. "I know who you are. What is it you want?"

Mrs. Castellano was a sturdy-looking woman, by no means glamorous but with a quiet poise and dignity of demeanor that suggested what a handsome and even imposing *bella donna* she must have been when Paul Castellano fell in love with her, almost fifty years before. Her posture, even in her late sixties, was wonderful. She had thick hair that was still dark, brushed simply back from a high, smooth forehead. She showed her age only in her eyes, which were somewhat hooded behind her glasses, and at the edges of her mouth, which were crisscrossed with tense lines, as if from too many years of pressing her lips together when there was something she was yearning to say.

"We'd like to see your husband," O'Brien said.

"He isn't here," said Nina Castellano, in a voice so perfectly neutral that it was impossible to tell if she was speaking the truth or lying, or if her husband was out for an hour, a week, or forever.

Mafia wives are almost always enigmatic, but the former Nina Manno, for all her grandmotherly calm, seemed more mysterious than most. What did she get from her liaison with the Godfather? A beautiful home, which was certainly more than most Mafia wives got. Mafiosi generally stayed in their old neighborhoods, parking their spouses in tenement apartments or, at best, forlorn side-by-side duplexes filled with garish furniture, too many televisions, ashtrays from Las Vegas, and terrifying reminders of the Crucifixion. Nina Castellano seemed unusually fortunate to have her grand house on Todt Hill—though of course, she wasn't really so fortunate at all. The mobsters with the crummy apartments at least kept their mistresses elsewhere, in the neighborhoods where they showed off and spent their money; Paul C., rather in the manner of a sultan, kept on the premises an alternate wife who was gradually elbowing out the lawfully wedded one.

"Do you know when he'll be back?" asked Wally Ticano.

"I don't think soon," said Nina Castellano.

Joe O'Brien looked at her patient face and tried to imagine why proud and presumably religious women got involved with Mafiosi to begin with. If the reason was some perverse excitement about being part of a criminal enterprise, they were surely disappointed, since Mob protocol strictly excluded wives from knowing the details of their husbands' business, let alone participating. No, the women were supposed to stay home, cook the red sauce, wait out the jail terms, and keep their mouths shut. So where was the payoff, where was the attraction? Could they just not conceive of any other life? Could they pretend they didn't know their husbands were thieves and murderers? Was it too much like a soap opera to think maybe they just fell in love, and then were trapped in whatever sort of farce or tragedy took off from there?

"No offense, Mrs. Castellano," said O'Brien, "but I hope your husband isn't ducking us."

"I can tell you he's not," she said. Then, for just an instant, a look of discomfort or perhaps embarrassment crossed her face. "My husband wouldn't do that."

Partly, maybe mainly, Joe O'Brien reasoned, honest women married mobsters as a way of giving their children a better life. Recent immigrants, after all, usually started poor and saw obstacles everywhere. Language. Prejudice. Tight, exclusive networks of better-established groups. Maybe one generation of violence and mortal risk seemed like an acceptable price for a long future of safety and respectability. That seemed to be the deal these women cut with their own morality. Usually, Mafia wives had what amounted to a prenuptial agreement guaranteeing that their children would be given quality educations and kept away from Mob associations.

Problem was, it usually didn't turn out that way. Criminality couldn't be so easily sloughed off in a single generation; you couldn't slip out of guilt as if it were a suit of clothes. More often than not, mobsters' kids found ways of screwing up. They got kicked out of one prep school too many—for drugs, fighting, or just not doing any work. They were accepted—perhaps with the help of a large donation—to top-tier colleges, only to drop out again. They made disastrous marriages that kept them mired in the sleazier precincts of life. And you didn't have to be a shrink to see that the kids' failures had a lot to do with spiting the parents, or with the fear of leaving them too far behind, coming to despise them too much.

"You know, Mrs. Castellano," Wally Ticano pressed, "some of your husband's friends made a kind of game of avoiding us. It's very unbecoming, and it doesn't change anything in the long run."

"What my husband's friends do is no concern of mine," she retorted. "Don't bother me about my husband's friends."

She said this not in anger but with a kind of bitter weariness in her voice, and Joe O'Brien felt that the bitterness was directed not at him and Ticano but rather at the whole web of associations that had dictated the shape of her own life, and the lives of her children. Paul Castellano used to brag that not only was he a millionaire many times over but he had made millionaires of each of his kids. This, while true, seemed to be thoroughly beside the point, as far as Nina Castellano was concerned. She wanted her children to become something fine. She wanted to see them graduate from college, use good grammar, have diplomas on office walls, run charities, go to yacht clubs. These things they would never do.

Of the three Castellano sons, only Paul junior had even started college. Unable to handle the academic and social pressures, he dropped out after one semester. Along with his brother Joe, he was then given his father's original business—Blue Ribbon Meats, which eventually blossomed into Dial Poultry. The youngest son, Philip, was also set up in a business of his own—Scara-Mix, a company that made cement on Staten Island. Cement? Without question it was a profitable enterprise, but if the intention was to break away from the taint of gangsterhood into the clear bright sunshine of legitimate capitalism, the cement business in New York City was a dubious way to go.

Just as the paths of the Castellano sons underscored the difficulty of truly flying free of a Mob nest, the fate of the only daughter, Connie, showed how uncharmed the life of a Mafia Princess can be. Tall, lean, pretty, and very rich, Connie Castellano should have had her pick of available young men. Yet when it came to selecting a first husband, she ended up with a small-time thug and occasional hijacker named Frank Amato, who was employed as a butcher at Dial Poultry. A worse match could hardly be imagined. Not only was Amato a flake and a nobody, he was a liar, philanderer, and bully. He also, apparently, had a serious death wish, which he implemented quite cleverly by beating up on the daughter of the Godfather. Some time after the couple divorced, in 1973, Frank Amato disappeared, and the former son-in-law of the Boss of Bosses has not been seen or heard from since.

When Connie Castellano remarried, it was to Joe Catalonotti, a man her father set up in the construction business. Paul also built his daughter a house directly across the street from his own. Connie overlooked her father's swimming pool and bocce courts. He, in turn, overlooked every detail of his daughter's life, making sure she wouldn't get into trouble again, making sure, as well, that she would never really have an adult existence of her own.

"Well," said Joe O'Brien, "I guess we'll just wait here till your husband returns."

Nina Castellano shrugged. She was accustomed to seeing people waste their time, do crazy things for crazy reasons, or for no reason at all. If the two FBI men wanted to waste a perfectly nice fall day waiting in a driveway for a man who wasn't coming home, it was all the same to her. She went back into the house.

O'Brien and Ticano descended the stairs and leaned against their beat-up car. The fluid it was leaking had slithered out from under and was running in a viscous stream toward Paul Castellano's perfect lawn.

"Nice old lady," said Wally Ticano. "And tough."

"Very nice," said Joe O'Brien. "Very tough."

CHAPTER 17

ONLY THE LUCKIEST and most diplomatically gifted Mob leaders enjoy the luxury of dying in bed. One of those who did was Carlo Gambino, and a central reason he was able to leave this world serenely was the tact and astuteness he had shown in the matter of family succession. Not that Gambino ended his days with his house perfectly in order—far from it. He had bought peace in his own lifetime at the cost of a factionalism that would later haunt his cousin Paul.

Born with the century, Gambino in the last year of his life— 1976—was physically wasted but mentally acute. Flesh had fallen from his small frame and his long face, leaving him a visage that was all wrinkles, big ears, red-rimmed, droopy eyes, and banana nose. Gambino has been described as resembling a fruit peddler, and the characterization is apt. One could imagine the old man in front of a cartful of apples, bending down slowly, painfully, to hand a Golden Delicious to a little girl while pinching her cheek and inquiring about her behavior at school.

To look at Cousin Carlo, one would never guess at the quiet yet untiring ruthlessness that had kept him on top for so long. Gambino managed by process of elimination. Anyone who challenged his leadership or, for that matter, simply brought unwelcome publicity to Mafia affairs was eliminated. Joe Colombo, who had made the Mafia a media event and was becoming both a star and an ever-greater embarrassment, was shot in the head and ended up in a coma. "Crazy Joey" Gallo (no relation to Joe N.) made a mockery of Mob decorum by stealing fifty thousand dollars from the safe at Ferrara's pastry shop in Little Italy, and was promptly mowed down at Umbertos Clam House, just up the street.

And all the while, smiling, soft-spoken Cousin Carlo carried on. How was he able to do it? Why did the other Bosses allow it? The answer would seem to be that Gambino was thoroughly reasonable, even statesmanlike, in his violence. His targets were the right targets, as far as maintaining order and efficiency within New York's crime families was concerned. Gambino did not strike out of pettiness or temper or spite. He built consensus. He had a vision.

That vision was very much in evidence in Cousin Carlo's deathbed choice of Paul Castellano as his successor.

Castellano, it should be understood, was by no means a sure bet to inherit the Boss's job. He did not yet have a big title within the family, and as far as blood bonds went, there were closer relatives available—among them, Carlo's own son Tommy.

But the smart money seemed to be on family underboss Aniello Dellacroce—known also as Neil, Mr. Neil, Mr. O'Neill, the Tall Guy, and, for some reason, the Polack. Dellacroce had served the family long and well. His tenure went back to the trigger-happy days of Albert Anastasia, and Dellacroce's cooperation had been a key element in keeping the intrafamily peace when Carlo Gambino first took power. Moreover, it was no secret that Dellacroce commanded the personal loyalties of probably the largest and toughest street crew in the entire Mob—the crew later inherited by John Gotti. If the question of succession came down to war, Mr. Neil would win, the Castellano faction would lose, there would be much blood in the streets, and much revenue would be lost. Other families would seize the opportunity to muscle in on Gambino strongholds, and Cousin Carlo's painstakingly assembled empire would be torn to shreds.

Gambino himself, in perhaps the only major strategic error he ever committed as Godfather, had laid the foundation for this possible calamity. He had allowed his carefully built crime machine to develop a seam that ran right down the middle of it. Like King Lear, he had in essence divided his holdings while he was still alive.

Dellacroce, the cigar-chomping, pug-faced, thick-necked, old-time mobster, handled the old-time rackets of loan-sharking and extortion; he also seemed to have no qualms about heavy involvement in the narcotics business. Gambino gave his underboss virtual independence in these matters, partly to keep him rich and friendly, but also to keep him away from the *other* side of the enterprise—the side that seemed to represent the Mob's growth sector.

Infiltration of legitimate businesses, control of unions and industry associations, money laundering—this, Gambino realized, was the next phase of Mafia evolution. It called for sophistication rather than—no, in addition to—intimidation, and Cousin Carlo wanted his own favored faction to inherit this brave new world.

Aniello Dellacroce, then, was in the same situation that not infrequently befalls the number-two guy in legitimate corporations. He seemed to be next in line for the corner office, yet he was fated never to get there, because he represented the organization's past rather than its future.

Still, it would have been very difficult for Carlo Gambino to pass over Mr. Neil were it not for the fortunate circumstance that, as Gambino lay dying, Dellacroce was in prison—serving a five-year stint for not paying taxes on $123,000 worth of stock he'd been given in a labor shakedown. Mr. Neil's incarceration armed Cousin Carlo with two persuasive arguments. First, Dellacroce was too well known to law enforcement agencies; the cops were onto his scent, and he was likely to be under constant and irritating scrutiny in the future. Castellano, on the other hand, had kept his nose clean and was all but unknown to the authorities. Besides, whatever happened in the longer term, the family needed an acting boss, and Mr. Neil was otherwise engaged.

So Big Paul was it. Beginning his tenure with Gambino still alive, he had the inestimable benefits of the old man's clear approval and reflected prestige. He quickly won the acceptance of the other New York family Bosses, at least one of whom—Funzie Tieri of the Genovese clan—was quite vocal in his relief at not having the blustery Dellacroce on the ruling Commission. By 1977, Paul was a figure to be reckoned with nationally; when a territorial dispute developed between the New York and Los Angeles Mobs, it was Castellano who sat down with then–Los Angeles acting

Boss (and later FBI informant) Jimmy "the Weasel" Fratianno.

But it would have been an inexcusable breach of Mob etiquette to officially anoint Castellano without the blessing of Dellacroce. Such an insult would practically have forced the underboss to stage a coup, merely for the purpose of saving face. So Castellano's actual "confirmation hearing" had to wait until November 24, 1976, by which time the elder man had been paroled. Associating with mobsters, of course, was strictly prohibited under the terms of Dellacroce's release, and his mere presence at the meeting would have been enough to return him to the slammer for an additional five years. Nonetheless, Mr. Neil was pleased to attend.

The meeting was held on a quiet, tree-lined street in Bensonhurst, at the home of Gambino *capo* Anthony Gaggi. In attendance were *consigliere* Joe N. Gallo, acting underboss Jimmy Failla, and several other *capos* who comprised the Gambino executive committee.

Present, too, though discreetly hidden from the other guests, was a nephew of Gaggi's named Dominick Montiglio. Montiglio was an ex–Green Beret and an expert marksman. Unlike thousands of other Vietnam vets, who wanted nothing more than to banish the memories of the horrors they had seen, Montiglio seemed to view his wartime experience as valuable job training. He'd loved it over there. He'd kept his skills sharp and his reflexes combat-ready.

On the evening of Paul Castellano's coronation, Montiglio's uncle Anthony handed him an automatic rifle and secreted him in an attic window with a clear view of the street. Gaggi himself used gray duct tape to affix a handgun to the underside of the kitchen table around which the meeting would be held. The host's instructions to his nephew were simple: "Listen. If you don't hear nothin', don't do nothin'. If you hear shots, kill anyone who runs out the front door." Gaggi had advised his own faction to exit, in case of trouble, by the back door.

Montiglio smiled and went to his post.

But the meeting that night went smoothly, as informants would later reveal. The assembled delegates nibbled roasted peppers and pecorino cheese. They poured Valpolicella and toasted the memory of Carlo Gambino. Aniello Dellacroce boasted about what a soft hitch he'd been able to buy for himself in prison. Paul Castellano, who had learned the wisdom of modesty from his cousin Carlo, let his adversary make the noise and get the laughs. Castellano knew that the most powerful man was the man who needed to say the least. Neil's carrying on, his slapping of backs— it had a certain gruff charm, but it did not speak of power. True power resided in the lift of the eyebrow, the barely discernible nod of the head. If Dellacroce wanted to play the emcee, fine—that only showed the relative weakness of his position.

When Castellano did address the gathering, he had nothing but praise and reassurance for Mr. Neil. "Nobody knows the streets like you. Nobody can do your job of holding things together. So here's what I'm suggesting. Anything you had with Carlo, you keep. Anything more you want, we talk."

Dellacroce accepted the proposal, though his reasons for doing so have remained in the realm of conjecture. Perhaps he felt he would make as much money with fewer headaches in the number-two position. Perhaps, just recently out of jail, he didn't have the stomach for a fight. Perhaps he relished the leverage of being an ostensible ally who still needed to be feared. Perhaps—who knows—he simply respected Gambino's deathbed wish.

Still, however the pill was sweetened up, the fact remained that Aniello Dellacroce had been slighted, passed over, and the peace he made with Big Paul was never really more than an armed truce. Egos aside, another huge issue divided the two men. That issue was narcotics, and while it was too explosive a subject to be discussed at the Bensonhurst meeting, it would smolder throughout Paul Castellano's tenure.

This, then, was the lingering curse that came with leadership of Carlo Gambino's divided kingdom. Alongside the faction that might be thought of as the modernizers, there was the more blatantly thuggish faction that had grown powerful on broken knees and very rich on drugs, and wasn't about to give up those time-honored practices just because some new Boss had a different idea about how the crime business should be run. Everything being relative, Big Paul Castellano, former butcher with an eighth-grade education, was effete. His schemes were too abstract. They involved bookkeeping, sometimes even Wall Street. And some of his scruples seemed hypocritical if not bizarre.

So the balance within the Gambino family was not likely to be a stable one. The wing represented by Cousin Carlo and Big Paul seemed doomed to alternate in power with the wing personified by Albert Anastasia, Aniello Dellacroce, and one of Mr. Neil's most impatient and assertive boys, John Gotti.

That evening in Bensonhurst was Paul Castellano's moment, make no mistake. But even though the Green Beret in the attic saw no action that night, the stage was already set for later violence.

CHAPTER 18

THERE WAS SOMETHING about doing nothing that made Joe O'Brien hungry. He sat in the beat-up government car parked in Paul Castellano's driveway, and he began to think of rare roast beef. He thought of Russian dressing. He thought of poppy seeds tumbling off the crown of a crisp roll. Around noon, he flipped a coin. Wally Ticano lost the toss and went for sandwiches. O'Brien sat on the Godfather's front steps and read the *New York Times*.

By midafternoon, nothing whatsoever had happened. The newspaper had been read. It was too early to eat again. There was no sign of Big Paul. O'Brien and Ticano had relived their glory moments in sports, talked about the trouble they got into at school, bragged about their kids. Stakeouts were boring.

Then two women emerged from a side door of the Castellano house, a door near the garage. They were wearing dowdy jackets and flat shoes. One of them had on a kerchief and carried a plastic shopping bag with big blue flowers stamped on it.

"The maids," said Joe O'Brien. "I'm going after them."

He waited until they were well out of sight of the house, having headed down the steep slope of Benedict Road; then he followed on foot. As the road wound down from the summit of Todt Hill the homes became less grand, the ambience more middle-class. O'Brien caught up with the two women on a street corner flanked by small brick houses whose yards featured scraggly rhododendrons and plaster birdbaths. Standing there, the maids themselves seemed somehow birdlike—small, frail outsiders foraging for food and shelter in a country full of mysteries and dangers.

"Excuse me," said the agent, presenting his credentials. "I'm Joe O'Brien from the FBI."

"Excuse me," said the maid without the kerchief. "I'm Gloria Olarte from Bogotá, Colombia."

There was nothing meek or frail about her voice and manner, and in spite of her imperfect English, there was both wit and challenge in her reply. A natural mimic, she had the knack of picking up on people's speech patterns and rhythms and throwing them right back. This could be hilarious. It could also be infuriating.

"And who's your friend?" O'Brien asked.

"Her name ees María Eugenia Estrada. Also from Bogotá. Also legal immigrant. You can check. No problem. But her Eengleesh ees no so good like mine."

The maid with the kerchief and the plastic shopping bag smiled weakly and executed a small and awkward curtsy.

"And your employer—you know who he is?"

"He's Meester Paul."

"Right. And you know what he does for a living?"

"He's beeznessman. Berry beeg beeznessman."

"Yes, but do you know what sort of business?"

"Talking beezness," said Gloria Olarte.

"Talking business?"

"Yes. Always talking beezness. Always people coming to talk."

"Who comes, Gloria? What do they talk about?"

The Colombian maid fell silent and stared down at her flat shoes. She certainly did not look the part of the femme fatale. She was thin and rather shapeless. She had coarse dark hair, cut short and arranged in no particular style. Her black eyebrows nearly met in the middle, and there was a hint of shadow on her upper lip. Her nose was slightly bulbous. Only the eyes could be called beautiful—very wide-spaced, intensely brown, as alert as those of a forest animal.

"I don't talk to you now," she said. "We must go chopping for Meesus Nina. She be berry mad weeth us eef we take too long. Goodbye, Meester Joe."

And she started walking, with María Eugenia Estrada right alongside.

"Wait, Gloria," said O'Brien, reaching in his wallet for a business card. "Will you call me on your day off? We'll have coffee."

The maid took the card and studied it. "Who pays for these?" she asked. "You or the payers of the taxes? I bet the payers of the taxes, eh? You geeve away a lot of them. Meester Paul, he has three, four, five."

"Well, Gloria," said O'Brien, "now you have one of your own. Will you call?"

"I theenk about eet."

"Oh, and Gloria, don't tell Mr. or Mrs. Castellano that we talked. I don't think they would like it."

"Hokay," said Gloria Olarte, and she continued down Benedict Road, swaying her hips just slightly.

CHAPTER 19

THREE QUARTERS OF AN HOUR LATER, O'Brien was back in the passenger seat of the government car, shooting the breeze with Ticano, when the two maids, each laden with big bags of groceries, reentered the house by the servants' door.

Shortly thereafter, Nina Castellano appeared at the main entrance. She seemed agitated, and she was waving something in her right hand.

It was Joe O'Brien's business card.

She descended the broad stairs and approached the rusted Plymouth. "Mr. O'Brien," she began.

"Joe."

"Joe, then," she said, standing close to his elbow, which rested on the window frame. "I don't appreciate you upsetting my maids. They're poor girls. They're foreign. They're ignorant. And they couldn't possibly be of any help to the FBI."

"Then why do you care if I talk to them?"

The question threw Nina Castellano, though only for an instant. "Because . . . because what if they get frightened and quit? Then I have to worry about new maids. And think about them! Listen, Joe, we took these girls out of a hovel in South America. Off a dirt farm. They ate weeds. We gave them a nice place to live. Steady work. Dignity. You bother them, you scare them, all that goes right down the drain."

O'Brien hesitated, weighing his response. Later, when he'd learned about the true dynamics of the Castellano household, he'd be both impressed and baffled by Nina's performance. Did Mafia wives have their own ultrastringent and slightly bizarre codes of behavior? Who was she really protecting? Was it conceivable that she was trying to shield her husband from the annoyance of having an upset mistress? Or was she acting out of pride, clinging to the appearance that she was still in charge? O'Brien decided to steer toward a different subject rather than argue.

"Listen, Mrs. Castellano, I wouldn't need to do this kind of thing if we had more cooperation from your husband."

This, of course, was an absurd concept. *Cooperation from the Boss of Bosses!* Still, the change of focus served to deflect Nina Castellano's anger. "I don't tell my husband how to run his business," she said. "I think you know that."

"Of course," said O'Brien, in his most conciliatory tone. "And I'm sorry if I upset your maids."

A little bit of politeness went a long way with Nina Castellano. Her face softened, and her expression was almost playful as she handed O'Brien's card through the open window of the Plymouth. It was an expression one might wear while scolding a child for the sort of clever naughtiness a parent was secretly proud of. "You know," said Mrs. Castellano, "I have a son named Joe. He's tall. He doesn't talk loud. He has nice manners. You remind me of him a little."

O'Brien almost blushed at what, coming from a mother, was a lofty compliment. But still, he had to tell her. "I know your son. I've spoken to him."

Nina Castellano's face collapsed, her mouth tightening and her eyes clinching at the corners. She recoiled a step from the government car and struck a posture of defense. "Why'd you have to talk to Joe?" she snapped. "My son Joe's a good boy."

"I'm not saying he isn't," said O'Brien. "I talked to him about the meat business. About chickens."

The mother was not reassured. Her hands flew up nervously, the fingers, as if by reflex, intertwined. "I don't see why you had to talk to my son Joe."

O'Brien felt a sudden impulse to get out of the car and put his arm around the old woman's shoulders. She probably wished she were back in Brooklyn, married to the neighborhood butcher, living in a cramped apartment. No big house. No Cadillacs. No maids. Just big family meals on Sundays, and plenty of grandchildren to spoil.

"Listen, Mrs. Castellano. Try to understand. Joe isn't only your son. He's your husband's son as well."

She turned, uncomforted, and went up the stairs to the enormous house.

CHAPTER 20

WALLY TICANO let out a long, slow, whistling breath and drummed his fingers lightly on the steering wheel. "Oh, what a friend we have in Gloria Olarte," he said.

And of course, it was clear that the Colombian maid was not to be trusted. What was not clear as yet, however, was that Gloria's manipulation of Joe O'Brien was not prompted exclusively or even primarily by her loyalty to the Castellano family. No—Gloria manipulated everyone, up to and including Mr. Paul himself. Moreover, as the FBI would later learn, she could barely be held accountable for her remarkable deviousness, two-facedness, and cynicism. The poor woman was a psychological disaster.

She was born on October 18, 1949, in Sevilla, a village of four thousand people, located some two hundred miles south of the notorious drug capital, Medellín. Her family was poor, and her father was politically radical; he became embroiled in Colombia's unrelenting battles between conservatives and liberals, and enthusiastic conservatives spent a lot of time trying to hunt him down and kill him. Gloria spent much of her childhood hiding out in other people's houses, wondering if *Padre* would make it back alive from his various caves and stakeouts in the hills.

Capping this girlhood of insecurity and mistrust was an incident of particular brutality: at the age of fourteen, Gloria was raped. The episode left her in a schizoid catatonic state, physically rigid, unwilling or unable to speak, seemingly oblivious. She was institutionalized in a convent, where she spent several years sitting silently in a nearly empty room, staring at a shaft of sunlight that moved with the hours across the whitewashed walls. Nuns came and went, talking to her, praying over her, brushing her hair, and Gloria Olarte made no response.

Her mind, however, does not seem to have been idle. The abused young woman was formulating a strategy for survival in an appalling and senseless world. At the center of the strategy was an insulating selfishness that made Gloria a nation of one, an entity at war with all others. People had to be kept off balance, played off one against the other, so that Gloria might prevail. Lying was a good way to accomplish this, but there were subtler ways as well. Humor worked sometimes. Charm helped, if it had a bitter edge to it. But most effective of all was sex.

Sitting in her convent room, Gloria Olarte must have come to the precocious and perverse conclusion that the same drive that had been so cruelly used as a weapon against her could in fact become *her* weapon. Sex—men thought it made them strong, but in truth it made them weak. It made them foolish. It made them into little boys, into puppy dogs. The act itself, Gloria realized, was the least of it. There was the teasing, the withholding, the jealousy. There were the compliments, the threats, the complaints that could so easily and deeply wound. She could use all that. She wasn't beautiful, wasn't voluptuous, wasn't even stylish—but what did that matter? Appetite was blind, stupid, faceless; that much she had learned. As sex had been the vehicle of her injury, so it would be the vehicle of her general revenge against the world.

One morning at the convent, after several years of almost totally silent residence, Gloria Olarte announced that she was ready to go home. She spoke normally. She made it clear that she was perfectly aware of what was going on around her. Gloria knew she wasn't "cured"; she still had her demons and her rage. But she also knew that if she *acted* cured, she could walk out the door.

So she was released, and that provided evidence of just how easy people were to fool.

In this, of course, Gloria sold her doctors short. They knew the difference between true healing and the formation of a serviceable scar. But what could they do? They kept Gloria as an outpatient. They dosed her with those great American inventions, tranquilizers and antidepressants. Even after she went to the United States, Gloria stayed in close touch with her therapist in

Bogotá. The FBI knew this because of the extraordinary long-distance charges rung up on Paul Castellano's private line. Hundreds, sometimes thousands of dollars a month were invested in phone calls in the name of keeping the Godfather's maid and mistress just this side of emotional collapse.

The stanchions of the Verrazano-Narrows Bridge were taking on the golden glow of late afternoon, and rush hour traffic was beginning to stack up on the approaches to the tolls. Joe O'Brien shifted in his seat to uncramp his legs. He was starting to feel like he'd been wearing his suit too many hours. He itched.

Static crackled on the car radio. Then a dispatcher's voice advised that Agent Joe O'Brien was to call his supervisor immediately. Repeat: immediately.

"Wonder what's up," said Wally Ticano.

"Anything's better than nothing," said O'Brien.

He slid across the front seat of the Plymouth as Ticano slipped out and installed himself on the front steps; then he drove down Benedict Road to a pay phone. Bruce Mouw picked up on the very first ring.

"LaRossa's threatening to sue you," he said.

"LaRossa" was James LaRossa, Paul Castellano's attorney, and Mouw pronounced the name with that special snarl he reserved for high-priced Mafia mouthpieces, with their sprayed silver hair, their Hermès ties, their shirts so white they scalded the retina.

"Again?" said O'Brien. It was a standard threat. Agent gets too close to a major mobster, especially if it's near said mobster's family, and major mobster's lawyer threatens to sue for harassment. No doubt this is a great fantasy for the lawyer, who can envision running up staggering fees and also having the fun of being the plaintiff for a change. But did anyone really believe that a known Mafioso would go out of his way to take the FBI to court?

"Yup," said Mouw. "He wants me to tell you that if you don't cease and desist and all that other bullshit, he's filing."

"Fine," said O'Brien. "But you didn't tell me that, because I can't be reached. LaRossa wants to talk to me, he can come to his client's house and talk to me. I'll be in the driveway."

"How long do you intend to be there?" asked Mouw.

"Until Castellano comes home so I can serve the fucking subpoena."

"What if he doesn't come home?"

"Look, Bruce, this is a man who likes his house. He'll come home."

"You got a sleeping bag?" asked Mouw.

CHAPTER 21

IT GOT DARK. Lights came on inside the Castellano mansion and across the water in Brooklyn. On the highway far below Todt Hill, headlamps threw yellow rays at clashing angles across the pavement.

"Chinese?" said Wally Ticano.

"Doesn't work so well in the car," said Joe O'Brien. "Slides off the chopsticks. Stains."

"Italian?"

"I'm kind of sick of Italian. Aren't you?"

"You're talking about my heritage," said Ticano, pretending to be affronted.

"Bullshit," said O'Brien. "I'm talking about dried-out, lukewarm, crusty ziti in aluminum containers. I'm talking about fake veal cutlets like the nuns used to—"

Dim lights came on on the Castellano porch. The big oak door swung open, and in a triangle of brightness stood Nina Castellano and a younger woman. The younger woman was holding a pair of Doberman pinschers by their leather collars.

"Joe," said the Boss's wife, "could we talk to you a minute?"

O'Brien slid out of the battered Plymouth and gingerly climbed the steps, keeping his eyes on the dogs. They weren't growling, but they seemed more interested than the agent would have liked. They strained forward against their collars; their haunches were quivering. Their eyes, devilishly marked with bright brown against the prevailing black, were avid. Their tongues glistened; their mouths were open, showing a lot of teeth.

"They won't bother you," said the younger woman, in a voice that seemed intended to be more taunting than reassuring. "As long as I hold them."

O'Brien, planted now between the huge columns of the portico, let his eyes slide away from the dogs, and up the arm of the woman who was restraining them. She was a slender blonde with dark eyebrows, and she was wearing tight-fitting leather pants with semi-high-heeled shoes to match. Her blouse was white and rather sheer, and in the fractured light of the porch there was something structural, architectural, about the outline of her bra. "I'm Connie Catalonotti," she said. "We've just been speaking with our attorney."

She was trying to sound officious and tough, but the act was not persuasive. Dobermans or no Dobermans, leather pants or no leather pants, Paul Castellano's daughter did not come across as a strong woman. Shielded from many things, avenged for others, she had not developed her mother's stoicism.

"Oh?" said O'Brien, as if this were the first he'd ever heard of Castellano's lawyer.

"Mr. LaRossa," Connie said. "He advised us that you have no right to be here. You're trespassing. If you don't contact him immediately to explain your actions, you'll be risking a lawsuit."

"I see," said O'Brien, slipping into the hey-bear-with-me-I'm-just-a-cop tone that on certain occasions served him very well. "Hmm. Well, that sort of puts me between a rock and a hard place, because my orders are not to leave until I've served this subpoena. Do you mind if I confer with my partner about this?"

The Castellano women, mother and daughter, murmured that they did not mind. O'Brien motioned for Ticano to join him on the porch.

"Nice dogs," Ticano said. "Do they like to be petted?"

He tentatively reached out a hand. The dog opened its mouth wider.

"I wouldn't," said Connie.

"So what it comes down to, Wally," O'Brien concluded, after sketching in the situation, "is that Mr. LaRossa says we can't stay, and headquarters says we can't leave."

"Hmm," said Ticano. He picked up fast. "I guess we should speak with Mr. LaRossa."

117

"Yes," said Connie Catalonotti, the dog-free hand planted on her hip. "That's exactly what Mr. LaRossa suggested."

"Too bad there's no phone in the car," O'Brien said.

"Yeah," said Ticano. "Especially since, if we spoke to Mr. LaRossa and he agreed to accept the subpoena for Mr. Castellano, we could stop bothering these people and go home."

The Castellano women brightened at the thought.

"Hmm," said O'Brien.

"So *call Mr. LaRossa*," Nina Castellano said. She had put on a cardigan against the evening chill, and the style of it made her look older than she'd seemed that afternoon.

"Well, that's the thing," said Joe O'Brien. "We can't leave to make the call."

"*One* of you could leave," Connie suggested.

"Not after dark," said Wally Ticano. "Can't separate after dark. Regulations."

"So we're back where we started from," said O'Brien.

"Can't leave."

"Can't call."

"Gotta stay."

"Sorry."

Nina and Connie Castellano shuffled their feet. The dogs rubbed their flanks together and clicked their paws against the portico floor.

"Unless," continued Joe O'Brien, as blandly as he could, "you'd let us use your phone to make the call."

Mother and daughter looked at each other. One of the dogs whined, as if in warning; O'Brien wanted to kick it. "Excuse us a sec," said Connie, and the two women slipped into the house.

O'Brien and Ticano didn't meet each other's eyes and didn't breathe more than they had to.

The door reopened, wider this time. Connie kept one hand on the doorknob and the other on the Dobes. "Okay. You can come in," she said, "if you promise that you'll never, ever tell my father that we let you in his house."

The agents agreed, and in fact it was a promise they kept to the end of Paul Castellano's life.

The Boss's daughter led them through a cavernous entrance hall, floored in marble, hung with enormous gilt-framed mirrors. This foyer gave onto a formal living room, of the sort that usually goes unlived in. Heavy brocaded sofas with cushions fat as clouds glared at each other across a glass-topped coffee table. There were vases tall as people and statues that turned out to be lamps. You could turn an ankle in the carpeting, it was so deep. On the opposite side of the corridor was a dining room with a long mahogany table that looked like something out of the captain's cabin of a cruise ship. It probably sat twenty, and it was flanked by breakfronts full of crystal and cupboards of the same deep-grained wood, inlaid with ebony and teak.

The agents hung back half a step, strolling at a museum pace, gawking at the silver trays, the somber paintings, the spiral staircase that led up to the bedroom level, but Connie Catalonotti, pulled along by the dogs, walked briskly down the tunnel-like hallway to the kitchen. Huge and bright, with milky recessed lights and a terra-cotta tile floor, the room did nothing to dispel the notion of Italian-American culture as centering on food. Outsize freezers loomed along one wall. Across from the rank of appliances was a vast counter that small planes could have landed on; jars of olive oil gleamed warmly next to a hedgehog of a knife block. A pile of heroic steaks, red and thick as bricks, was stacked up on a butcher's slab. Beyond the counter was a large informal dining space, with a blond wood table and glass doors leading to a terrace.

Against this backdrop of prosperous domesticity, a bizarre scene was being played: Gloria Olarte, wearing a frumpy apron like a proper household servant, was preparing dinner, while Nina Castellano sat idly by, fidgeting. Joe O'Brien watched the older woman's hands; they made little dicing and chopping motions in her lap—probably she'd rather be doing the cooking herself. Connie, meanwhile, dragged the dogs across the room, to lock them away in the laundry. Whining, they hunkered down, their claws skidding and scratching over the tile floor. They cast resentful looks at the FBI men, as if promising to remember who had been the cause of their chagrin.

119

For an instant, Joe O'Brien felt that the moral ground was slipping away under his feet. Nothing was what it seemed in this house of lies. Everyone kept secrets; no one ever told a story honest and entire. The master of the house, of course, never gave a clear account of anything to anyone. What about the secrecy the daughter had exacted from Ticano and O'Brien? Wouldn't Gloria tell Paul about their visit? Wouldn't LaRossa? Did anyone really expect to get away with all this shamming that seemed to come as naturally as breath? And was there perhaps some mortal spite in the Castellano women's letting them in in the first place?

"There's the phone," said Connie, grudgingly. It hung on the wall next to a braided string of garlic. The room was silent except for the soft splutter of onions and mushrooms sautéing slowly in olive oil.

O'Brien dialed Bruce Mouw's direct line.

"Supervisor Mouw," he said, "this is Agent O'Brien."

"What's this 'supervisor' shit?" said Mouw. "Are you telling me you can't talk?"

"Yes, sir. I'm calling from the Castellano residence, sir."

"Don't yank my chain, O'Brien. It's late."

"I understand, sir. But there seems to be a problem here." And he spun out the lawsuit threat all over again.

"Jesus Christ, Joe. You're not kidding? You're in his house?"

"That's correct. We can call Mr. LaRossa from here, if you agree."

"In his *house,* Joe? You must be pissing in your pants."

"Affirmative, sir."

"Well, for Christ's sake, use your eyes. Focus. Remember. Potted plants. Hanging baskets. Fixed shelves. Sketch it when you leave."

"Then I'll contact Mr. LaRossa? Fine."

He hung up. Gloria Olarte took a break from her cooking to shoot him an accusing look; he shot it right back. Ticano leaned against the counter, his eyes flicking left and right. The dogs clawed at the louvered door of the laundry room. Nina Castellano had turned her back. Connie Catalonotti slid a piece of yellow paper with James LaRossa's number on it across the counter.

"Joe O'Brien for James LaRossa, please."

"O'Brien," said the attorney, "I want you off my client's property. You're out of line."

"I've got a subpoena to serve, Mr. LaRossa. If your client wasn't ducking me, we could all be home by now."

"He isn't ducking. He's in the hospital."

"What a coincidence," said O'Brien. "What is it this time? Shortness of breath, or chest pains?"

"It's surgery, O'Brien. Elective surgery that was planned weeks ago."

"What kind of surgery?" O'Brien pressed. He'd learned to be skeptical about the medical claims of mobsters under pressure. Their physicians were not always above strategic misrepresentations.

"I don't have to tell you that," said LaRossa, "and I'm not going to."

"Then tell me this: When can he travel? Because surgery or no surgery, we want him in Florida."

LaRossa yawned in O'Brien's ear. "Look, you tell the U.S. Attorney that if it's worth the government's time and money to force my client to fly to Florida just to invoke the Fifth Amendment, he should call me. Now, will you leave the property, or shall we initiate proceedings?"

"Will you accept the subpoena?"

"You know I will."

"Ice the champagne, then. We'll be there soon."

He hung up the phone. No one spoke. Connie Catalonotti put her hands on the hips of her leather pants, in a gesture that was apparently meant to be defiant but came off as merely petulant. Just then Gloria Olarte picked up an enormous sirloin and dropped it into the hot oil. It sizzled like a soul in hell.

"Sorry we can't stay for dinner," said Wally Ticano, gesturing across the gigantic counter at the blond wood table. At the head of it was a chair with a higher back than all the others, and a tall chrome lamp that threw a diffuse light into the corner of the room. "We've still got these papers to serve."

Nina Castellano looked drawn and worried now, aware, perhaps, that she had made a big mistake, or maybe had acted on a masked vengeful impulse for which she would find it difficult to forgive herself. But she mustered her dignity for one final flex of her power as the mistress of the house.

"Gloria," she said in a firm, commanding voice, "show these gentlemen to the door."

CHAPTER 22

TWO DAYS LATER, a one-page medical document, forwarded by the U.S. Attorney's Office in Tampa, landed on Joe O'Brien's desk. The document confirmed that Paul Castellano had in fact been hospitalized for elective surgery. The procedure he'd undergone was known as a penile implant.

"Penile implant?" said Andy Kurins. "What the hell is that?"

"Beats me," said O'Brien, "but it doesn't sound pleasant. Maybe the guy can't take a leak or something."

As a bit of research revealed, however, the operation elected by the Godfather concerned not the excretory but the sexual function of the male organ. In essence, he'd had an artificial erection installed under his skin.

"Jesus," said Kurins, when the nature of the procedure had settled in. "Why?"

"Why what?" said O'Brien.

"Why does he need it? And why does he want it? I mean, we know enough about him to know he's not a womanizer. He barely goes out. If there's any romance left between him and Nina, it doesn't show."

"He's a complicated man," said Joe O'Brien.

And so the matter of the penile implant became yet another riddle in the enigmatic character of the Godfather. An old man, not a skirt chaser, subjects himself to a painful and rather bizarre operation to recapture a semblance of sexual prowess. What for? Who for?

Only later would it become clear that the motivating force behind Big Paul's decision was the unlikely yet inevitable figure of Gloria Olarte. This was strange—but then, everything about the Colombian woman's sojourn in America was strange.

When Gloria Olarte first came to the United States, in January 1979, she had no idea of the odd things that would happen to her in her adopted land. She spoke virtually no English, and even in Spanish her education was severely limited. She lived at first with her older sister Nellie, who had emigrated some years earlier and had an apartment in Corona, Queens. Nellie helped Gloria get a job in a factory, but the socially ambitious younger woman wasn't satisfied. She didn't want to limit her circle of contacts to fellow Hispanics, whom she considered low-class; she wanted to mingle with real Americans, rich people. When she heard through the Colombian grapevine that a wealthy couple who lived in a mansion were looking for a maid, she told her sister she wanted the job.

"But Gloria," Nellie said to her in Spanish, "you don't speak English."

"I learn."

"And you've never been a maid before."

"*No importa.* These people, I make them love me."

The habits and methods of the American rich were an utter mystery to Gloria, so it did not strike her as odd when, one Saturday that summer, a Castellano flunky came to Queens to pick her up in a gleaming Lincoln, gave her a new dress, drove her to a White Castle hamburger joint, and told her to change in the ladies' room, then wait for another Lincoln to pick her up. The second Lincoln was powder blue and was driven by no less a personage than "Joe Red" Gambino, a grandson of the illustrious Carlo. The would-be maid was impressed with the car, but not by the lineage of the driver—she barely knew what the Mafia was, let alone the fabled names on its roster.

Joe Red crossed the Verrazano Bridge, climbed Todt Hill, and nosed into the Castellano driveway.

"Why you take Gloria to church?" she asked.

"This ain't no church, *chiquita*," Joe Red informed her. "This is where they live."

Dios mío.

The job interview was brief, conducted by Nina Castellano and her daughter, Connie. The Godfather happened to be sitting in the kitchen at the time, but he did not speak. Gloria's first impression was that he was a sad and bitter man.

When Gloria began working for the Castellanos, her English was so limited that her chores had to be acted out in sign language. The distinguished Mrs. Nina had to perform grotesque contortions to tell her maid to put the clothes in the dryer or to iron some shirts. To end this tiresome game of charades, the Godfather one day brought home a hand-held bilingual computer. *Do the dishes* could be punched in in English; *Lave los platos* would appear on the readout, and Gloria would march to the sink.

After several months, however, unexpected messages began appearing on the little language machine. *Me encanta su sonrisa* would appear: *I like your smile.* And: *Qué bonitos ojos tiene: What pretty eyes you have.* Gloria was confused. Was Mr. Paul flirting with her, or had the inscrutable translator gone haywire?

The matter was settled one evening after dinner. Gloria was doing dishes, when the Godfather came up behind her and put his huge hands on her waist. He turned her toward him, gently took her wrists, and placed her hands on his shoulders. In a strangely sacramental gesture, he raised his own hands to her head, the fingers splaying out over her coarse and springy hair. According to Gloria Olarte's version of events, his eyes were moist.

"I wish I could be like you," the Godfather said.

The maid stood rigid and silent.

"You have nothing, and you are happy. I have everything, and I am sad."

Sadness amid luxury was to the maid as profound a mystery as was the little language machine. She said nothing.

"I like to see you here. Please stay."

Now Gloria was really confused. She claimed, and still claims, to love Mrs. Nina like a mother. True, she was aware that the Castellano marriage was far from ideal. Mr. and Mrs. slept in separate rooms, and there were no nighttime footsteps in the hallway. What passion Paul and Nina had for each other came out only in the form of raging arguments—arguments in which one didn't need English to hear the hate. Was it a sin to come between a husband and wife who did nothing but make each other miserable?

Gloria wrestled with the question. She told her sister Nellie that Meester Paul was making passes at her and she was going to quit her job. Nellie said she was imagining things—what would a rich, important man like Castellano want with a frumpy little nobody like her? Nellie, it should be understood, had reasons of her own to advise her little sister to stay. The Castellanos were very generous to Gloria. They gave her dresses, men's suits, expensive shoes, many of them never worn; the maid brought these lavish discards to Corona on her Wednesday visits, playing Santa Claus to the Colombian enclave there. If Gloria's virtue needed to be sacrificed in order to keep the largess flowing, well, that's how it was between rich and poor, in North America as in South.

So Gloria went back to the Todt Hill mansion and allowed things to take their course. But if she chose to portray her alliance with Paul Castellano as the selfless sacrifice of her body, that sacrifice, for many months, went uncompleted. The quasi-lovers would kiss, press, pet, and then—nothing. They would stroke and fondle, only to have their arousal drift off and dissipate like the steam above a pot of boiling pasta. Gloria was again confused. Was this how people made love in the United States? Or was such exceptional restraint a refinement practiced only by the very rich?

Although the Colombian maid was baffled by her lover's holding back from carnal union, the Godfather understood precisely what was going on. Paul Castellano had been diabetic for many years, and in some very small proportion of cases, diabetes causes a kind of neural damage that leads, in turn, to impotence. Castellano had been unable to achieve an erection since 1976—ironically, the same year he had become the omnipotent Godfather. The disability apparently had not greatly bothered him until the Colombian maid entered his life. Then he began to find it intolerable.

"Ah, Gloria," he would sigh as one of their long petting sessions was drifting toward its anticlimax, "I wish I could make you happy."

"I happy, Meester Paul."

"I not so happy," the Godfather acknowledged, slipping into the pidgin English he often used when speaking with his paramour. "I very angry with this old body of mine."

One evening some months later, the Godfather made an announcement.

"Gloria," he said, "there's an operation they can do."

"Operation?" said the maid. The word scared her.

"They put a rod in."

She said nothing.

"They make a cut, down here . . ."

She averted her eyes and cringed. "No, don't tell Gloria."

But the Godfather was full of bravado that night. "No big deal. They make a cut, then they take a small drill and make a tunnel. The rod goes in, and then, *zhup*, it works just like a . . . like a gooseneck lamp."

"Gooseneck?" said the maid. "What ees gooseneck?"

"Gooseneck," repeated the Godfather. He found it was a difficult thing to explain. "Like, flexible. But not too flexible. Like, you can make it turn up, or you can make it turn down."

The maid blushed. "Eet must hurt."

"I wouldn't hurt you, little Gloria."

"No, Meester Paul. Eet must hurt *you*."

The Godfather chuckled. Apparently, going through the pain was to him an integral part of seizing back his manhood. "Maybe," he said, "but only for a little while."

"No, Meester Paul. Eef eet will hurt, you should not do thees for Gloria."

"I've already made up my mind," said Castellano. "I'm having it done. Soon."

"When, Meester Paul?" asked Gloria, surprised to find that her body was celebrating the impending change even as her conscience dreaded it.

"As soon as the parts come in," said the Godfather. "We're just waiting for the parts."

CHAPTER 23

THE PLANTING of a residential bug is the Rolls-Royce of surveillance techniques.

On the scale that runs from casual observation, to systematic study, to the development of informants, to the tapping of phone lines, the bugging of a house reaches an entirely different level of intimacy. It is about as close as law enforcement can ever come to getting inside the criminal's head, to seeing the person and the process whole. As far as organized crime is concerned, a high-level bug is probably the strongest medicine there is for stopping the sickness cold—or at least radically altering the course of the disease.

But strong medicines call for cautious use, and the American judiciary takes a very conservative stance on matters like slipping into the homes of citizens, planting hidden microphones, and monitoring personal chitchat held on private property. Whole books could be written on the moral and constitutional issues of planting a microphone in someone's house—though all the questions finally come down to this: Where, precisely, is the dividing line between, on the one hand, individual rights and guarantees of privacy, and, on the other, government's responsibility to protect its citizens from crime?

The answer to that will vary according to who is asked, as well as when—since there are fashions in judicial thinking as in everything else. In terms of getting court authorization to plant a residential bug, however, certain things are definite. First, "probable cause" must be established beyond a reasonable doubt. It must be shown, that is, *before the fact,* that there is a real likelihood that criminal activity is being planned at the target residence. This probable cause may be established through informants or direct observation, or through references on other bugs. It must be backed up by specifics with airtight documentation. It is not good enough simply to demonstrate that a person has a criminal background, or to say that Paul Castellano is head of the Gambino crime family and everybody knows it.

Second, it is a sad fact of life—sad for FBI agents, that is—that affidavits in request of Title III searches must be couched in formal and faultless legalese. The documents come under merciless scrutiny—first by FBI headquarters, then by the Justice Department, sometimes by the Attorney General himself. These reviews are in anticipation of the equally merciless scrutiny practiced by defense attorneys who, in their endless search for technical loopholes, are certain to try to discredit the affidavit, thereby discrediting the bug, thereby disallowing the evidence.

Finally, since there have been instances of bugs being compromised before they were even placed—either by unintentional law enforcement leaks or by organized crime moles in various administrative jobs—the preparation of a surveillance request must be a closely held secret.

For all these reasons, once the bugging of the Staten Island White House came to be seen as a real possibility—a moonshot, yes, but a plausible moonshot—the whole tenor of the Castellano investigation changed. No longer did it have the freewheeling, antic character of the Wreak Havoc campaign, whose idea had been to make a bunch of noise and see who flinched. No longer did the Brooklyn-Queens Resident Agency resound with after-work bull sessions about how Andy Kurins had been cursed out by Tommy Agro or how Joe O'Brien had gotten George Remini to smile for the camera. Information was now on a need-to-know basis. Discretion was of the essence.

To be sure, street contact with Gambino family members would continue, but its purpose was now precisely the opposite of the original intent. Initially, the idea was to make the mobsters imagine that more was going on than really was; now the aim was to make them think there was *less* going on. Let the Gambino family think the FBI was still groping, spray-hitting, firing blind; that would help deflect attention from what was becoming an ever-more-focused strategy with an ever-more-singular aim—catching Castellano in his own voice, in his own words, in his own house.

As the target came more clearly into focus the team pursuing it was trimmed. Agents not directly engaged in the Castellano surveillance—even some with long experience on the Gambino squad—were kept in the dark as to plans for the Staten Island bug. It would have done no one any good to have them know about it.

With exclusivity comes esprit, and a new closeness and intensity developed among those few agents now gathering intelligence in support of the Title III surveillance. Joe O'Brien dubbed the project Operation Castaway, and in its service, to his own surprise, he seemed never to get tired; full days of regular duty would lead seamlessly into long evenings spent with Assistant U.S. Attorney James Harmon, of the Organized Crime Strike Force of the Eastern District of New York, who helped see him through the daunting technicalities of preparing the affidavit. Andy Kurins, through Joe Gallo and the Home Run investigation, traced lines of influence up and down the Gambino organization, unearthing dozens of veiled allusions to "the Boss" or "the Pope"—allusions that would help establish probable cause. Supervisor Bruce Mouw dropped his habitual mirthless laugh in favor of an almost breathless whisper that greeted each new bit of information as a watershed event.

Frank Spero, the agent in whose company Joe O'Brien had first come face-to-face with the Godfather, stepped up his observation of the Castellano home, documenting visitors, tracing vehicles, constructing a detailed flow-chart of known and suspected mobsters in and out of the big house. With his partner, Matty Tricorico, Spero compiled a portrait whose implication no reasonable judge would be able to deny: that Paul Castellano's Todt Hill mansion was the de facto headquarters and nerve center of the Mafia in America.

CHAPTER 24

ANDY KURINS stood in the shadow of a shoe store awning on Crescent Street in Astoria, Queens. He wasn't hiding, mind you, but if standing in the shade at noon on a clear, sunny May day gave him the chance to see before being seen, well, that was okay.

Joe Gallo, who was almost as regular as a working stiff in his daytime habits, usually shambled up the street to Sperrazza's Luncheonette just around this time. Grandfatherly Joe—with his finger-curled white hair and his neatly tied running shoes, his gracious manners and his foul vocabulary, his seeming candor and his artful way of lying. Kurins had come to like him—sort of. Gallo was elegant in his dishonesty, a worthy opponent in debate. He was a lot brighter than most of his associates, and it had occurred to Kurins that the old *consigliere* actually liked being hounded by the FBI, if for no other reason than that it gave him an opportunity to talk with people who could follow a line of logic and had an attention span longer than ten seconds. What, after all, was Gallo's typical business conversation like? *Go here. See Sal. Pick up the money. Bring it there. Take X. Hand in Y. What if Sal doesn't have the money? Okay, smack him. No, don't whack him. Smack him.* Intellectually stimulating it was not. In fact, Andy Kurins thought, being a Mob *consigliere* was a little like being a kindergarten teacher; the difference was that you didn't have the pleasure of seeing your students grow up. The typical street thug hit a certain level of functional capacity, and there he stuck like a rock in mud.

A city bus went by, belching acrid smoke. Half a block away, an old man in a baggy pale blue shirt was almost run down by a kid on a skateboard. The old man was Joe Gallo, and Andy Kurins

131

had to chuckle at the limits of Mob power—maybe they could keep the streets safe from muggers, but not from city kids for whom kamikaze skateboarding was the closest thing to outdoor adventure.

The *consigliere* recovered his poise and resumed walking toward the agent. He got within fifteen yards before he noticed him, and then he did a somewhat odd thing. He stopped in his tracks, reached deep into his pants pocket, and, with a gesture that was casual but not casual enough, he tossed a fistful of scraps into a trash can. They rained down in a blizzard of paper, fluttering and tumbling. Andy Kurins could see exactly what they were.

"Joe," he said, "maybe you've got a winner there."

Gallo said nothing.

"OTB's *legal*, Joe," Kurins continued. "Why'd ya throw them away?"

Gallo didn't even shrug, didn't even acknowledge the question. It was a free country, and if he wanted to trash a few hundred dollars' worth of pari-mutuel tickets, that was his business. No doubt he dumped the chits as part of his lifelong habit of excessive caution and radical self-effacement. He was just a pensioner from the neighborhood, after all. How could he support a horse habit of several hundred dollars every day?

"Lurking in the shadows like a pimp," he said to the FBI agent. "Not very classy, Andy."

"Just staying out of the glare," replied Kurins. "Buy you a cup of coffee?"

They walked together to Sperrazza's, where no one ever seemed to pay for coffee or anything else. They slid into Gallo's regular booth at the back—a booth whose green vinyl upholstery had split here and there, showing a kind of oily straw stuffing.

"Whaddya hear from Joe junior?" Kurins asked.

It was a cordial but not a kind opening gambit, since Gallo's eldest son, Joseph Carl, was in jail. He had been caught, not by the FBI but by New York City's finest, selling heroin. He'd copped a plea but had still received a tough sentence—eight and two-thirds years to life—under the provisions of New York's Rockefeller Law.

"The cocksuckers don't want to grant him parole," said the *consigliere*. "It's a bullshit case to begin with, they framed him, now they're diddling their own rules on parole. It stinks."

Andy Kurins stirred his coffee. He'd learned the drill with Gallo by now. You took a breath, counted to five, and more information, or disinformation, would be forthcoming.

"Asshole lawyers. I tell them, 'Listen, your name is Gallo, you don't plea-bargain. You plea-bargain, you get fucked right up the ass.' So what do they do? They plea-bargain. And Joey gets fucked."

"But Joe, they caught him dealing junk."

"That's a lie!" said the *consigliere*, although the evidence in his son's case had been airtight. The old man slapped the table, and his espresso spoon jumped, flipped, and clattered down against his saucer. No one in Sperrazza's looked around. When Joe N. Gallo got upset, it was better not to notice. "They framed him because I'm the one they want, and they can't get me."

This argument was one that, in various contexts, Andy Kurins had heard before, and it always struck him as curious. Mobsters liked to claim that the Mafia was only a figment of the government's imagination, but sometimes it seemed that the reverse was true: that law enforcement was a figment of the Mafia's imagination. Mobsters imagined some vast, single-minded "they" bent on destroying them, and, ironically, in their paranoid detestation of law enforcement, they sometimes gave law enforcement too much credit. Did Joe Gallo imagine that the NYPD was so seamlessly meshed with the FBI that the locals would persecute the son because the feds wanted the father? Did he fancy, further, that the court system and the parole board paid rapt attention to the goings-on at Sperrazza's Luncheonette in deciding the fate of one more midlevel heroin dealer? Sometimes, to be sure, various agencies coordinated their efforts, and when they did so unjealously and well, law enforcement was a beautiful machine. But usually it wasn't quite so neat.

"Are you sure, Joe?" Kurins asked.

"Sure of what?" asked the *consigliere*, his forehead looking very pink against his silver hair. Flushing—that was phase one of

Gallo getting agitated. Phase two was a very slight tremor in the fingers of the right hand. Phase three was reaching, almost convulsively, for the angina pills.

"Sure that it's you they want?"

No doubt it is difficult for any father to think clearly and reasonably about the jailing of his son; in addition, Joe junior's drug offense created complications for Joe senior that had nothing to do with the police. During the tenure of Paul Castellano, Gambino family members and associates were barred from the narcotics business. In Paul's personal war on drugs, the rules were simple: You deal, you die.

It is moot how effectively this edict was actually applied, or how often and willingly exceptions were made. But the Boss wasn't grandstanding when he laid it down. He had the sincere if deluded idea that members of La Cosa Nostra were well on their way to becoming gentlemen, smooth business operators in tasteful ties, whereas drugs were the realm of street trash. Of course, Castellano's idea of being a gentleman was to snarl, in regard to drugs: "Let the spicks control that shit. It's nigger business anyway." His racism aside, Paul seemed not to understand that the then-burgeoning part of the narcotics racket—cocaine—had as its typical end user a member of the white middle class.

In any case, Joe Gallo had a problem. If you are the number-three man in the Gambino organization, how do you explain away the inconvenient fact of your firstborn being in the slammer for what the Boss considered the sleaziest, unmanliest, and stupidest form of unlawful activity? And how do you protect the kid when he's back on the street?

Looking at it from the kid's point of view, it must be tough to have a Mafioso for a father. If your old man is already a loan shark, a shakedown artist, a con man, a fence, and probably a murderer, how do you act out the need to rebel? What can you do in the line of misbehavior that won't be a pale emulation of Dad's accomplishments? For Joe Gallo, Jr., dealing junk was probably a way of assuring himself that he wasn't just going into the family business, he was doing something on his own.

"Let's say you're right, Joe," Andy Kurins continued. "Let's for argument's sake say the city cops, the FBI, the parole guys—they all get together to bust the chops of guys named Gallo. Now, with all due respect, Joe, I can think of a few people they'd rather have. Can't you?"

The *consigliere* flushed a shade darker and splayed his manicured fingers on the Formica table. He pressed down until his nails went from pink to white, and Kurins knew that he was wrestling with the awful conflict between demands of family and of Family, the one code natural and eternal, the other contrived but, for made men, no less compelling.

"Don't ever offer me a deal, Andy. Don't say a fucking word about a deal."

"I haven't."

Joe Gallo went on as if he hadn't heard. "I'd rather not hate you. Don't ever dangle a deal in front of me. And don't talk to me anymore about my son."

CHAPTER 25

ONE WAY OF APPRAISING a leader is through the characters and talents of the people he carries with him to the top. Does he have the savvy to select associates whose abilities complement his own? Does he have the confidence to surround himself with people who are strong and impressive in their own right? Does he have the vision and the generosity to nurture underlings who will grow into bigger responsibilities? Or does he pad his ranks with nonthreatening mediocrities who do more for his ego than for the organization?

In the case of Paul Castellano, it must be said that the men he promoted, and one of them in particular, did not reflect well on his judgment. The capable people in the Gambino organization—Dellacroce, Gallo, *capos* like Pasquale Conte, John Gotti, and Joe Armone—had been in place before Big Paul's ascension. They had no real peers among the new regime. Why? One likes to think the Mafia's "talent pool" was shrinking as more mobsters went to jail and the new generation decided there were easier ways to make a living.

But it also seems that some shortcoming in Castellano prevented him from building a top-quality team. Lawyers, accountants, sure—he went for the very best, and got them. When it came to actual Mob associates, however, the story was different. Paul didn't seem at ease with anyone too ambitious or too clever. He didn't deal well with opinions different from his own, and made enemies of certain strong personalities—Gotti, for one—by barring them from the councils of power; a savvier leader would have neutralized these potential rivals by keeping them close. Finally, and perversely, even as Big Paul was striving to move the Mafia into a purportedly sanitized future, he felt compelled to surround himself with characters who reminded him of the Mob's—and his own—grimy, gutterish past.

Nowhere was this clearer than in Big Paul's choice of Tommy Bilotti as his favorite and protégé—a choice that gave the lie to the sophisticated image Castellano tried so hard to cultivate. True, the Boss had his conservative suits, with lapels of a width that would not draw glances at Manhattan's tonier men's clubs. He had his tables at midtown restaurants frequented by folks who were educated at boarding school rather than in prison. He had brainy advisers who steered him toward income opportunities involving initial public offerings of stock.

But he also had Tommy, and that sort of blew the whole effect.

Bilotti was Castellano's darling—and even among his own ranks this was regarded as bizarre. What did the man have? He was basically a pit bull with shoes on. If he had any business ability beyond choreographing a shakedown or calculating the interest owed on shylock loans, it didn't show. In a milieu not known for its conversational finesse, Bilotti distinguished himself by his spluttering inarticulateness. He was short—five feet seven. He was stubby—a rock-solid two-twenty. He wore a bad toupee. He had no tact, no charm, no sense of humor. He had a big mouth, and his piggish eyes were too close together. To the concept of self-control he was a stranger.

He had begun his rise as Paul Castellano's driver and bodyguard, and that was in fact the perfect job for him. Bilotti, to give fair credit, was vigilant, hardworking, fearless, and, above all, loyal. His capacity for devotion had been stretched by certain excruciating events in his personal life. His first wife, Catherine, died a slow death from cancer in her middle thirties; Bilotti had watched her fade away. Remarried now, he still brought flowers to her grave. Catherine and Tommy had an autistic son, who had been institutionalized since toddlerhood. Bilotti loved the boy dearly and visited him regularly, though he never spoke of him. Either he felt the disease somehow reflected badly on his manhood, or he dimly perceived some unbearable irony in his own violent nature being passed on to his child in the form of a compulsion toward self-inflicted hurt. Maybe he just found the subject too painful to discuss. As some people keep their brutal sides a secret, so Bilotti hid those very few things that called forth tenderness in him.

In any case, as the small circle of his caring shrank, Tommy became ever more fanatically dedicated to the Boss. He defended him with a stoic solicitude, and would almost certainly have sacrificed his own life to save him. He was programmed not for malice, exactly, but for combat-readiness. He didn't seem to connect violence with a reason for violence. It was just something that happened, and you had to have a jump on it. The only time Tommy *didn't* have a jump on it, he and his Boss ended up dead.

As long as he was waiting on Paul Castellano, Tommy Bilotti was deferential, subdued, watchful yet calm, like a dog on a rug. His self-esteem derived from adoration of the master, and he could afford to be well-behaved. Problems occurred, however, when Bilotti was sent on errands of his own. Out of sight of the Boss, he got rambunctious. He tried to play the big shot; he overdid things. He got creative in a sadistic sort of way, and embroidered gratuitous cruelty through what should have been straightforward business transactions.

Once, for instance, Bilotti was sent to collect some overdue loan interest from a Staten Island bar owner. This bar owner, as it happened, had been badly beaten up some weeks before—the last time he'd gotten behind in his "vig" payments. The beating had led to medical bills and time lost from work—the guy was less able than ever to pay. Still, Tommy Bilotti would either collect or register a protest. So he went into the guy's establishment one afternoon, carrying a baseball bat.

Four or five customers were sitting at the bar, wearing flannel shirts, drinking shots and beers. They glanced around, the way people do when an open tavern door lets in an unwanted wedge of sunlight. Seeing the barrel-chested Bilotti standing there with his weapon of choice, a few made discreet movements toward the exit.

"No one leaves," Bilotti said. The voice was flat and final. Then he turned his attention to the proprietor, who had already blanched dead white and was trying to disappear among the back-bar shelves. "You, fuckface, get your sorry ass out here."

The bartender hesitated, then very slowly came around the bar. It wasn't clear whether he still limped from his beating or his legs were locked with fear.

"Get on your fucking knees."

The bar owner didn't. It wasn't defiance—he just couldn't move. Bilotti lifted the bat. The man knelt, quickly.

Castellano's darling now turned to the customers. "Why do you assholes drink at a place run by a scumbag who doesn't pay his bills? A fucking deadbeat. How can you do business with a fucking piece of shit like this? And he's a faggot besides. You guys didn't know that?"

The place was utterly silent except for the metallic rasp of Tommy Bilotti's fly being opened, tooth by tooth.

"Take it in your mouth, you piece of shit."

The kneeling man recoiled, his head involuntarily snapping back like that of a boxer who's been nailed.

"I said take it in your mouth."

The bar owner closed his eyes, held his breath, and did as he was told.

"You see?" Bilotti said to the customers. "He likes it."

Stepping gingerly away, he put his small and almost dainty foot squarely on the man's chest and kicked him backward across the floor. "Faggot cocksucker," he said, zipped his pants, and left.

This was the man Paul Castellano regarded as top executive material in a modern Mafia that had supposedly outgrown thuggishness and now made its money through prudent and shrewd investments. This man was to be a cabinet-level administrator in a kinder, gentler Mob.

CHAPTER 26

J

OE O'BRIEN had been warned about the Boss's hotheaded
sidekick.

He had been told about his multiple arrests for assault and
weapons possession, his indiscreet boasting about the hits he'd
performed—eleven and counting, according to street sources.

"Don't ever talk to Tommy Bilotti alone," Bruce Mouw had
advised. "He doesn't play by the rules. He's monstrously strong
and he'll go after anybody. Very short fuse. Always keeps a bat
under the front seat of his car. Ends conversations by breaking
things. Heads and legs, usually."

Well, O'Brien didn't intend having any street-corner confrontations with Tommy. But things don't always turn out as one
intends.

On a mild Sunday morning in the spring of 1982, O'Brien was
doing surveillance on the Staten Island White House, jotting down
license plate numbers, observing familiar faces, gathering whatever scraps he could in support of the Title III affidavit. Around
noon, he saw Tommy Bilotti come wheeling out of the horseshoe
driveway in his mauve Buick, license plate number 5348APG. He
decided to follow. At that time, he knew little of Tommy's patterns
when he wasn't playing chauffeur. It couldn't hurt to see where he
went.

Bilotti wound down from the affluent heights of Todt Hill to
the neat but dowdy working-class neighborhoods that comprise
much of Staten Island. Staten Island, all in all, is a quiet place. Not
so long ago, before the Verrazano Bridge went up, there were
farms there. People caught striped bass from its beaches, and lived
in villages that fanned out from old-style commercial streets, with
one- or two-story red brick buildings containing Italian delis, Jew-

ish bakeries, German wurst houses. It wasn't like the rest of New York City. Little kids could walk around alone. Strangers would help them cross the street.

Tommy Bilotti was now heading toward one of those village centers, Hylan Boulevard in the Grasmere section. He parked in front of a small, dark shop that stood alone. It was a beauty parlor called Faces, and it was clearly not open for streaking, frosting, or permanent waves. Bilotti took a key from a pants pocket, unceremoniously opened the door, and went inside.

O'Brien parked on a residential side street, half a block away, and wondered what brought a lone man to a locked beauty parlor on a springtime Sunday. Did he hide cash there? Did he work from a pay phone inside? Maybe he was expecting company. O'Brien daydreamed the scenario of choice: Bilotti had just received instructions—for a shakedown, a hijacking, perhaps even a hit—from Paul Castellano; he was now meeting a soldier, to pass the instructions down the line of command. O'Brien would intercept the transaction, the trail would lead straight back up the hill to the White House, and—bingo, the missing link.

He waited twenty minutes. Virtually all the Hylan Boulevard shops were closed, and the street was nearly empty. Far off, the sound of lawn mowers could be heard, and there were even traces of that rarest urban sound, birdsong. It was lulling. O'Brien peered through his windshield at the beauty parlor door, and yawned.

"Hello, asshole."

The voice was loud, menacing, and practically in Joe O'Brien's left ear. He flinched, then spun his head to see Tommy Bilotti behind the wheel of a blue Ford that had slowly pulled up cheek by jowl with his old government Plymouth. Bilotti's fat face was not more than four feet away; O'Brien could smell his aftershave filling the car. The mobster flashed a smirk full of crooked teeth and gave a single snort of a laugh. "You can't tail me, O'Brien. I'm a fucking professional. I'm the best. I coulda lost you anytime."

"Congratulations," said O'Brien, trying to deny the spurt of fear that had started him instantly sweating and sent a milky feeling coursing through his stomach and down his legs. Bilotti had killer's eyes, black, vacant, opaque as stones. His left hand was on the steering wheel, but the right was hidden, and this was not reassuring. O'Brien's .38 was in its shoulder holster, beneath his moistening jacket. Reaching for it would signal a level of commitment the agent would rather avoid. More to the point, it would take too long. Bullets travel faster than fingers. "Is this your regular beauty parlor?"

"It's my wife's place," said Bilotti "You got a problem with that?"

"No," said O'Brien. "Just curious."

"Too fucking curious," said Bilotti. "You're pissing off some big people, O'Brien. This bullshit with sending cards. You might think that's cute. Other people don't. All this hanging around the Hill, like you own the place. All this talking, talking, talking. All this cat-and-mouse bullshit. So-and-so says this-and-such to what's-his-face. This asshole went here and did this-and-so to some other scumbag. You fuckers with your piece-of-shit cars and your fucking goddamn neckties always so neat, you come around making trouble, you don't know shit, you think you're smart, you can't even follow me six blocks without I know you're there, asshole . . ."

Now, most people, when they are building up to a fit of rage, need some give-and-take, some goading, to get them really psyched. Not Tommy Bilotti. When he got mad, it was like a nuclear reactor going into meltdown. Once a certain threshold was reached, the process just fed on itself, the voltage increasing exponentially until the fuel was all used up and everything within a certain radius had been leveled. His voice got louder and louder, he made less and less sense. Soon he was just spitting out curses wrapped in random phrases, his face purple, his nostrils distended, ropy veins standing out on his pit-bull neck.

"Come on, Tommy," Joe O'Brien said during a brief pause for breath, "don't hold back. Tell me what's really on your mind."

"Prick!" screamed Bilotti, the word slicing through the still air and bouncing off the brick walls of the shops. "On my mind? My hair, you asshole. You nosy, prying scumbag. It's no one's business. No one knew. I do what I like. No one fucks with me, O'Brien. Then you tell people. You spread it around like horse manure. Who the fuck are you to tell people? You're nothing. You're a government drone. You're a fucking mailman! Who the fuck are you to embarrass Tommy Bilotti?"

Gradually and with great difficulty, O'Brien found his way through the tangled wreckage that Bilotti made of the English language. So *that's* what was upsetting him: he seemed to think no one had known he wore a toupee, until Joe O'Brien began chatting up Gambino family members. The agent, in spite of his fear, in spite of his clammy shirt, almost laughed. Bilotti's rug had shelves where it joined his own hair on the sides; it overhung like a miniature version of a World War I German helmet. It gleamed like a soaked cat, and the color was not a perfect match. *Everybody* knew Bilotti wore a toup.

So now O'Brien had a strategic decision on his hands. He was sitting alone and exposed on an empty street with a known killer who might or might not be armed, and who was in the midst of a tantrum. He could stay silent and hope the storm would pass, or he could provoke Bilotti further, trying to confuse or exhaust him in his rage. He decided on the latter course. Probably the pit bull wouldn't bite as long as he was barking.

"Tommy, you're wrong."

"Fuck you, I'm wrong. I'm right. Word gets back. Don't deny it, chickenshit. You call me 'Wig.' I should rip your fucking throat out for that."

"You give me too much credit, Tommy. You think I made that up? I'll tell you where I heard it: wiretaps. That's what your *friends* call you, Tommy, when they're talking on the phone."

"You're lying. You're full of shit." Bilotti's face got more purple still. His pupils shrank to pinpoints of black light, and pulsing blood seemed to make his forehead crawl.

"Tommy, it's on tape. When we indict you, you'll get to listen. *The Wig said this. The Wig did that.* It's your family nickname. Didn't you know?"

The news put Bilotti's fury over the top. For one brief instant, his face went weirdly calm as he shifted gears from words to action. With the heightened alertness of imminent battle, O'Brien took in everything at once. Bilotti's left hand slid from the steering wheel to the door handle. The hidden, dreaded right darted down beneath the seat: that meant Bilotti had no gun and was opting for the baseball bat. O'Brien reached under his damp jacket and pulled his pistol from its holster; the metal was hot, the butt of the weapon moist. He sidled toward the middle of the seat, giving himself room to aim and shoot.

Then, in the same heartbeat, Tommy Bilotti and Joe O'Brien both remembered a certain small detail: Castellano's favorite had changed cars. There was no bat.

Bilotti sat bolt upright, grabbed his steering wheel with both hands, and yanked on it as if he meant to rip it off its stem. His toupee was disheveled, gross rings of perspiration were spreading from the armpits of his shirt, and breath was whistling through his nose. For a moment, it looked like he might burst into tears like a fat, squalling baby.

"Look at the bright side, Tommy," said O'Brien. "You just spared yourself a whole lot of trouble."

The other man only pulled his upper lip back from his teeth and snarled. O'Brien decided to press his advantage. Bilotti had made him look bad, after all, sneaking up on him like that. The agent owed him one.

"And Tommy," he said, "just so it doesn't take you by surprise—I'm gonna have to let Paul know about your bad manners. He doesn't like his guys threatening the FBI, and you know it. He's not gonna be pleased."

Incurring the displeasure of the master—this, for Tommy Bilotti, was the ultimate agony, maybe the only thing left that really hurt. He tried to curse and couldn't get the words out; he just passed a lot of air over his gums. Then he started his car and gunned the engine. He pointed a finger at Joe O'Brien. The finger was stubby and thick, armored with wrinkles and crowned by a talonlike nail that seemed designed for clawing out eyes. "If it comes down to it, O'Brien, me and you, you'll see heaven before I do."

"There you go again, Tommy. That sounds distinctly like a threat."

"You take it any fucking way you want."

"Okay. But Tommy—just for that, no more greeting cards."

Bilotti gave a final snarl and barreled off. O'Brien winced at the ugly screech of the tires.

CHAPTER 27

PROBABLE CAUSE. The slipperiness of the concept, its openness to a range of interpretations, made Joe O'Brien nervous.

Paul Castellano, with his satin bathrobe, his swimming pool, his two-inch-thick steaks, his gooseneck penis, and his mistress culled from the ranks of domestic servants, lived the life of a decadent and reclusive feudal lord while doing no form of demonstrable, legal work. Did that establish probable cause that he was a racketeer?

Tommy Bilotti went straight from Sunday morning meetings at the Staten Island White House to spluttering confrontations with the FBI. Did that establish probable cause that Big Paul presided over a criminal enterprise?

Mobsters, of both the reputed and the convicted varieties, regularly appeared at Castellano's house, their waxed black Cadillacs lending a funereal aspect to the grounds. Did that establish probable cause that the Todt Hall mansion was the nerve center of Mob activities?

Damn straight it did, as far as Joe O'Brien was concerned. But Joe O'Brien was not the one who would grant permission for a Title III surveillance. That determination would be left to a federal judge, and federal judges were a difficult and inscrutable breed.

Most—not all—of them were brilliant, with yards upon yards of leather-bound books crammed into their heads. As a group, they believed deeply in the sanctity of their work, yet their behavior on the bench was not infrequently bizarre. They'd read the *Wall Street Journal* in the midst of testimony. They'd yawn so loud their microphones would ring with feedback. Then, just when it seemed they'd lost all track of what was going on, they'd zing a lawyer on some obscure and all but inaudible point. Decades of practice apparently gave them an uncanny gift for passively absorbing the ninety-eight percent of courtroom goings-on that consists of mere procedures, repetitions, empty formalities—and saving their active attention for the two percent that mattered.

This was a skill Joe O'Brien admired greatly, yet he also understood that it did not do to be in awe of judges. They were human underneath the robes; they had their own ambitions and their own agendas. Aside from respecting their own high scruples, they had their own soft butts to cover. If you wanted to persuade a judge, you had to convince him not only that *you* were right but that *he* would be right for seeing things your way. You had to make him more than sure. You had to arm him against defense attorneys playing the civil rights violin, their cynical manipulation of constitutional guarantees. Above all, you had to make the judge feel secure against reversals by higher judges. Reversed on appeal— to the layman these are temperate words, suggesting a calm and measured difference of opinion; to a judge they are a devastating rebuke, a phrase that conjures battered egos and, sometimes, stalled careers. Around the Brooklyn-Queens Resident Agency of the FBI, then, the rule of thumb was this: Figure out how much evidence you need, then triple it.

So Joe O'Brien continued piling up his justifications for the bugging of the Castellano house—examining documents, reading grand jury transcripts, reviewing wiretaps—and in June 1982, his efforts were rewarded with a discovery whose implications went far beyond the question of the affidavit. What he found were the first faint but unmistakable rumblings of civil war within the Gambino organization.

In March of that year, the FBI had bugged the Cedarhurst, Long Island, home of Gambino soldier Angelo Ruggiero. Ruggiero was a nephew of Aniello Dellacroce; one of his closest associates was Eugene Gotti, brother of John. He represented the faction of the Gambino family that had been cut off from the mainstream of power ever since Cousin Carlo divided his kingdom into two pieces of roughly equal wealth but quite unequal prestige. The out-of-power faction had never had a very high regard for Paul Castellano, with his newfangled money schemes, his lack of flamboyance. By 1982, as recorded on the Ruggiero bug, they were saying things about him that were crude, insubordinate, and un-forgivable. They called him a "milk drinker" and a "pansy." They called his sons "the chicken men," and referred to his business advisers as "the Jew club." They conjectured that he spent his evenings "whackin' off with Tommy."

But beneath the mockery of Castellano was an edge of hard, cold fear. Sometime in the early 1980s—no one knows precisely when—the Boss had handed down a pair of edicts that came to be known as the Two Commandments. The first of these executive orders stated that no one caught dealing drugs after 1962 (the reason for this cutoff date remains unclear) could ever become an initiated member of the Gambino family. The second proclaimed that anyone caught dealing drugs, and whose activities in any way implicated other family members, would be whacked.

As it happened, both Angelo Ruggiero and Eugene Gotti were heavily involved in heroin trafficking, and would be arrested in 1983. In the meantime, they did not lack for evidence that Paul Castellano was prepared to follow through on his threat. On April 22, 1982, the Boss chaired a meeting to decide the fate of a soldier named Pete Tambone, who had been identified by an intrafamily informer as a dealer in smack. The verdict, delivered by Big Paul in a calm, gruff, uninflected voice: Clip him.

On April 25, against all Mob protocol, Ruggiero warned his drug traffic colleague about the impending hit. "Pete," he said, as the surveillance tape was running, "listen to me, listen to me like a brother. I'm tellin' ya, worse comes to worse, get your wife and take off." Tambone did.

But if Angelo Ruggiero was doing all he could behind the scenes to subvert Paul Castellano's leadership, to all outward ap-pearances he was still a loyal family member. He never acknowl-edged dealing drugs, and even after his arrest he devoted as much time to protecting his in-family reputation as to preparing his legal defense. So brazen was he in his two-facedness that in 1982 he borrowed a hundred thousand dollars in cash—at an interest rate of half a point a week—from the Boss he so despised. Ruggiero claimed that the money was needed for a gambit in pornography;

in fact, it was used to bankroll a major drug buy, thus creating a very ironic situation: Castellano was now implicated in a narcotics deal, the perpetrators of which he would have executed, had he known their true intentions.

In any case, as Joe O'Brien realized, what was now shaping up was a Byzantine web of threats, insults, and accusations—incendiary things said by each faction that should never be heard by the other. Yet, according to law, each side's tapes would *have* to be heard by the other; as soon as prosecutors announced their intention to use tapes or transcripts as evidence, those indicted had the right to review them.

So, then, given that the Ruggiero bug was background for the Castellano bug, Paul would someday have the pleasure of hearing his own troops call him a pansy with chicken salesmen for sons and a mutual masturbator for an aide-de-camp. If, in turn, the Castellano bug led to arrests within the opposite faction of the family, Ruggiero, Eugene Gotti, and company would learn of the Boss's opinion of them as brainless gorillas, and of his blithe readiness to have them rubbed out.

O'Brien thought Mouw should know about the potential mayhem. "Bruce," he said, "when the courts order these transcripts to be circulated, all hell is going to break loose."

Mouw smiled. There were some days when he felt the American legal system was truly the most marvelous thing in the world.

CHAPTER 28

WHERE DOES the Godfather sit?

If the question sounds like the opening of a very old joke, the answer was of serious consequence to the FBI. A wireless transmitting microphone is a nifty little piece of technology, but its capabilities are limited. It can't walk to the scene of conversations, and it doesn't hear very well through walls. It can be made extraordinarily sensitive, but does a very imperfect job of filtering ambient noise. Therefore it has to be placed in just the right spot, or it is virtually useless.

Paul Castellano's mansion had seventeen rooms. Some of them were bedrooms, and could be ruled out. With his own eyes, however, Joe O'Brien had seen a living room, a dining room, a huge kitchen with a less formal sitting area—any of which was suitable for chitchats. Moreover, Agent Frank Spero, in a brilliant bit of foresight, had a couple of years before subpoenaed the blueprints of Castellano's house from the architect who designed it. Included in the plans was a room marked study, a large basement area identified as the bar, and an apparently glassed-in porch back by the pool. None of these places could be dismissed as the site of Paul's meetings, and of course, there was no guarantee he favored the same spot all the time. He had seven thousand square feet to rattle around in, after all.

So Joe O'Brien had to figure out where the Boss sat, and in seeking the information he ran into a not unfamiliar paradox: those who were eager to blab didn't know, and those who knew he couldn't ask.

The FBI, by mid-1982, had a pretty good network of informants among associates of the Gambino family. Some were buying their way out of prison terms, some were ratting for revenge. Like most people, the informants liked to feel important, and imagined that the intelligence they provided, much of which was either re-dundant or garbage, was of the deepest significance. True, they occasionally provided valuable insights into what was going on in the social clubs or on the street corners, but as to the inner work-ings of the Castellano stronghold, the stoolies who were so avid to help were also embarrassed to admit they'd never crossed the Boss's threshold. These were low-level hoods, not even initiated soldiers. They had about as much chance of getting invited to a sit-down at Paul Castellano's as does John Q. Citizen of attending a conference in the Oval Office.

Then there were the full-fledged family members on whom O'Brien and Andy Kurins were still paying social calls. *They* knew where the sit-downs were held. Given their famous paranoia, how-ever, it would be folly to try to work them around to discussing the subject. They'd run to Paul and tell him something was up, making installation of the bug that much dicier. A poised and practiced liar like Joe Gallo might even have the presence of mind to ad-lib a misleading story, the upshot of which might be a surveillance of Gloria Olarte listening to soap operas on Telemundo.

No, what O'Brien needed was someone who was inside, but not *too* loyal. Someone with a guilty conscience, but not, in his own mind, a criminal. He needed a set-up guy, a pigeon.

Now, at the FBI office on Queens Boulevard in Rego Park, there was a little wooden box in which were kept three-by-five index cards recording the name, car description, and license plate number of everyone who visited the Castellano residence. The dates and times of each observed visit were marked on these cards, and some guys had spilled over onto page two.

Joe O'Brien looked through this file, and decided to eliminate as prospects anyone with an Italian name; since only Italians could become initiates in La Cosa Nostra, this got rid of all made men or those who might be angling to become soldiers. Of course, it also got rid of gardeners, dog trainers, tile layers, upholsterers, and housepainters, since Paul Castellano was visited by a steady stream of service people, and did business with *paisan*s whenever possible.

In any case, the agent found himself left with a few Jewish

names and a couple of Irish ones, and he started interviewing potential sources of information. While he succeeded in making some businessmen, union officials, and urologists very nervous, he did not find out where Big Paul Castellano sat. Then he called a man named Julie Miron, of whom little was known at that point, except that he drove a black Mercedes 560 SEL and appeared at the Staten Island White House on an average of once a month. Miron turned out to be of invaluable assistance, mainly because he liked to doodle.

He was head of the Miron Lumber Company, based in Brooklyn, and, like many people in and around the construction trades, he was something of a frustrated architect. If his family had had the money to keep him in school, chances are he would have designed skyscrapers. As it turned out, he presided over a multimillion-dollar building materials operation, while constantly sketching bridges, facades, and spacecraft on a pad of letterhead kept next to his telephone. His office was connected to his lumberyard, and had the slightly burned, resiny, astringent smell of fresh-sawn wood.

"Ah, Mr. O'Brien," Miron said, rising from his desk, dropping his pencil. He was a natty little man, thin and balding; with him was a younger fellow, also thin, also balding, dressed in a pin-striped suit and striped suspenders. "This is my son Stephen. He's an attorney. He's not representing me. Just looking out for my interests."

O'Brien wasn't quite sure he grasped the fine distinction, but he shook hands with both men and sat down in an old-fashioned oak chair with a spindle back. Outside, saw blades rang and forklifts clattered by. The agent took out a Bic pen and a small notebook. The younger Miron took out a legal pad and a Mont Blanc. Miron senior picked up his pencil and resumed doodling; his trim fingernails and slightly hairy knuckles became something of a blur. He seemed to be working on a multilevel shopping mall, or maybe it was modular housing.

"Mr. Miron, how long have you known Paul Castellano?"

"Oh," said Miron, glancing at the agent while continuing right on with the pencil, "around five years, I think. Six years, maybe."

"And how did you first meet him?"

"Through his sons. They were building houses on Staten Island. They came to me for materials."

"I thought his sons were in wholesale meat," said Joe O'Brien. He felt Stephen Miron's eyes turned on him, even as the attorney's fountain pen kept scratching out notes on the yellow pad. Apparently the talent for scribbling without looking ran in the family.

"They are," said Julie Miron.

"So what were they doing building houses?"

"For themselves," said Miron. "Houses for themselves. They were their own contractors."

"Ah," said O'Brien. "Isn't that a lot of work and time for people who are running a substantial business?"

Miron lifted his pencil, traced quick circles in the air, and smiled benignly. "Not for people who love houses."

"Right," said O'Brien. "But okay, that was five or six years ago, I believe you still see Paul Castellano."

"Occasionally. But that's different. That's on catalog business."

"Catalog business?"

"Yeah, I run a mail order catalog."

O'Brien sniffed the sawdust and listened to the forklifts. "I thought you were in building supplies."

"I am."

"Well, isn't it a lot of trouble to run a building supplies company *and* a catalog operation?"

Miron smiled. "Not for people who love mail order. And fine design. We sell appliances, glassware, lighting, jewelry. European mostly. High-end. Sometimes, if Paul Castellano orders something, I bring it to his house. Stephen, give Mr. O'Brien a catalog."

The son reached into a bookshelf behind him, then handed the agent a richly produced booklet. On the cover it said Miron's Desirables. O'Brien leafed through it absently, noticed some travel alarms and some fancied-up Mixmasters, then dropped it into his briefcase. "Mr. Miron, let me make sure I have this straight. You are the president of a large company, a busy man. On the side, you run a mail order catalog. And you, the boss, personally deliver

153

merchandise? If I order a toaster from you, you jump in the Merc and bring it to my house?"

"We have a wonderful toaster," said the design buff. "German. The outside never gets hot. And it adjusts automatically to the thickness of the bread."

"That's terrific. And you'll bring it to my house and show me how to make toast?"

"No, no, no," said Miron. "I obviously can't do that for everyone. But for certain regular customers, if I happen to be in the neighborhood . . ."

"Or for friends. Would you say that you and Paul Castellano are friends?"

Stephen Miron, the attorney-who-was-not-functioning-as-an-attorney, coughed softly, and this seemed to be a signal that his father should dodge the question by launching into another of his picayune and even Talmudic distinctions.

"Friend?" he said. "What's a friend? Just someone you like? Someone you trust with your wife, with your wallet? Paul Castellano is an acquaintance I stay in touch with. I don't know how else to put it."

"Are you aware of his connections to organized crime?"

Julie Miron put down his pencil, noticed it was at a jarring angle to the paper, and moved it slightly. "You know, Mr. O'Brien, I don't like prejudice. Italian guy has a big house, right away it's organized crime."

"I don't like prejudice either," said O'Brien. "But you didn't answer the question."

"No," said Miron. "I don't know anything about Paul Castellano and organized crime. Okay?"

"Okay," said O'Brien. He raised his hands in a gesture almost of surrender, and with a motion just slightly more expansive than was absolutely necessary, he put notebook and pen into his jacket pocket. The interview was over, or so it appeared. Stephen Miron, rather suddenly, seemed to make a point of looking bored or annoyed; no doubt he wanted to suggest he was missing all sorts of exciting business in Manhattan. He put his yellow pad in his attaché case and started leafing through the *New York Times*. Julie

Miron retrieved his pencil and started on a fresh sheet of paper, doodling something interplanetary.

"It *is* a big house, though, isn't it?" said Joe O'Brien, trying to muster a tone of awe.

Julie Miron smiled warmly. The notebooks were put away, the pressure was off, and O'Brien was talking about the frustrated architect's favorite subject. "Yes," he said, "it's quite a place."

"I can hardly imagine what it must be like inside."

"Very lavish," Miron volunteered. "Not, between us, in the best of taste. A little . . ." He tilted his head in syncopation with a wagging hand. "A little . . ."

"Mafioso?"

In spite of himself, Miron laughed. "All right, have it your way. A little Mafioso. But everything the best. Carrara marble. Inlaid woods. Notching moldings. The kind of detail work you just don't see anymore."

"Still," O'Brien said, "when I see a house that big, I feel a little overwhelmed. I can imagine getting lost in there."

Julie Miron was quick to correct him. Professorially, he raised a finger. "In a well-designed house, one is never ill at ease, and never lost. A good house has a logic that carries you through. It's like music. In a good piece of music, you may be surprised, but you are never lost."

"If you say so," said O'Brien. "But me, I see a mansion like Castellano's, I'm intimidated."

"From the outside, yes," said Miron. "That's the idea. To impress. But from the inside, no." He tore off his space station drawing and put his pencil point onto a clean sheet of letterhead. The son rattled his newspaper, but did not come out from behind it. Like most sons of most fathers, he'd probably stopped listening to what the old man was droning on about.

"From the inside," Julie Miron continued, beginning the practiced, steady movement of his pencil, "it's human-scaled and comfy. Forget the columns and all that monumental crap. That's just real estate. Now we're talking life.

"Look, here's the doorway. Then there's an entrance hall. It's big, sure, but it's for getting out of big coats; it makes sense. Then you come down this corridor that gives you just two choices—you dogleg into the living room, or you continue back. Two choices—that's not overwhelming, is it? Then over here's the dining room—again, you can enter or pass it by. But you know what makes this such a good design? The hallway is really pulling you toward the kitchen, which is where people always want to go anyway."

O'Brien watched the sketch emerging under Julie Miron's lithe hand. It matched his own recollection of the Castellano house; it jibed very well with the blueprints. The man knew whereof he spoke.

"But still," said O'Brien. "So many rooms."

"Sure," said Miron. "But when you're in the house, you forget about them. The bedrooms are tucked away upstairs—you don't have to think about all those canopies gathering dust. The den, the rec room—again, they're off by themselves. Ninety-eight percent of the time, you forget about them."

"Okay, but that still leaves the decision about which of all those rooms you want to *be* in."

"Ah," said Miron, with almost voluptuous satisfaction, as if he'd just been proved utterly correct in his very fondest theory. "That's where human nature comes in. People are creatures of habit. They might have a hundred chairs, a hundred coffee mugs—they'll use the same one every time. The rest are for ego, for show. It's the same with rooms in a house."

"So you're telling me Paul Castellano has all these empty rooms and only lives in one?"

"Not exactly," said Miron. He looked down at his drawing, then started scratching in vector lines that ran from various points and converged with what seemed like scientific inevitability near the kitchen—specifically, it appeared to Joe O'Brien, in the dining nook defined by the runwaylike counter where Gloria Olarte had stacked the monstrous steaks. "What I'm telling you is that design is about psychology. Human beings are really all alike. You think we're so different from the caveman? Certain things we take comfort from. The hearth. Seeing what the womenfolk are up to. And no one who has a choice likes to be very far away from his refrigerator."

CHAPTER 29

ON NOVEMBER 12, 1982—after the Operation Castaway affidavit had been vetted by FBI headquarters in Washington and reviewed by the Attorney General of the United States—district court judge Henry Bramwell signed an order authorizing the installation of an electronic eavesdropping device at the Staten Island residence of Paul Castellano.

At the Brooklyn-Queens Resident Agency of the FBI, there was a closely held sense of satisfaction and relief, but no celebration. There wasn't time for one. Judge Bramwell's order gave the Bureau thirty days to get the bug installed. Thirty days to devise and execute a strategy for an undetected entry into the Godfather's house. Thirty days to figure out how to neutralize the Dobermans, hide from the closed-circuit security cameras, baffle the alarm system, defeat the purportedly tamper-proof locks, escape the notice of both family and household staff, leave the bug right under the noses of some of the most suspicious individuals on the face of the earth, and get out again without leaving so much as a footprint in a Castellano carpet. This, moreover, at the home of a man who was slightly famous for staying home, lounging in his red satin robe, taking his goosenecked pleasure exactly when it suited him, entertaining friends and supplicants in his slippers.

It was fortunate that the Bureau had a running start in the project.

Shortly after his meeting with the doodling Julie Miron, Joe O'Brien, to corroborate Miron's information, had paid a visit to Gloria Olarte. This was on a Wednesday, the day that Gloria still visited her sister Nellie in Corona. Corona—with its gray tenements, street-corner *bodegas,* and twenty-year-old Chevys and Pontiacs—was a far cry from the luxury of Todt Hill, yet it seemed to be the only place Gloria really relaxed. With Nellie, she'd drink coffee and gossip, or sometimes see a Spanish movie or shop at one of those stores where dish towels and underpants are displayed in huge open bins. Often she brought food from the Castellano larder—bags of frozen shrimp, roasts of a quality not available in poorer neighborhoods—but whether the food was pilfered or freely offered at the largess of Big Paul, Joe O'Brien could not be sure.

"Gloria," the agent said, as the maid descended the birdcage stairway of the El, "what a coincidence." He'd been leaning against an orange wire trash can for three hours.

She looked up from the dirty sidewalk and regarded him. "Meester Joe," she said, in a tone that was not at all unfriendly, and not terribly surprised. Her alert eyes scanned his face. "Ees no coincidence," she announced. "You want to talk with Gloria. Ees hokay. You like *café con leche?*"

They ducked into a Cuban luncheonette and sat down at the counter, making small talk over the hiss of the milk steamer. Gloria, seeming suddenly rather girlish, propped her elbows on the cool Formica with the boomerang design and let her plain but mobile face rest on her fists. She smiled. Sipping her coffee, she glanced up at the agent through her eyelashes, which were matted with mascara. "So, Meester Joe, what you like to talk about?"

"Your family in Colombia."

For an instant, Gloria's expression seemed to float free of the bones of her face, as if the circuitry of her mistrust had to process these unexpected words before she could allow herself to respond in any way. "My family good people. Berry poor. But proud, honest. You no make trouble for my family, Meester Joe."

"I wasn't thinking of making trouble," said O'Brien. "I was thinking maybe I could help them."

"How you help?"

"Visas? Green cards? Maybe they'd like to come to this country."

Gloria laughed. It was the relieved laugh of a child who has felt out of her depth in some new game, then suddenly figured it out. "Oh, I see," she said, singing out the syllables like the NBC network chimes. "I help Meester Joe. Meester Joe help me. Yes?"

She put her hand on O'Brien's arm and swiveled on her stool, letting the motion rock her clear up to her shoulders. Gradually, a somewhat absurd fact was getting through to the agent: Paul Castellano's maid was flirting with him. This, O'Brien didn't need; her playfulness embarrassed him, and had he known at the time about Gloria's true relationship with the Godfather, it would have made him nervous as well. On the other hand, Gloria Olarte's goodwill could prove quite important. "Yes," he said. "Maybe we can help each other."

"So how I help?"

"First of all, you don't go running back and tell Mrs. Nina that we talked."

Gloria wrinkled her nose. "Meesus Nina, I no tell her nothing. Me and Meesus Nina, we feenish. *Nada*."

O'Brien took a sip of the thick, sweet coffee. Recent surveillances of the Todt Hill mansion had indicated that Castellano's second maid, María Eugenia Estrada, was no longer around; as O'Brien would later confirm, she had in fact gone back to Bogotá. And as he would also learn, this left two women vying for supremacy in Paul Castellano's house. Not that Nina was contending for her husband's affections—that contest she seemed to have conceded. But she was not ready to surrender her authority, her place of honor. She was still the lawful partner, and not above savoring the acid pleasure of humiliating her husband's paramour, who was still, after all, on the payroll. Between the ever-bitterer wife and the ever-bolder maid and mistress, the hatred was heating up.

"And you don't tell Mr. Paul, either," Joe O'Brien said.

The maid put on her most elfin look, all wide brown eyes and innocent lips. "Thees ees hard for Gloria to promise."

"Then don't promise. Just don't do it."

Gloria responded to this bit of sternness by making her expression still more kittenish. For a moment, O'Brien had the distressing thought that she was about to lay her head against his shoulder. "So what you want Gloria to do?"

"I want you to tell me who visits Mr. Paul and what they talk about."

"I no hear what they talk about," she said.

"Gloria," said O'Brien, "no lies today, okay? Mr. Paul holds his meetings in the kitchen. You serve coffee, drinks. You cook. Don't tell me you don't hear."

If Gloria was nonplussed at what Joe O'Brien claimed to know already, it didn't show. "Ees far," she protested.

"How far could it be?" said the agent.

"*Far.* Gloria, she work over here." She stabbed at the Formica counter with a stubby index finger. "Meester Paul, he talk his beezness *here.*" She traced a wide loop, and O'Brien saw clear as day the divider between the Castellano kitchen and the dining area.

Still, he wanted to be a notch surer that Big Paul in fact sat at the far end of the long blond table. He gently nudged Gloria Olarte's knee with his own. "Your legs must get tired, bringing the cannoli all the way around."

Gloria gave a languorous little groan, the universal sound made by a person who'd like something rubbed. "Oh, yes, Meester Joe. Sometimes Gloria's legs they get berry tired."

O'Brien looked down at his coffee. He tried to decide if Gloria Olarte was in fact leaning closer to him, or if he only imagined that the almost-empty luncheonette was suddenly getting crowded. "So, Gloria, you'll listen? You'll tell me?"

"You geeve me beezness card again?"

"No," said O'Brien. He didn't especially want to furnish Paul Castellano with concrete evidence of his visit. "I can reach you."

"On Wednesdays."

"Yes, I know."

"My seester . . ."

"Nellie."

"She sometimes go out," said Gloria, swiveling her hips, letting the twist run all the way up her torso. "She sometimes leave Gloria all by herself in the apartment. Sometimes Gloria get berry lonely, Meester Joe."

Top, Paul Castellano's first mug shot of record. He was nineteen years old at the time. *Above,* Castellano's mug shot at the time of the Roy DeMeo case in 1984.

Castellano's Todt Hill mansion on New York's Staten Island. He had the house built to specification and moved in in 1980. His wife and daughter still live there.

"The Plant." Agents Kurins and O'Brien operated from an apartment on the second and third floors of this building, monitoring the bug they had planted in Castellano's nearby house. *Right,* Julie Miron, a successful businessman and personal friend of Castellano, inadvertently provided a floor plan of the Godfather's kitchen where he held court. His information enabled the FBI to successfully place a bug in the house.

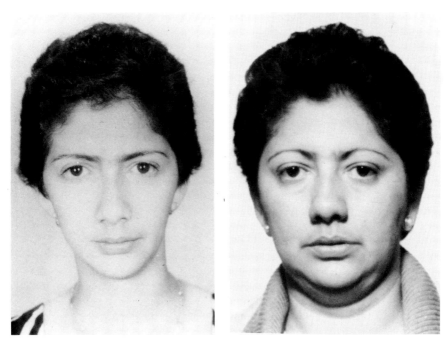

Left, Gloria Olarte in 1978, newly arrived in the United States from Colombia, looking for work. *Right,* Gloria in 1986, shortly after the death of Paul Castellano. His demise marked the end of their love affair as well as of her employment.

Gloria and Big Paul, circa 1983, in one of the very few
pictures showing Castellano smiling. Obviously their affair had
begun.

Left, Castellano with his daughter, Connie, in the dining room of his home. *Below,* Castellano holding his granddaughter, Connie's child.

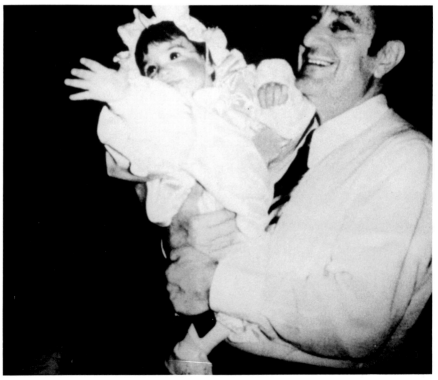

Top, Paul Castellano, at home, holding court. At Castellano's left is Joe Watts, a Gambino associate. To his right is Frank De Cicco, captain in the Gambino family. De Cicco is credited with setting up Castellano's assassination. De Cicco himself was blown up in a car bombing in April of 1986 on a Brooklyn Street. *Above,* A smiling Julie Miron seated next to Castellano. Ducking out of the photo is James Failla, Gambino *capo* and one of the men who helped plan the Godfather's death.

Above, Tommy Bilotti relaxing at the Godfather's condo in Pompano Beach, Florida. His bat is nowhere in sight. *Left,* Bilotti at work—with Castellano and Gambino soldier Frank Di Stefano, captured by surveillance outside Martini's Seafood Restaurant in Bay Ridge, Brooklyn.

Joe Gallo at work in his Astoria, Queens, neighborhood—in front of Sperrazza's Luncheonette.

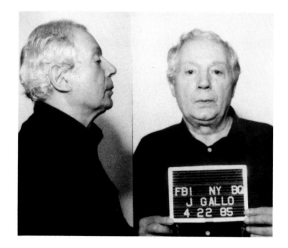

Left, Joseph N. Gallo at the time of his arrest in 1985. *Below,* surveillance photo, left to right: Frankie Di Stefano, Gambino soldier; John Gotti, then Gambino *capo;* and the elder statesman, Joseph Gallo, *consigliere.* The photograph was taken shortly after these men had lunch with Castellano at Martini's Seafood Restaurant.

Above, Aniello Dellacroce, Gambino LCN underboss, with his protégé John Gotti, outside J's Villa Restaurant on Staten Island. *Right,* Alphonse "Funzie" Mosca, a soldier in the Gambino family, was the money courier for construction payoffs. These mug shots, taken only ten months apart, show what a little time in the slammer can do to some people.

Above, Café Biondo, 141 Mulberry Street in Little Italy, owned by Gambino captain Joe "Butch" Corrao, served as a favorite meeting place. The restaurant is the building in the center. *Left,* Mildred Russo, a grandmother and the mother-in-law of "Big Gus" Augustus Sclafini, worked in the sealed records department of the Southern District of the New York Federal Court system. She served as an informer for the mob.

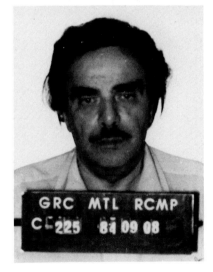

Top, Thomas Agro and Joseph "Piney" Armone outside Larry's Restaurant on First Avenue in Manhattan. Agro was a Gambino soldier in the crew of *capo* Armone. *Above left,* An early arrest of Tommy Agro in Nassau County, Long Island, on bookmaking charges. *Above right,* Agro's court photograph taken by Canadian Royal Mounted Police in Montreal. At the time of his arrest, Agro had been an FBI fugitive for one year.

Top, The house on Staten Island's Cameron Avenue that served as site of the Commission meeting, later dubbed Apalachin II. *Above left*, Anthony "Fat Tony" Salerno, boss of the Genovese family, emerging from the meeting on Cameron Avenue. *Above right*, Gennaro Langella (Gerry Lang), acting boss of the Columbo family, followed by Tommy Bilotti and Ralph Scopo, Columbo soldier, leaving the Commission meeting.

A Gambino family portrait, taken by Gloria Olarte. From the left: Thomas Gambino, Tommy Bilotti, Joseph Corrao, Joe Delmonico, Paul Castellano, Frank DePolito, Frank De Cicco, and James Failla. Of all these shown, only Delmonico did not rank as captain or higher.

Tommy Bilotti took six shots to the head and body as he emerged from his car on Manhattan's East 46th Street. His boss Paul Castellano was also shot six times. Unfortunately the entire staff of Sparks Steak House was in a meeting at the rear of the restaurant at the time, so no one there witnessed the historic event.

CHAPTER 30

ON THE DAY the Title III authorization was handed down, Joe O'Brien stopped shaving and started breaking in a pair of enormous wing-tip shoes. He also began acclimating himself to wearing glasses with horn frames and noncorrective lenses, and took to sporting a charcoal-gray fedora.

He was cultivating an undercover identity as one Joseph P. Greenberg, of Syracuse, an attorney who was now seeking employment at one of New York's Wall Street firms. While job-hunting—so the story was concocted—O'Brien/Greenberg would live in Staten Island's Todt Hill neighborhood. Like tens of thousands of other Staten Islanders, he'd commute by ferry to lower Manhattan, there to seek his fortune.

O'Brien/Greenberg's digs, of course, would serve as the monitoring station for the Castellano bug, and there were several requirements the location had to fulfill. First, it had to lie within the radius of effective transmission that had been laid out by FBI technicians.

This requirement already posed problems. Castellano lived in an enclave of million-dollar-plus, owner-occupied, single-family dwellings. No one rented. Nor did anyone park on the street, which scotched another possibility: the beat-up vans fitted out as state-of-the-art sound trucks for inner-city use would have been discovered in a minute here. In theory, the Bureau might have bought a house, and sold it again at the end of the surveillance. But even aside from the awkwardness of explaining to Washington why Joe O'Brien needed a million and a half in petty cash, this would have been a dubious tactic. A Todt Hill house coming on the market was a rare and gossip-worthy event, with neighbors rabid to assess the source and extent of potential buyers' wealth.

A six-foot-five Irishman posing as a Jewish lawyer and trying not to attract attention did not want to be seen perusing real estate in those immediate environs.

So O'Brien/Greenberg moved down the hill, toward the perimeter of the listening area. He now had another factor to consider: sight lines. Especially at the beginning, matching voices to names would be a difficult chore for the agents monitoring the bug. It was important, therefore, to provide a vantage point that covered the main access route to and from the White House. License plates could then be used to corroborate who was speaking.

Security was the final requirement for the FBI plant, and it was more of a problem than one might at first imagine. People sometimes assume, to their cost, that all solid citizens are of course on the side of law enforcement in the fight against organized crime. This assumption is woefully naive. America has always had a perverse affection for its outlaws, as well as a deep ambivalence toward its authorities. There is little doubt that some of the good people of Staten Island would not have minded helping Paul Castellano at the expense of the FBI. Maybe they knew he was Mafia, but they didn't see the blood on his hands. They didn't feel the crushed kneecaps. They thought of Castellano as a quiet neighbor who gave money to the Church and helped keep the streets safe. No one—least of all O'Brien/Greenberg's eventual landlord—could be assumed to be an ally against the rich old man from the top of the hill. The plant, then, needed to be snoop-resistant.

Finding a New York apartment is an ordeal under any circumstances, and given the parameters within which O'Brien/Greenberg had to work, the process was more irritating still. Finally, however, he found the perfect place.

It was a lovingly restored Victorian house located at 1510 Richmond Road—the main boulevard leading to Todt Hill. The building was owned by a surgeon named Robert Vitolo, who used the ground floor as his medical offices. The place was thus unoccupied at night. For a thousand dollars a month, plus a month's security deposit, O'Brien/Greenberg rented the second-floor apartment, which also included a loft-dormer that was ideal for the stashing of the monitoring gear.

As a final detail of his cover, O'Brien/Greenberg told Vitolo he would have a roommate, an airline pilot who was between marriages. Since, conveniently enough, the roommate was just then flying to Hawaii, he could neither sign the lease nor be introduced. The "pilot," then, could be anybody—Andy Kurins, Frank Spero, or any of the other agents who would be working at the plant. And if Dr. Vitolo, or his staff, or his neighbors, happened to notice a number of different males coming and going from the Greenberg apartment at strange hours of the night, and if they felt the need to conjecture as to why, they were free to surmise that the quiet blue-eyed Jewish lawyer was one of those ultradiscreet white-collar gays who were button-down conventional during daylight hours but led a not uneventful social life.

CHAPTER 31

HOW ABOUT WE gas 'em?" said the surveillance specialist who had been sent up from D.C.

"Gas who?" Bruce Mouw asked, chewing on his pipe. "The people or the dogs?"

"Everybody," said the surveillance guy. "Shoot the gas in through the heating vents. We go in with masks. In the morning, no one remembers a thing."

"The gas," said Andy Kurins. "Dangerous?"

"A little," confessed the expert.

"Great," said Joe O'Brien. "We plant the bug. We're psyched. Next morning, we put on the headphones. Nothing. Everybody's brain-dead."

"And the Dobes have rigor mortis," Kurins said. "Stiff as carousel horses. Timmy Bilotti comes over. Lights a match. Place explodes."

"It's not that kind of gas," said the expert.

"What else ya got," Mouw asked him.

Undaunted, the surveillance man reviewed the notes on his clipboard and went on. "For the dogs, we got knockout meat. We gauge the dosage to the size of the animals, shoot the steaks full of tranquilizers, then throw them over the fence or something, one per dog."

"What if one dog gets both steaks?" asked O'Brien.

"That dog is dead."

"Plus the other dog is really pissed," said Kurins. Reflexively, he covered up his groin.

"All right," said the man from Washington, "we'll come back to the dogs. What about getting in the house? We have anyone cooperating inside?"

"I wouldn't count on it," Mouw said.

"You said there was a maid?"

"Yeah, but she won't help us," replied O'Brien.

"Why not?"

O'Brien searched for words to express a rather sudden hunch about Gloria's allegiance to her boss and benefactor. Instead, he decided on a more neutral reply: "She's squirrelly, I guess."

"How about lifting her keys when she's out shopping?" suggested the expert. "We could have someone grab them, make a wax impression, and return them to her purse. Takes twelve seconds."

"Iffy," said Kurins. "She's well known in the neighborhood. People keep an eye on her. Everyone's eager to do a favor for Big Paul."

"What about we send guys in as workmen?" asked the surveillance man. "Exterminators? Pool maintenance? Rug shampooers?"

"No good," O'Brien said. "Castellano knows all those companies. Probably controls most of them. Besides, we know that Tommy Bilotti checks up on everyone who comes in. If it's not the regular guy, he calls the office."

"Hmm," said the man from Washington to the now-bearded Joe O'Brien. "You've gotten inside once already, right?"

The agent nodded.

"Well, if you can get inside again, we can buy you some time. We can crash some cars outside. Send some ambulances. Maybe run down a power line."

"I don't think they'd let me in again," said O'Brien. "I think they know they screwed up, letting me in the first time."

The surveillance expert put down his clipboard and drummed lightly on the edge of Bruce Mouw's desk. "Well then, gents," he said, "it looks like it has to be a good old-fashioned break-in. What do we know about the alarm system?"

"We know you need a code to deactivate it," said O'Brien.

"And that there's a siren on the roof over the garage," added Kurins.

"It probably has motion sensors," said the surveillance man. "Which means that the dogs have to be penned in at night."

165

"I think they stay in the laundry room," O'Brien said.

"Good," said the man from D.C. "But there's a few more things we have to find out. We have to learn if there's a remote alarm, and what sort of security service it goes to. We have to check their response time. We have to see what direction they come from, and what kind of manpower they bring."

"Fine," said Mouw, chomping down on his pipe. "So how do we find that out?"

The surveillance expert locked his fingers across his tummy and leaned back in his chair. "Well, by setting off some false alarms, of course."

CHAPTER 32

O N DECEMBER 2, 1982, at 12:46 A.M., Andy Kurins, dressed in black from head to foot, climbed the portico steps of Paul Castellano's Todt Hill mansion. Floodlights stretched his zigzagged shadow across the stairs. Security cameras panned slowly, serene as oscillating fans. Inside, the house was dark and utterly silent.

Kurins paused for just an instant, and looked behind him. In the near distance, the trees and hedges of Benedict Road were etched black and flat against the cool sky; beyond, the Verrazano Bridge twinkled blue against the orange streetlamps of Brooklyn.

The agent sidled over to one of the Godfather's windows. At its corners, small, clear suction cups held delicate wires that would be tripped if the window was opened, smashed, or too firmly shaken, even by the wind. Kurins put the heels of his hands against the frame, took a deep breath, and gave a quick hard thrust.

The roof alarm exploded into a wail as abrupt and piercing as a blast of air on the root of a tooth. Inside, the Dobermans bayed, a sound that conjured racing blood and glinting fangs. Andy Kurins moved quickly down the steps, across the Castellano driveway, and into the dimness of Benedict Road.

And now the FBI surveillance team, arrayed around the neighborhood, went to school on the Godfather's defenses.

In quick succession, two upstairs lights came on, separated by a dark window. Paul and Nina Castellano in their separate bedrooms.

At the back of the house, from a narrow portal cut into the slope of Todt Hill, came another slice of yellow light. It must have come from Gloria's room in the servants' quarters.

No doors opened; there was no bodyguard or watchman on the premises.

Twelve minutes and twenty-six seconds after the first blast of the alarm, a single black sedan screeched into Castellano's driveway, having approached from the direction of Four Corners Road. The sedan, though unmarked, was later traced to a firm called Community Security Service. CSS was headed by a registered private investigator named Salvatore Barbato, who sometimes filled in for Tommy Bilotti as Paul Castellano's driver. CSS, it seemed clear, could not be worked with.

Some thirty seconds after Barbato's arrival, Bilotti himself appeared in his mauve Buick. Castellano met them at the door. Barbato went inside, and Bilotti, carrying a flashlight in one hand and a baseball bat in the other, explored the grounds. By twenty after one, the Messrs. B. had left and the house was dark again.

"Very helpful," said the surveillance expert, reviewing the caper next day in Bruce Mouw's office. "In four, five days we'll do it again."

"What more do we need to know?" asked Joe O'Brien.

"Nothing," said the surveillance man with a smile. "In fact, we'll just have one guy looking on."

"Then why are we doing it?" asked Mouw.

"Cry wolf. Make the security guy tired."

Several nights later, the CSS response time ballooned to eighteen minutes and seven seconds.

Joe O'Brien and Wally Ticano were riding the Metroliner to Washington, where, at an FBI acoustics lab, a close facsimile of Paul Castellano's kitchen and dining area was being constructed. Working from the subpoenaed blueprints, the technicians could easily duplicate room dimensions. But they needed the agents' recollections on details. The size, materials, and placement of the furniture. The location of appliances that could throw off radio interference. The existence of draperies that swallowed sound or naked glass that turned it thin and tinny. The most informed opinion possible as to where the Godfather sat. Even the typical volume of his speaking voice, that breathy rumble through a throat that never seemed quite open.

The train clattered on through New Jersey, past Philadelphia. Like other businessmen, O'Brien and Ticano sat with their attaché cases propped open on the tray tables in front of them, and when conversation wore thin, they riffled through their papers. Among the notes, directives, and loose sketches in Joe O'Brien's bag was the Miron's Desirables catalog. O'Brien had never bothered to look at it and had practically forgotten he had it. But now he took it out.

"Julie Miron's hobby," he said to Ticano. "In case he doesn't get rich enough from supplying lumber for Mob construction jobs."

Ticano took the booklet, thumbed through it. "Pricey stuff."

"Fine design," purred O'Brien, squeezing into the syllables a deep dislike of the fey, the precious, the overwrought.

"My ass," said Ticano. He pointed to a cobalt-blue enameled gizmo that called itself the Food Sculptor. "It's still a slicer-dicer to me."

He turned pages, shaking his head. "Hey, isn't this the lamp that stands next to Castellano's table?"

O'Brien took back the catalog. The item in question was a European chrome design—round base, hexagonal shaft, universal swivel at the shoulder; then, leading to a sleek triangular shade, a counterbalanced arm with a gooseneck extension. "Whaddya know," O'Brien said. "Miron really does deliver orders to Castellano's house."

He dog-eared the catalog page and returned it to his briefcase. It might be a worthwhile thing to show the fellows at the lab.

CHAPTER 33

WHEN A TITLE III court authorization runs out, there is no fanfare, no gong, no buzzer. There is only the quiet frustration of time lost, opportunity slipping away—that, and the bothersome necessity of updating the affidavit, and hoping the judge will grant a renewal.

At midnight on December 11, 1982, when the first permission to bug Castellano's house expired, there was still much to be done. In Washington, the simulated Castellano kitchen was now completed, and Andy Kurins and Joe O'Brien were just beginning the tedious and exacting exercise of practicing the mechanics of the installation. There was much to master, and it had to be mastered cold. The procedures were learned in daylight, then tested in pitch-blackness. Seconds were trimmed from every step. Gloved fingers became increasingly adept at handling lockpicks and tiny wrenches of surgical steel. Mouths and ears cultivated a taste for absolute silence.

Meanwhile, Christmas came to Staten Island, and for Paul Castellano it was as prosperous and apparently unthreatened a holiday season as he had ever known. For all the taxpayers' money being spent, all the manpower redirected, all the Byzantine schemes being hatched, the FBI had still not even ruffled the outward calm of the most powerful mobster in America.

He relished his holidays, the Godfather did. Delivery vans from Dial Poultry brought enormous slabs of meat and dozens of wing-tagged Perdue chickens to his door. Bakery trucks appeared with huge tiered and doilied trays of cookies, pastries, *biscotti*. The sons and daughters visited, they brought the grandkids, and no one left without getting stuffed full of macaroni, *baccalà*, salads of pecorino cheese and fennel.

Gambino *capo*s, flush with the spirit of Christmas giving, filed in with fat envelopes stuffed with cash for the Boss. Hundreds, thousands, tens of thousands—the top man's cut of the tens of millions of ill-gotten dollars circulating in a vast and dizzying gyre all around Mafia New York. Contractors were slipping cash-heavy greetings to union guys. Nightclub owners showed year-end appreciation to their liquor sources, their garbage haulers, their keepers-of-order. Cops, to be sure, got their Christmas bonuses; neighborhood enforcers got a little something extra for the kids. Paul Castellano took his tribute share of every dollar, and feasted on it. He kissed cheeks and pinched babies. He ate cheesecake and shot insulin. He played paterfamilias and bestowed largess on everyone around him.

It is not known what, if anything, the Godfather gave his wife that Christmas. To Gloria, however, he gave a sports car, a red Datsun 280Z. Gloria did not know how to drive. But she said she wanted to learn. In this, as apparently in many things, the Mob's most imperious man indulged her.

Among the men and women of the FBI, it is a point of pride that only college graduates may become agents of the Bureau. Still, it must be said that at certain moments, the connection between all that education and the task at hand gets a little blurred. Such a moment must have been experienced by the surveillance man who, in early 1983, was circling Todt Hill in a single-engine plane. His mission: to observe and chart where and when the Castellano dogs took dumps.

By this time, the second thirty-day authorization for the installing of the bug had expired, and the third was on the wane. Around the Brooklyn-Queens Resident Agency of the FBI, patience was wearing thin. To maintain appearances, Joe O'Brien/Greenberg had been spending most of his nights at the Richmond Road plant—away from his family, bored stiff, sleeping badly, and accomplishing, in the short term, nothing. Andy Kurins was on edge, his attempts at levity turning sourer and sourer. Bruce Mouw bit his pipe and winced a lot.

But it had been clear from the start that the Bureau would have one chance, and one chance only, to successfully install the microphone. The slightest miscue would inflame the ready paranoia of the Godfather and his minions, and that would be the end of the affair.

Through January and February, there was simply too much activity at the Castellano mansion to launch the operation. The Mercs and the Jags stacked up in the driveway. Tommy Bilotti haunted the premises like a squat and murderous gremlin.

When Joe O'Brien handed in a revised affidavit for a fourth authorization, Judge Henry Bramwell was sympathetic but firm. "There's a limit on these things, boys," he said. "This is the last one I can sign."

Then, toward the middle of March, the agents watching the Staten Island White House observed a strange and encouraging exodus. Tommy Bilotti appeared one morning in his mauve Buick, and left the engine running at the foot of the portico steps. He went into the house, and emerged a few minutes later carrying luggage. More trips, more suitcases. Finally, Paul Castellano appeared in the doorway. At his side, her arm almost touching his, stood a smiling woman. It was not Nina. It was Gloria Olarte, dressed in a new wool coat, freshly outfitted for vacation. The Godfather, headed for warmer climes, sported only a cashmere muffler over his gray suit; he was already wearing tinted glasses.

Miami-based agents would soon confirm that Paul Castellano was relaxing at his luxury condo in Pompano Beach. He was seen in a sport shirt with a palm tree motif, his arm around a woman with coarse dark hair and a downy upper lip. With them was a scowling man with a bad toupee who drove the golf cart around the grounds and looked possessive.

Back in New York, the weather was blustery and gray. At headquarters on Queens Boulevard, Joe O'Brien read the Miami dispatches and scratched his head.

"Andy," he said to his partner, "lemme ask you something. How many guys do you know buy sports cars for their maids?"

"Not many," said Kurins.

"How many take their maids on vacation?"

"Not many."

"Does it say anything to you that she's always in new clothes all of a sudden?"

"Joe, I know exactly what it says, but—"

"And one other thing," O'Brien interrupted. "How many old guys do you know who would get their dicks repaired so they could make love to old wives they pay no attention to?"

"Joe," said Andy Kurins, "I know how it looks, but it's impossible. It's against all the traditions, against all the rules."

"Yeah," said O'Brien, "but maybe it's love."

"Love," Kurins said. "The Godfather in love? Well, maybe. I guess I've heard stranger things."

PART 3

CHAPTER 34

S NOOPY ONE is squatting near the blue spruce. Over."

"Roger. Can you spot Snoopy Two? Over."

"Affirmative. Snoopy Two is sniffing around by the rhododendron. Appears to be preparing to squat. Over."

"Standing by. Over."

The FBI surveillance plane banked a tight circle over Todt Hill, the spotter straining to keep his binoculars steady against his eyes. On the ground, two "gardeners" lolled in the shrubbery beyond the Castellano fence. They carried pruning shears and, slung over their shoulders, burlap sacks for the cuttings. In these sacks were two slabs of sirloin steak, injected with a chemical called Rompun. Five millimeters per hundred pounds of dog would render the creatures somewhere between docile and comatose.

"Snoopy Two is lifting a leg," said the spotter's voice through the walkie-talkie. "Suggest you heave meat. Over."

The two gardeners, positioned some forty feet apart, held each other's eyes, nodded, then tossed the steaks over the eight-foot fence. Frisbee-like, the sirloins pinwheeled gaily against the dimming sky, then crashed down through the foliage where the Dobermans were scrabbling, each in its previously charted territory. The gardeners heard the tearing of sinew and the smacking of long tongues.

It was 5:22 P.M. on March 17, Saint Patrick's Day, 1983. In six hours, the dogs would fall into a deep drugged sleep that would, in turn, last six hours. During that time, Paul Castellano would be encouched with his maid, a thousand miles away. His bodyguard and security chief would be nursing his sunburn, watching TV, or treating himself, perhaps, to the services of a call girl. Only Nina Castellano would be at home on Staten Island, sleeping the fragile sleep of those with too much empty space around them.

"Shit," said Joe O'Brien. "The pants are too short."

At the main Staten Island post office, on Bay Street, O'Brien, Andy Kurins, and an eight-man FBI surveillance crew were eating buttered rolls and drinking coffee out of cardboard cups. It was 11:15 P.M., and the two agents were slipping into their black ninja outfits—roomy cotton pants, smocks that came down to midthigh, close-fitting caps, and rubber-soled canvas slippers that were as silent and supple as anything the Godfather himself might wear while prowling through his personal domain. But on the six-foot-five O'Brien, the pants didn't reach the shoe tops, and the effect of all that matte and disappearing black was undone by a flash of pale and as if stroboscopic leg.

"Magic-marker his ankle," said the chief of the surveillance crew. O'Brien submitted; the wick tickled. "So let's go through this once again."

The crew chief directed his attention toward the two men wearing the proud and sporty uniforms of the New York City Department of Sanitation. "The garbage truck will be stationed at the intersection of Todt Hill and Four Corners. If the alarm gets tripped, we put it broadside and yank off the distributor cap. The security car will have to loop all the way back down to Richmond Road. That's an extra four minutes. Got it?"

The garbagemen nodded.

"You," he said to a wiry little man in a charcoal turtleneck. "When Joe and Andy get into the garage, you rappel up onto the roof and stuff the horn. Stay there till they're out again. Then clean out the foam and trail them. Got it?"

The mountaineer said no problem.

"Okay," said the crew chief, and turned to two large men wearing jeans and studded leather jackets, with bandannas tied around their heads. "You guys take the lead van and reconnoiter. Go twice around the block, then park on Benedict and watch for lights. Remember, she's an old woman, and old women don't sleep so well. If a light comes on, we're gone. Got it?"

The van pirates said they understood.

"Joe, Andy. You clear?"

The agents said they were. They'd been waiting two years to penetrate Paul Castellano's sanctum. They'd been rehearsing the moves for three months. They were more than ready.

CHAPTER 35

THE LEAD VAN headed out at 12:55 A.M.

At 1:14 the report came back that the Castellano mansion was dark and silent, with nothing untoward in the surrounding neighborhood. So the rest of the convoy rolled, through streets that were nearly deserted except for the occasional Saint Paddy's Day reveler weaving his way home. Orion dominated the late-winter sky, and on the winding way up Todt Hill, the Verrazano seemed to be writhing under different vantage points.

At 1:31, half a block from the entrance to the Castellano driveway, Joe O'Brien, Andy Kurins, and the mountaineer slipped out of the van and into the knuckly shadow of a leafless sycamore. O'Brien wore a bellyband, into which was tucked a small-bore automatic pistol in nonreflective blue steel. Kurins carried a dart gun loaded with booster doses for restless Dobermans. Both men wore thin gloves, had safe-frequency walkie-talkies harnessed to their necks, and hoisted knapsacks holding tools.

They edged quickly through the intersecting yellow flood-lights toward the house. Skirting the portico steps, moving past the stately columns and the ranks of dark windows, they padded toward the six-car garage. Next to the double-width vehicle door, there was a pedestrian entrance. This was the entrance used by the maids, and it was not connected to the alarm system, since it led no farther than the garage. Still, this was a serious design flaw in the Godfather's security scheme. Within seconds, Joe O'Brien had picked the lock, and the agents were safely ensconced amid the smells of gasoline and wax, out of reach of the floodlights and the panning cameras. The next step could proceed at leisure. They could catch their breath, look around. Had their mission been to steal some cars, they could have chosen among a Cadillac, a Jaguar, a Mercedes, and Gloria's racy little Datsun.

The mountaineer planted his hook in the shingles of the flat garage roof, and proceeded to walk straight up the wall.

Kurins and O'Brien gave him twenty seconds to silence the electric bullhorn. They then turned to opening the purportedly unpickable lock on the door that led into the house itself. It took less than half a minute. The door swung silently open, and the agents stepped uninvited into La Cosa Nostra headquarters.

Inside the door, the control panel for the burglar alarm glowed an ominous red. If the agents could not make the indicator turn to green before the electronic delay ran out, several things would happen. The choked horn on the roof would turn hot from its own clenched breath. At the office of Community Security Service, a signal would ring out, and a car, destined to encounter a stalled garbage truck on Todt Hill Road, would race toward the White House; its driver would be armed, and legally so. A phone call might perhaps be made from CSS to Nina Castellano, waking her and aborting the mission. A call might also go out to Tommy Bilotti in Pompano Beach, alerting him to trouble, shortening the Boss's vacation perhaps, scotching a second attempt at the installation.

The agents had estimated that they had twenty-five seconds to deactivate the system. Four of those seconds had been spent getting through the door and reaching the controls. Andy Kurins didn't breathe as he flashed a computerized digital selector at the alarm system's brain. The scanner riffled at an inconceivable pace through the ten thousand possible combinations, then gave a four-digit readout that glowed blue in the dark entryway. Kurins punched the buttons with his gloved fingertips. The indicator turned to green. Three seconds remained of the twenty-five they'd allowed.

And now the agents became aware of the sound of heavy breathing. Stertorous and moist, the whoosh of sucked air was issuing from behind a pair of louvered doors. Gently, Andy Kurins pulled back on the brass handle of one of the panels—the Castellano Dobermans were sleeping deeply in front of the washing machine. Their black noses glinted dully in the dim light that filtered in from the exterior floods; their ears hung defeated against their skulls. His dart gun at the ready, Kurins gave the dogs an easy

181

nudge with the toe of his canvas shoe. There was an involuntary twitch of muscle; nothing more. He left them to their slumbers.

In the Castellano kitchen, Joe O'Brien took a moment to reorient himself and collect his thoughts. The bank of freezers hummed softly against one wall; the double-width refrigerator switched on suddenly with a motor noise that seemed improbably loud and rude. The room smelled of coffee, olive oil, dishwashing soap. A gauzy glow filtered in through the curtains—the Godfather's own beacons gave them a perfect light to work by.

The two agents rounded the vast counter and tiptoed the length of the long blond table where Paul Castellano did his business. At its head, the Boss's high-backed chair seemed to hold a palpable remnant of his presence—some dim echo of that squeezed and imperious voice, some faint whiff of expensive after-shave, some rustle of imperial satin as Big Paul swept his robe around him and tore open an envelope full of cash. In the diffuse light, the chair's arms gleamed from years of rubbing by Castellano's meaty hands.

Joe O'Brien reached into his knapsack and took out a cool chrome disk, twelve inches in diameter, with an ivory-colored eight-foot electric cord attached.

Andy Kurins gently tipped the European lamp from the Miron's Desirables catalog, and laid it on the floor. He unplugged it, unscrewed its base, and clipped the wire that ran from the wall plug, up the shaft, through the gooseneck, to the socket in the shade. Stripping off a half-inch of insulation, he then spliced the cord to its twin on the replacement base.

This new disk was from a lamp that had not been hand-delivered by Julie Miron but shipped by more conventional means. Fitted out with an omnidirectional microphone and a self-contained power pack, it made an admirable bug. Current from the wall plug would keep the battery charged. The shaft of the lamp would serve nicely as an antenna. After the new base was attached, the Castellano house looked precisely as it had looked before. No holes drilled. No paint disturbed. One item added, one item removed. Net change: zero.

Joe O'Brien put the original chrome wafer in his sack. Andy

Kurins stood the lamp exactly where it had been standing. The agents checked for tools, footprints, shreds of insulation. Then they went out the same way they had come. They reactivated the alarm, relocked the doors. They moved quickly down the floodlit Castellano driveway, sensing the mountaineer's light step a half-dozen paces behind. They climbed into the waiting van and were gone.

They had been inside the Staten Island White House for twelve and a half minutes. That small parcel of time came as the excruciatingly delayed consummation of months and years of maneuvering and waiting. But if the consummation was long deferred, it proved to be amazingly fertile. A more crucial quarter-hour would be difficult to locate in all the annals of the fight against organized crime in America.

At 7:35 that morning, Joe O'Brien and Andy Kurins were sitting in the third-floor dormer of the monitoring station at 1510 Richmond Road. The early light was smudged with clouds, and the agents' eyes burned with fatigue. Yet they could not sleep until they heard something—anything—from the bug.

There are strict rules for the monitoring of a surveillance microphone. Only those suspected of criminal activity, and identified as such on the authorization affidavit, may be listened in on. But the FBI is allowed to sample conversations, in order to test reception and to differentiate pertinent conversation from random chitchat. And monitoring agents have considerable discretion in determining what is, or could become, pertinent. For example, a suspected Mob kingpin talking to his maid would generally be considered nonpertinent. But if the maid were also the kingpin's mistress, and if the kingpin, because of a strange and lingering insecurity in spite of his vast wealth and power, should feel the need of impressing his importance upon her, well . . .

The first thing heard on the Todt Hill bug was Nina Castellano talking to her dogs. "My," she said to them, above what seemed to be the sound of perking coffee, "you're sleepy this morning. Don't even want to go outside? Look at you, so lazy . . ."

The voice came through clear, with a slight metallic ring but no problem with static. Kurins and O'Brien flipped the toggle that turned off the transmission and stopped the reel-to-reel. Nina Castellano was still talking to the animals, and the agents had the distinct impression that she would keep on chattering even after the dogs had shaken off their drowsiness and gone outside. But the bug was there to let the Mafia hang itself, not to eavesdrop on the mumbling of a proud old woman whose life in those very days was being disassembled.

CHAPTER 36

MULBERRY STREET, in Manhattan's Little Italy, is not a very appealing place in March. Cold winds tunnel in from the uptown side, whipping up torn and filthy newspapers, throwing acrid dust in people's eyes. The tenement buildings look grim and devoid of life, since this time of year the windows stay shut and no old Italian mamas are draped over the sills, shouting to their friends down on the sidewalk. No one sits on the stoops in March, and the tourist business is lousy. In Jersey and Long Island, they're home watching basketball, and famous joints like Angelo's and Benito's have empty tables; stuffed artichokes and oiled peppers pose in the windows, trying to lure in trade.

Still, not all the merchants of Mulberry Street seem bothered by the late-winter dip in revenues. Some of them seem oblivious to the inactivity around them, almost as if they don't need the money, as if their livings don't really depend on how much veal parmigiana they push each day. Some of them don't even seem to care if they alienate paying customers.

One of the more insouciant of the Mulberry Street merchants was named Joseph "Joe Butch" Corrao, proprietor of Café Biondo, located at number 141. While other restaurateurs were stroking their guests with mendacious singsong cries of *"Buona sera,"* Corrao was greeting one potential diner thusly:

"Get the fuck out of here, O'Brien."

"Is that nice, Mr. Corrao?" asked the agent. "I just want a cup of coffee."

"You won't like the coffee here. It's salty."

"I'll have tea."

"I piss in the tea," said Corrao.

"And I suppose you shit in the minestrone," said O'Brien. "No wonder this dump is empty."

And Café Biondo was, more or less, empty. At one table, two Chinese were sipping cappuccino and sharing a rum baba. At another, a man sat alone, munching a Caesar salad and trying to look at ease in his own company. As for the rest of the tables, they held only sugar shakers and canisters of grated cheese. Still, O'Brien's remark seemed to pique Corrao's professional pride.

"It's empty, jerk-off, because you're here too early. Who the fuck eats at six-thirty, except for Chinks and cops? You wanna see this place full, come back at ten. You'll see it full. Classy crowd, too. Well-dressed people, uptown people. SoHo people, not these Jersey assholes they get down here."

"But Mr. Corrao," said O'Brien, "I'm being considerate. If I come when it's crowded, you won't have time to talk to me."

"I don't have time for you now. Take a hike."

Corrao turned his back and headed toward the kitchen. He looked around just before he reached the swinging doors, and saw that O'Brien hadn't budged. He didn't like this. He took one tentative step toward the agent, put his hands on his hips, and initiated a stare-down across the vacant restaurant. Joe Butch was a very handsome man. He had somehow escaped the telltale signs of inbreeding—the piggish eyes, the sloping brows, the blotched skin that went with hypertension—that made many other mobsters into caricatures of thuggishness. He was tall—six feet five— and slender. His dark eyes were widely spaced, his lips full and sensual; women liked Joe Butch, not for the favors he might do them but as a man. He had charm. He had smooth, freshly shaven cheeks. He even had real hair—a thick and wavy crop of it, dark brown splotched becomingly with gray.

He was far and away the most presentable of the Gambino family *capo*s.

But for all the typical Mob characteristics that Corrao had been spared, there was one he had in full degree: the sort of temper that went from zero to sixty in about three seconds, and ran down anything in its path. Mafiosi were known, of course, for busting up the joints of barkeeps and club owners who didn't pay their bills; Joe Butch was one of those rare individuals who now and then trashed his own place. Once, twice a year, he splintered some chairs, shattered some glass, spattered some squid with marinara on the walls. Terrified customers bolted up Mulberry Street, sure they were about to join the ranks of innocent bystanders who got dead. City cops appeared. Presumably some bills changed hands, and everything was neatened up. Next day, a moving van brought new furniture.

"O'Brien," said Corrao, "I really want you out of here." The voice was controlled yet held enough menace so that the Chinese wiped their mouths and called for a check. The solitary guy with the Caesar salad crunched a leaf of romaine and edged closer to the wall; for him it was dinner and a show. Joe O'Brien stayed silent, held Corrao's eyes, and waited to see if the proprietor of Café Biondo would blow.

The irony was that, at that moment, there was nothing in particular for Joe Butch to get worked up about. It was March 19, 1983. The Castellano bug had been installed, but Big Paul was still down in Pompano. While action in the center ring hung suspended, the FBI was pursuing several objectives along the flanks. One of these was simply to make the Gambinos believe that nothing whatsoever had changed, that law enforcement tactics were proceeding just as before. Another was to freshen up memories of the mobsters' individual voices, in order to facilitate identification on the tapes.

True, there was a further, though as yet hazy, reason to drop in on Joe Butch Corrao. It had come to the FBI's attention that several organized crime figures knew they were being indicted in the Southern District of New York, before the information became public. This was not supposed to happen; that's why the documents in question were called *sealed* indictments. But someone had to do the sealing, and several dozen people were involved in the preparation of the papers. Someone—almost certainly someone on the government payroll—was leaking the information. The leaked information, in turn, gave mobsters extra time to destroy evidence, concoct alibis, get their passports renewed. It gave them time to plan long vacations in Palermo or Quebec, time to buy condos on the Costa del Sol. It led to long and expensive chases, and tiresome and complicated extradition fights.

The documents were not leaked directly to those indicted, of course. They were routed through a presentable and appropriate contact on the street. Someone with a respectable facade. Someone with easy access to people. Someone, maybe, like Joe Butch, whose café happened to be located four blocks from the Southern District offices in the federal courthouse at St. Andrew's Plaza.

But this, so far, was just a hunch, though one that was supported by the usual Byzantine kinship ties. It was nothing Joe O'Brien was ready to talk about. Nothing Joe Butch needed to get excited over. But as the stare-down wore on he seemed to be getting agitated anyway.

He hooked a finger into the collar of his shirt and tugged it away from his neck. He curled back his upper lip and showed some tooth. Then, slowly, he walked toward Joe O'Brien. Without hesitation he passed straight through the invisible boundary that defines the polite and fitting distance between people not intimately involved. He got close enough so that the two tall men could read the pores on the sides of each other's noses. O'Brien smelled espresso and anisette on the other man's breath.

"You're pissing me off," Corrao whispered.

"Really?" said O'Brien. "Sorry."

"Come on, jerk-off, hit me. I'll give you the first shot, clean." He pointed to his own chin. Jutting and just slightly cleft, it made a tempting target. Joe O'Brien imagined with pleasure the sharp sting of his knuckles compacting against it.

"I don't think so," said the agent. "Not today."

The refusal seemed to miff Joe Butch, as though he'd been denied a kiss. He got red between the eyebrows. His own fists clenched. "Then maybe I'll go first."

"That's a better idea," O'Brien said. "My boss said I should always let the other guy go first."

And now a certain line of thought could be read as it flitted across Corrao's handsome but contorted face. He badly wanted to whomp O'Brien, but he could picture the arrest, the lawyers' bills, the aggravation of a trial. He could hear Joe Gallo calling him a putz for getting suckered into hitting a fed; he could see the displeasure and fatherly disappointment in Paul Castellano's baggy but flint-hard eyes. Restraint. He dug deep for some, as though it were the last dime in the bottom of a huge pocket.

He backed off half a step, and tore his eyes away from the agent. He seemed to be looking for something to throw. He reached toward a canister of grated cheese, then jerkily stopped the movement of his hand. He grabbed the back of a chair, then forced his fingers to unclasp. He was a man at war with his own synapses, snuffing out impulses as fast as they arose. Finally, with unwonted good judgment, Joe Butch Corrao bolted through his own front door. If O'Brien wouldn't leave, *he* would, and he'd throw his shit-fit outside, where it wouldn't cost him money.

Out on the sidewalk, he kicked a rusty garbage can. The dented top flew off, and the can teetered and fell, spilling its mixture of red sauce and decomposing vegetables against somebody's tire. Then he found an empty cardboard box and started booting it uptown. Buffeted by the cold March wind, the box flew away from him, and he chased it down like a kid playing soccer. He kicked it again, and it rose from the sidewalk, pinwheeling and drifting up Mulberry Street.

Joe O'Brien, standing discreetly in Café Biondo's doorway, watched the suave, handsome restaurateur kick and curse his way up the block. Then O'Brien shook his head and walked the other way, downtown, toward the courthouse. He was a notch more persuaded that Joe Butch was involved with the leaked indictments. Clearly, the man had something on his mind.

CHAPTER 37

C
ONGRATULATIONS," said Andy Kurins.

It was a simple enough remark, calling for a simple thank you in response, but so ingrained was the paranoia of Joe N. Gallo, so complex and meandering his web of offhand lies, that the Gambino *consigliere* paused a long moment to consider whether he was being snared. He looked down at his neat hands, splayed against the Formica of his table at Sperrazza's Luncheonette. He rattled his tiny espresso spoon. "Congratulations for what?" he said at last.

"I heard you retired from the Association," said the agent.

The body in question was the Greater Blouse, Skirt, and Undergarment Association, located on West Thirty-fourth Street in Manhattan's garment district. Greater Blouse was one of those scam entities that modestly but unremittingly sucked blood out of free enterprise in New York. It did this by promulgating a sort of Alice-in-Wonderland logic which, over time, took on the granite authority of the-way-it's-always-been-done.

To do business in the city, garment manufacturers and jobbers had to use union labor. The union, however, ILGWU Local 23-25, would not negotiate with individual shops but only through the Association. Thus, roughly six hundred companies were essentially held hostage by Greater Blouse, coerced into paying dues of fifty to seventy-five dollars a month. Some fraction of this money went toward the furtherance of legitimate industry concerns. But much of it was in fact a kitty from which was dispensed a Mob largess in cars, expense accounts, and salaries for no-show jobs. Joe N. Gallo had been on the payroll there for more than twenty years, ostensibly as a "labor relations representative."

"Yeah," the old man offered blandly, "I decided enough was

enough. The trip in on the train. The crowds." He dismissed it all with a wave of his hand.

"Still," said Kurins, "it must have been tough to give it up. Four-fifty a week. Steady employment and straight recordkeeping to show the IRS. And the health benefits—they must've come in handy. Whenever I went in to visit you, they said you were on sick leave."

Gallo tapped his heart. "I haven't been a well man these last few years."

"I figured your colleagues must have missed you. So I went to some of the shops the Association represents. They'd never heard of you, Joe."

"People forget," said the *consigliere*. "You think everyone you do business with remembers you?"

"Frankly, yes," said Andy Kurins. Who, after all, forgot about dealings with the FBI? "But Joe, Mae Gallin, the bookkeeper who's been there for years—I showed her a picture of you. She didn't recognize it."

Gallo put on an expression of wounded vanity.

"She knew your name, though," Kurins resumed. "She said she's been mailing you checks forever."

"So what are you getting at, Andy?" Gallo said. It seemed he was weary of dodging and decided to go on the offensive. He signaled this by picking up his tiny spoon and using it to make gestures that were almost professorial.

"Are we getting into this old happy horseshit about legitimate enterprise and the good of society? Are we gonna get high and mighty about the idea of glomming a day's pay without putting in a day's work? If that's a crime, Andy, you better build a lot more jails, 'cause you're gonna have to lock up half the fucking country.

"Start with the little WASP faggots with their trust funds. Then get the stockbrokers. Then get the Jew doctors who charge two hundred bucks to stick a finger up your ass to diddle your prostate gland. Then, for Chrissake, get the eight-foot niggers who are handed a million bucks a year for dribbling a fucking basketball. And after that, if you've still got room in the fucking penitentiary, then come back and hassle a little pissant like me with his four-fifty a week."

"But Joe," said Andy Kurins, "you're talking pay scales. I'm talking criminal conspiracy."

"Conspiracy," hissed the white-haired Mafioso. "Conspiracy. That's the magic word with you guys. That's the word that gives you a righteous hard-on. But lemme ask you something—what *isn't* a conspiracy? The Bar Association? How many cocks you have to suck to get in *that* club? Politics? Cut me a break. Wall Street? We both know that's a license to steal. No, Andy, it's *all* conspiracies, and the only difference is that some conspiracies you bust, and some you don't."

"That's not the only difference," said Kurins. "Some conspiracies break knees."

"And some break neighborhoods. And some break hearts," countered Gallo. "Let's not take out the fucking violin. You want the story on the Blouse Association, here it is: I used to work there, I don't anymore. End of story."

"And what about James Clemenza?"

"What about him?"

"He used to work there too."

"That's correct. What does that prove?"

"And he's a *capo* in the Colombo family."

"*Capo?* Colombo family? Andy, that's all made up by you and the FBI."

"Let's pretend it isn't," Kurins said, "because I have this theory. The theory says that the Greater Blouse, Skirt, and Undergarment Association is a kind of skeleton key to the whole rag trade. Figure out how the Association is divvied up, and you've got a pretty fair idea of how the whole industry is fingered. You're a Gambino and you've got a piece of it. Clemenza's a Colombo and he's got a piece of it. I have reason to believe the Genoveses are in there too."

"That's bullshit, Andy. All bullshit."

"Again, let's pretend it isn't," said Kurins. "Now follow this. The Mob likes its arithmetic simple. You don't find them taking square roots. If Greater Blouse is a third, a third, and a third, chances are trucking is a third, a third, and a third. Chances are it's thirds up and down the line. The guys who push the racks. The women in the sweatshops. All thirds."

"Horseshit," said Gallo. He pushed his espresso cup away and smiled pleasantly. At the back of Sperrazza's a pay phone rang. A moment later, a lackey tiptoed over and told the *consigliere* it was for him. Long distance. "Later," he said. "Got any other theories, Andy?"

"Well, actually," said the agent, "I do. I have a theory about how bribe money circulates through the penal system."

"Oh really?"

"Yeah. I think of it sort of like a big travel agency. X amount buys you a nice vacation in the form of early parole. Y amount gets you a cruise to a low-security Club Fed. Z amount takes you home free, first-class: unconditional release. Money sticks to different hands along the way. You know, like commissions. The only difference is, you can't buy your own ticket. You need someone outside, a relative maybe, to book your passage. Whaddya think?"

"I think you had a gassy lunch," said Joe N. Gallo, pulling on his knuckles. "You're full of whimsy today."

"I guess you're right," said Andy Kurins, sliding out of the torn green vinyl booth. "I just get these notions sometimes. But by the way, is Joe junior still in Attica?"

CHAPTER 38

S O, YOU DID GOOD this morning?" said Paul Castellano, the most powerful mobster in America.

A mile away, Joe O'Brien and Andy Kurins, wearing headphones and drinking coffee, suspended their game of gin rummy and hunkered forward, listening intently. Behind them, the reel-to-reel serenely turned.

The date was March 23, 1983. Castellano had gotten back from Pompano Beach just the night before. He was tan. He was rested. His voice, always breathy through a tight throat and suspicious lips, was a shade less clenched than usual. From the quality of sound issuing through the FBI surveillance microphone, it seemed he was sitting in his tall chair at the head of the blond table near the kitchen counter. Julie Miron's observations about houses and human nature were holding up nicely: home for barely a dozen hours, already the Godfather was reestablished in his Todt Hill routine, running the Gambino family and his own odd ménage from his favorite ten square feet out of the seven thousand at his disposal.

"Yes," said an unmistakable female voice. "I do berry good."

"Confidence is what you need, Gloria. Confidence is everything."

"Yes. I getting more conpident."

"You didn't hit the cones today?"

A quick shrill laugh crackled through the headphones. "Well, Meester Paul, I almost don't heet the cones today."

O'Brien lifted his phones off one ear. "Unbelievable! They're talking about her driving lessons."

"Nonpertinent," said Kurins.

"Let's give it a few more seconds," said O'Brien. But when the conversation turned to directional signals, he agreed that they should terminate the session.

Thus began the monitoring of the Godfather himself.

CHAPTER 39

FUCKING MORON," said Paul Castellano. "I got a headache. Gloria, bring me some aspirin. That cheap jerk. He don't know what the fuck he's getting involved in. Pain in the ass."

"Pain in the ass," echoed Tommy Bilotti, in the high, reedy tenor that contrasted drolly with his squat and bullish frame.

"He don't know," said another voice, a more conciliatory one. "It's a dumb mistake, but it's only a mistake."

Joe O'Brien and Andy Kurins, listening in from their third-floor dormer, went to work on this new voice. Strange things happen when you do audio surveillance. The ear takes on functions usually performed by other organs. It reads character. It has to; it's all you have to go on. This new voice seemed to convey a reasonable intelligence but no power. It was a rather soft voice, pleasant but at the same time wheedling, deferential. It sought to soothe, to placate, even while sounding suitably gruff. It was a voice that seemed almost to expect that it would be interrupted—a voice, so to speak, with one foot on the brake.

"Mistake, mistake," squeaked Tommy Bilotti. "It's still a pain in the ass and it's still this asshole's fault."

"He gotta pay," said Paul Castellano. "And he gotta be clued in. Over two, forget it, he sits out. That's club. Under a deuce, we talk. Maybe he gets some. But he pays the two points. First. None of this 'you'll have it in a few days' bullshit."

"You want I should talk to the fat guy?" said the one with the conciliatory voice.

"Talk to the fucking President for all I care," said the Godfather. "Just get me my money."

Reluctantly, like a spectator pulling himself away from a football game, Andy Kurins slipped off his headset, went to the telephone, and dialed Frank Spero's beeper. Twenty seconds later, Spero called back from a pay phone at the base of Todt Hill. Kurins asked him to identify the vehicle of Paul Castellano's morning guest. The date was March 24, and the Godfather was getting back to business. He already had his usual headache to prove it.

"I don't see where this fucking guy should get nothing," piped Bilotti, the perennial hard-liner, the little man who showed his doglike fealty by urging the master to exercise his mastery on every possible occasion. "We set it up. We did the work."

"What work?" said Castellano, and there was a laugh.

Now, it should be understood that at this point, the monitoring agents had only the vaguest idea what the three Mafiosi were talking about. The public has a fantasy—law enforcement is sometimes guilty of believing in it too—that if you could only listen in on criminals, they would reveal their schemes and methods whole and entire, with names named and specific capers unmistakably referred to. It's something that almost never happens.

First of all, these people make such a bludgeoned pulp of the English language that their meaning would seldom be clear even if they intended it to be. Which of course they don't. They have suspicion where other people have livers; they tend to speak in code even in the presumed privacy of their homes. A shrink might conjecture that more than just security is behind this—maybe they try to lessen their guilt by avoiding such opprobrious terms as "bribe," "shakedown," "kickback," "threat," and "murder." Then, too, there is the simple fact that the participants in these conversations already know what's being discussed; they leave out all the antecedents. What emerges from the surveillance, then, is no clear outline but a dizzying array of hints and impressions which swim in the mind like one of those novelty drawings that look like random nonsense and only gradually resolve themselves into pictures.

"If you're calling the fat guy," said Castellano, "call the Chin."

"Meester Tommy," said Gloria Olarte, "you feeneesh all the cookies."

"Ah shit," said the third man, God knows why. Maybe he

wanted more pignolia biscuits. Maybe he spilled hot coffee in his lap.

The phone rang at the monitoring plant. It was Frank Spero, and he told Kurins that Paul Castellano's guest that morning was almost certainly Alphonse "Funzie" Mosca.

O'Brien and Kurins knew Mosca only from pictures and by reputation. He was a Gambino soldier of the subspecies bagman. He had reddish hair and hazel eyes, a yellowish complexion and soft little belly that correlated closely with many peaceful evenings of television watching. He was not, at this stage of his career at least, a tough guy; in fact, he seemed to go out of his way to look like a nebbish. He dressed in suits that were not very sharp and not very nice, and wore with them conservative ties that didn't quite go. He missed places when he shaved. In all, he looked like a clerk who hoped to be mistaken for an executive. He carried an attaché case which, while it was of crummy imitation leather glued onto slabs of cardboard, was generally stuffed with large amounts of cash. He brought money from building contractors to union officials, from union officials to the Hill. You saw Funzie coming, the only question was deposit or withdrawal.

This much of Mosca's role was known thanks to the 1982 racketeering prosecution of John Cody, president of Local 282 of the International Brotherhood of Teamsters. Cody's trial had shed a partial but significant light on why building costs in New York were increasing by twenty percent a year. The man sold labor peace like Florsheim sells penny loafers.

You wanted cement trucks to keep delivering while a foundation was being poured, you paid; if you didn't pay, the mixers mysteriously stopped appearing, and you were left with a very expensive hole in the ground. You wanted I-beams carted in while you were bleeding money to keep a crane and a crew of sky-boys on the site, you slipped fifty or a hundred grand to Cody; if you didn't, the materials got lost somewhere and your crew drew wages for sitting on the sidewalk, making sucking noises at passing secretaries and eating Drake's cakes. One contractor gave Cody's mistress a luxury apartment, capping the gift with that most precious of Manhattan commodities—two free parking spaces. Another carried three Teamsters on the payroll, to serve as Cody's bodyguards and chauffeurs.

In any case, Cody had been Castellano's boy, and 282 had been Castellano's union. In 1983, the Teamster boss was appealing his conviction; he would lose the appeal and end up in prison. But the rest hadn't changed, although the new boss, Bobby Sasso, said it had, much to the amusement of law enforcement and the media. Two eighty-two, it appeared, was still a Gambino family local, and Funzie Mosca still carried messages and money.

"So he says take it for six million nine," the bagman was saying, over what sounded like the rush of water in the Godfather's kitchen sink. A touching domestic tableau: the maid washing dishes, while the big boys steal. "Cody says take it for six seven-fifty, a hundred seventy-five grand under. Something like that. Plus some jobs."

"Twelve men, fifteen days," said Castellano. Big Paul did not always sound like a leader. Sometimes he waffled, sometimes he doubled back on himself. But occasionally he made pronouncements that were almost military in their clipped precision and finality. Why twelve men? Why fifteen jobs? It didn't matter why. Because Castellano said it, that's why.

"Yeah," parroted Tommy Bilotti. "Twelve. Fifteen."

"And the money comes up thirty percent," said the Godfather. "We do things on our own. We gotta think of our own. Tell it to the fat guy. Tell Chin."

"It might get a little raw," said Funzie Mosca.

"It does, it does," said Castellano. "What're they gonna do, sue me?"

Bilotti laughed. Gloria laughed. Big Paul's claque was well rehearsed.

Through their headsets, Joe O'Brien and Andy Kurins heard the clatter of coffee cups, the scraping of chairs. There was talk of weather and of lamb chops, Florida sun and Gloria's upcoming driver's test.

The agents switched off the reel-to-reel. They were sweating. They had the pent-up, restless feeling that comes from sitting too long, breathless, over a chessboard. Hard listening is hard work;

hard listening points up how sloppy and intermittent is the attention we usually pay.

Certain things they had already figured out, and those certain things made their fingers itch. "The fat guy" was Anthony "Fat Tony" Salerno, cigar-chomping Boss of the Genovese family. "Chin" was Vincente Gigante, once the failed assassin of Frank Costello, now the real power behind Salerno's throne. Funzie Mosca was being dispatched as an emissary at the very highest levels of the Mob pyramid, on interfamily matters where tens of millions of dollars were concerned. This was no quarter-and-a-half numbers racket. This was no protection money shakedown at the corner bakery. This seemed to be about control over the building of skyscrapers on prime real estate in midtown. This was serious money.

CHAPTER 40

"ES YOUR WIFE gets better?" chirped the bright and increasingly confident voice of Gloria Olarte.

"Good days, bad days," said a deep baritone which, while uneducated in its accent, was almost courtly in its intonation. "She suffers. For what she has there is no medication."

"Hot towels," said the maid. "You get the steam from the towels, you know, the . . ."

"The vapor," said the deep, mellow voice.

"Yes. The bapor. Sometimes, you know, when I cooking, and the water, eet boils, I put my nose like thees. . . . Yes, almost in the pot."

"Yes, Gloria," said the gentle voice, a little wearily, it seemed to the listening agents.

"Well, Meester Paul, he be right down. You like some coffee?"

Sitting in the plant on Richmond Road, Joe O'Brien reached forward and scrawled a question mark on a yellow pad. But Andy Kurins knew the mellifluous baritone to be that of Joseph Armone, a long-standing Gambino *capo* who later, in the time of troubles, would have his brief shot at being underboss.

Armone was in many ways a throwback to a more gracious and romantic time, a time when Mafia hoods could still lay somewhat persuasive claim to being Robin Hoods. Piney Armone got his nickname way back in the late 1930s, when, as a young tough on the Lower East Side, he coerced the men who sold Christmas trees on the sidewalks into giving small pines, gratis, to the poorer families. That was the "rent" they paid for doing business in the neighborhood, and while such kindhearted brands of extortion hardly defined the range of Armone's later criminal career—he did time for heroin trafficking in the notorious French Connection case—the episode did say something about the man. He had his own morality. He wanted to do his bit to make life fairer. He didn't believe decent people should have to do without Christmas trees, especially given the fact that surplus merchandise would be burned.

In other ways as well, Armone was a far more sympathetic figure than most of the opportunists, cynics, and bullies who surrounded Paul Castellano. He was a devoted family man who, amazingly enough, did not seem to keep a mistress; he was sometimes seen taking his own wife out for dinner. They made a rather touching sight: the gray, slight Mafioso—sixty-six years old in 1983—with thick glasses for his failing eyes and a worsening limp from an ancient gunshot wound, and on his arm a sick old lady, clearly stretched to the limits of her strength by the act of getting into clothes a quarter-century out of fashion, putting on her rouge, and flinging a fox stole over her shrunken shoulders. One surveillance photo had them holding hands.

Alone among Gambino members, Joe Armone almost never cursed, and his speech, while not necessarily grammatical, had a certain high-flown formality to it; you could think of it as Mob Shakespearean. He took seriously—perhaps even more seriously than did Big Paul himself—the Mafia codes of silence and of honor. On the occasions when Andy Kurins had approached him, the old *capo* always made himself available, and never said more than he wanted to. He was respectful of the FBI, and comported himself as an amiable enemy totally devoid of personal malice.

But now Piney had a problem.

"I read that article in the Miami newspaper," he was saying to Big Paul Castellano. "The *Herald*. About Tommy Agro. And the fact is, Paul, there is going to be a lot of heat this spring."

"Fuck," said the Godfather.

"It's a big investigation. They connected him with everything they wanted to—gambling, bribery, loan-sharking, all of it. And the other guy refused to give back the connection."

"Fuck," Castellano said again.

"So now he's sitting there, he's feeling the wind, and it seems that he is making up his mind. And you know his mind, Paul. It isn't something you'd bank on."

"You talk to him?"

"No, but I hear, and he's plenty concerned."

"How's he leaning?"

Piney answered with a frustrating silence: maybe he was making some decisive gesture, maybe only shrugging. But shrugs and gestures don't show up on audio tape.

In the present instance, however, the monitoring agents had the great luxury of knowing more about the subject under discussion than did the mobsters who were discussing it. It was the Home Run investigation—the case launched by Tommy Agro's 1981 assault on Joseph Iannuzzi, the case that, indirectly, had first allowed Joe O'Brien to gain admission to the Godfather's kitchen. Of all the various nets that law enforcement had been casting over the Gambino family, Operation Home Run was the first to tighten down. In the spring of 1983, it was almost time to start hauling in the catch.

"So what I need to ask you, Paul," said the courtly Armone, "is, if he asks our blessing and our help to take it on the lam, then what is our position?"

Castellano belched. "I got indigestion. Gloria, you got some Tums over there?"

"We don't need to decide right now," said the *capo*. "But, you know, he might ask our permission, he might bolt without it. Either way, we oughtta have a plan."

Tommy Agro, of course, had been the most proximate target of "Joe Dogs" Iannuzzi's revenge against the Mob. It was not surprising that Iannuzzi turned informer after his near death at Don Ritz's Pizzeria. What may seem odd to some, however, is that Agro continued to trust Joe Dogs after having almost killed him. Iannuzzi, his nose rearranged and his viscera permanently damaged, got out of the hospital, and the two men—literally—kissed and made up.

Not that it was so unusual for someone victimized by the Mob to reembrace the Mob. If he didn't, how would he make his living? Almost more important, who would his friends be? Still, the readiness with which Agro welcomed Iannuzzi back into his confidence showed a lack of judgment bordering on lunacy. Wired for sound, Joe Dogs resumed his role as Tommy A.'s eyes and ears in Florida. If anything, Agro confided in him more than before, as if the episode at Don Ritz's had constituted some perverse rite of friendship, or perhaps dominion.

So Iannuzzi's microphone recorded everything from Tommy A.'s medical complaints, to evidence of his ongoing shylock operations, to instructions for shakedowns, to loud avowals of his pronounced and in fact rather crazed enthusiasm for anal penetration of his wives and girlfriends. These traits were not the sort that got a jury on one's side. Agro, legally speaking, was dead meat.

"He runs, what does it cost us?" asked the Godfather.

"In money or in trouble?" Piney asked. As Agro's *capo*, he was responsible for his soldier's grace, or lack thereof, under pressure. This could not have been an easy conversation for him.

"Both," said Castellano.

"Trouble, the feds will be annoyed. They'll come asking where he is. They'll ask me, they'll ask you, they'll ask Joe [Gallo]. If there's any way they can nail us for harboring or abetting, they'll jump on it. Money, it depends. You want him to be comfortable, maybe fifty thousand."

"*Marrone,*" said the Godfather. "That comfortable he don't need to be."

"He could be killed and have it done," said Armone.

"You suggesting that?"

"We're talking options."

"No," said Castellano. "Tommy A., he's good people. Some guys get jammed up, they get afraid, they're worth shit, fuck 'em, forget about it. Tommy A., this guy we help out best we can. It ain't that bad."

The fact was, however, it was considerably worse than Paul Castellano and Joe Armone realized. The managed leak to the *Miami Herald* did not give the whole story. It was a teaser, that article, a little flash of leg; the truth about the Home Run case extended much farther up the Gambino family tenderloin.

"Nah," said Joe Armone, in a tone that did not seem totally convinced. "It's unfortunate, but it's manageable. And in the meantime, everything else is status quo. The boys all send you their best."

"They send me anything else?" Paul Castellano asked.

"Oh yeah," said Piney, as if it was an afterthought. A light slapping sound came through Joe O'Brien's and Andy Kurins's headsets—the sound, it seemed, of a small parcel being dropped onto the long blond table. "There's nine thousand in the envelope."

CHAPTER 41

THERE ARE TWO SORTS of men in the world—those who outdo the accomplishments of their fathers and those who remain forever in the patriarchal shadows. The first sort of man appropriates the family name as his very own property, his birthright, and he exalts or soils it in accordance with the dictates of his own untrammeled character. The second sort carries the name like a hod of bricks. It stays, so to speak, outside of him. He picks it up, he bears up bravely, or sags, under the weight of it, but it is never really his.

Tommy Gambino, the son of Carlo, was, it seems fair to say, this second sort of man. In superficial ways, he bore a remarkable resemblance to his father—the same lean build, long face, Durante nose, and the flat dark eyes that seemed to move a millimeter closer together with each succeeding generation. But there the similarities ended. Gambino *padre* was in every way an outsize figure—legendary in his ruthlessness, mythic in his guile, monumental, even, in his mistakes. He was a tough act to follow, and Tommy didn't really try to follow him. He hung back, remained a modest, unassertive family *capo*, and seemed not just content but greatly relieved to have his uncle Paul Castellano interposed in the dynastic line of the Gambino clan.

Not that Tommy Gambino was inclined to make himself a life away from family ties. His sense of kinship was stronger than most people's, since his mother and father had been first cousins. Moreover, in an arrangement reminiscent of the peacemaking gestures of medieval kings, he had been married off to the daughter of Thomas Lucchese, late boss of the competing crime family that still bears his name.

But if family ties had held Tommy Gambino back from truly

becoming his own man, the perks that went with the kinship bonds provided a considerable compensation. Gambino *figlio* was a millionaire many times over. He lived in a penthouse that spanned two brownstones on an ultrafashionable block off Fifth Avenue; Al Pacino lived across the street. As proprietor of a garment-transporting firm called Consolidated Trucking, Gambino had all the benefits of working in a traditional Mob stronghold, while at the same time he was well placed to oversee family interests throughout the rag trade.

In the spring of 1983, however, those interests were in some disarray, and during the early evening of May 6, Gambino visited Paul Castellano to talk about them.

"So I says to him, Paul, I says, 'Hey, wait a second, Jimmy, just wait a second. Your guy retires, he gets fifty thousand a year for three years. Joe Gallo, when he gets out, walks away with thirteen cents. I mean, where's the fairness here?' "

"Yeah," said Castellano, "where's the equity? I don't see it."

"That's because it ain't there," said Tommy Bilotti, his voice piping up sudden and squeaky, like an ill-played clarinet. "This is bullshit."

"Then there's this business with the car," Gambino went on. "I say Augie should get a car. They say no. I say *Jimmy* has a car, so what the fuck? They say Augie's job never called for a car. I says, 'What's this never shit? So we change the rules, what's the big deal?' That's when they start crying the blues about there's not enough money coming in."

"What comes in?" asked the Godfather.

"Figure conservative," said Tommy Gambino. "Figure six hundred shops at fifty bucks a month."

"Thirty thousand," put in Bilotti, with the abruptness of the hyper kid who always wants to get his hand up first in class.

Sitting in the Richmond Road attic, Joe O'Brien checked his arithmetic on a yellow pad. You had to say this much for Mafiosi—their grammar stank, they couldn't tell you the capital of Pennsylvania or the chemical symbol for water or what year the Battle of Hastings was fought, but they were quick and accurate at toting up money.

"So where does it go?" asked Castellano.

"Well, there's Jimmy, and his car. There's Augie. Neil gets a slice. There's Clemenza's pension. . . ."

"All right," said Castellano. "So if we pay some money in, we're just paying it to ourselves."

"No, Paul," Gambino said, "because what's different is that now some of it is going to fight the Chinese."

At this, Joe O'Brien and Andy Kurins mugged at each other and cranked up their concentration another notch. This was a new angle, at least as it pertained to the Greater Blouse, Skirt, and Undergarment Association—though interethnic strife was becoming an ever-more-pronounced feature in virtually every aspect of organized crime. Between Chinese and Italian mobsters there seemed to exist a special, almost salacious sort of hatred. This mutual loathing had its roots in the fact that Little Italy and Chinatown shared the common border of Canal Street. The Chinese traditionally stayed south of it, the Italians north, and no barbed wire was required to convey the idea of a frontier between two countries at a seething truce. Before, say, 1975, Chinese went "uptown" at their considerable peril, and Italians, for reasons of pride, wouldn't be caught dead among "the slants." As for the relative prestige of the Mafia and the Tong, that was no contest. Mafia was big-time, a second government, whereas Chinese gangs were generally thought of as a few scrawny thugs with hand-rolled cigarettes and dirty undershirts, running mid-stakes mah-jongg games in the backs of teahouses and dealing a little opium to fat old immigrant ladies in loud sarongs.

More recently, however, the Chinese gangs, like the Chinese community overall, had been expanding in both population and economic clout, while both the fortunes and numbers of the Italians were stagnating. Legitimate Chinese businesses on Mulberry Street, crooked Chinese influence in the garment district—both were blows to the Sicilian ego, and both were painfully clear hints about how the future was trending. The money coming out of Taiwan and Hong Kong was daunting; the ethnic shift in New York's small-business power structure was dramatic and still ongoing.

"You gotta be strong with the Chinese," Tommy Bilotti sagely advised. "They sense weakness, they get brave. You gotta push their skinny asses into a chair and stick your fingers in their face. Keep your fucking chopsticks outa my plate, you little slant cocksucker. You savvy?"

"It isn't that easy," said Gambino. "It ain't the streets down there. It's business. And who do we got to deal with? We got our people, fine. Then we got a bunch of Jews. Okay, strictly on a business basis, we control them. But you think there's loyalty there? Forget it. You got more and more Chinese in the shops. Get too many of 'em, they can outlaw us, and boom, there goes your Association. You can kiss it goodbye."

"Kiss *this* goodbye, you yellow bastards," said Tommy Bilotti. Kurins and O'Brien tried to picture the accompanying gesture. Was it just the middle finger, or the whole stubby forearm popping up in defiance?

"So, are you telling me that people are gonna get hurt down there?" the Godfather asked.

"For now, no. We sat down. There's been an accommodation. But it costs, Paul. The rent went up. What I'm telling you is that you ought to see to your share of what's left."

"All right," said Castellano. "So lemme make sure I understand what our interests are in there. Are we at a third, all at a third, or what?"

"Well, it ain't exactly that simple," Tommy Gambino said. "There's three partners, yeah. You got a third in, the West Side [Genovese family] got a third in, and—"

"And Gerry," put in Tommy Bilotti. "Gerry Lang got a third." Gerry Lang was the street name of Colombo family underboss Gennaro Langella.

"Right," said Gambino. "Now, in jobs, it's all a third. You put your man in, they put their man in. But in money it ain't exactly equal."

"Why ain't it?" demanded Bilotti.

"I'm just telling you what *they* say," said Gambino. "They say they've had their man in there for thirty years. They say they've been active. They've been building something, pounding away. Us—well, I'm not being critical of Joe [Gallo], don't get me wrong.

But the fact is, he'd go in every now and then on Friday to pick up a check, and that was it. While he was there, okay, they wouldn't jerk him around. But when he retired—"

Paul Castellano interrupted, sounding suddenly like a harried CEO. Explanations were for the *Wall Street Journal;* he just wanted the bottom number. "So what's the fucking story on the money, Tommy?"

Gambino seemed to brace himself. "Their guy gets six-fifty a week and a car. Our guy gets four-fifty and no car."

Now, by the sixth of May, Joe O'Brien and Andy Kurins had heard enough of Big Paul's conversations to know that he seldom raised his voice. At this moment he did. Initially at least, it did not seem to be raised in anger but incredulity. A law as fundamental as gravity in Paul Castellano's universe was being violated. "You're telling me that their guys get more fucking money than you and I?"

"Yeah," said Gambino, sounding relieved to get the awful truth off his narrow chest. "Yeah, yeah."

"What the fuck!" said the Godfather.

"Jesus Christ," said Bilotti.

"Well, here's how it seems to me," Castellano said, embarking on a slow burn the likes of which the monitoring agents had not heard before. "If it's thirds, it's thirds, and cut the bullshit excuses. Look, we got a third of the jobs, and I want a third of the money. A third of the jobs and a third of the responsibility. I want a third of everything, get it? It's rightfully mine, and I want it. Fuck the Chinese, fuck the Jews, and fuck the fucking *paisans* who are grabbing more than their share. It's our Association to reap the benefits."

He seemed quite honestly to have forgotten that Greater Blouse had anything to do with New York's garment workers or manufacturers.

"Listen, Paul," purred Tommy Gambino, "lemme say something here. Just food for thought, okay? I know you're upset. I understand. But let's say you wanna make a stink about this. You wanna, you can. You got the power. So you sit down with Gerry Lang and Jimmy Brown [James Clemenza], you stand up for your rights, and now you're the heavy. You won, but what did you win? And maybe you opened up a can of worms. Maybe Gerry says, 'Hey, wait a minute, Paul—if it's thirds over here, why is it that, over in construction, anything over two mil goes to you, like automatic?' So now you gotta argue with the fucking guy. What I'm saying is, maybe you're risking something big to get something small."

But the Godfather was not to be so easily placated on what was, to him, a matter of principle. "Big, small, who gives a fuck? I want my third. Gloria, bring me some aspirin. So where does it stand right now? What did you say to them?"

With this, Gambino launched into an exercise in butt-covering and buck-passing that any middle manager in America would have been proud of. "I . . . I told them I didn't think it was justified. That much I declared, Paul. I didn't, you know, play the middle of the road. But I said, 'Look, I gotta talk to my uncle about this. That's the rules. I'm goin' by the book.' So here I am. I'm not coming here, you know, to give up the responsibility. I'm just coming here to get some guidelines. You can say to me, 'Tommy, go along with it,' or 'Tommy, stick to your guns.' I'm just asking if you wanna take it any further."

"Who wants macaroni?" asked Gloria Olarte. A loud clanging accompanied the question—it sounded as though the maid, military style, was beating a wooden spoon against a pot to signal chowtime. O'Brien pictured her marching around the kitchen, playing the utensil like a drum.

"What does Joe Gallo say?" asked the Godfather.

"You got sausage?" asked Tommy Bilotti.

"I'm seeing him on Monday," said Gambino.

"Yes, Meester Tommy, hot and sweet."

"Sounds like somebody I know," said Castellano. His audience dutifully laughed.

Then there was a sound like Niagara Falls, which must have been Gloria filling up the huge spaghetti pot from the tap. The cascading noise drowned out conversation for a minute or so, and by the time it stopped, the discussion about the Greater Blouse, Skirt, and Undergarment Association had been either concluded or shelved. When the words became audible again, the chat was cozier, more personal, more appropriate for dinner hour. Tommy Gambino, meek son of an imperious father, was giving a capsule account of the story of his life.

"Me," he was saying, "I never had the chance to say, 'Well, I'm going to do something I want to do.' I always did it for my family, for my children, for my father, for my mother. Matter of fact, always, even when I spoke, it was always, how does it affect other people? I wish I had your independence, Paul. In my life, in my fifties, I still haven't reached it. Where I could do something that I want to do and the hell with anybody else. Understand, I don't begrudge it to you. I'm glad you have that leverage, that privilege. You wear it well. God bless you, Paul."

CHAPTER 42

ON BRUCE MOUW'S rather stoic face, large differences in frame of mind were reflected in small changes of expression.

Before the installation of the Castellano bug, when the tension of waiting for the opportune moment had made everybody edgy, the supervisor's frazzled nerves had given rise to no more than the occasional wince when he bit down on his pipestem. Now, with the microphone in place and yielding results that surpassed all sober expectations, he allowed himself no more flamboyant a display of satisfaction than the occasional small smile that just barely opened up around his teeth and etched small crinkles at the corners of his eyes. More than native reticence was behind this understatement: even within the Bureau, the Castellano bug was still a secret, kept that way to minimize the chances of its being compromised.

When Andy Kurins and Joe O'Brien briefed their boss on what was being heard, they did so behind closed doors in Mouw's office on Queens Boulevard. These weekly meetings always seemed to start the same way—with Bruce Mouw smiling slightly around his pipe and saying, "So, guys, what do we know?"

Andy Kurins's answer, at one such meeting in mid-May, was, "Well, we know Gloria cuts his toenails."

"Now how do we know that?"

"We heard him ask her to," said Joe O'Brien. He did what was becoming a quite proficient Castellano imitation. " 'Gloria, baby, my toenails is rubbin' against duh topsa my shoes. I ripped a ten-dollar paira socks the other day. Oleg Cassini. Would ya clip 'em for me, honey?' And she goes down on him right at the table there. Goes down to do his nails, I mean."

"And how do we know *that*?" asked the supervisor.

"We hear the clipping," said Kurins. "It happens right down at mike level. Sounds like gunshots."

"And we also know that Castellano feels her up while she does it," said O'Brien.

"I don't think I even want to know how we know that."

But Joe O'Brien was determined to tell him anyway, even though his Gloria Olarte imitation was not nearly so proficient as his impression of the Godfather. " 'Oh, Meester Paul, if you do that, I no can concentrate. I scared I cut your toe off, Meester Paul.' "

"All right, all right," said Mouw, groping for a more official tone. "Enough of the nonpertinent gossip."

"Gossip, yes," said Andy Kurins. "Nonpertinent, no."

Mouw urged him on with a lift of his chin.

"It says a lot about what's going on over there. He's getting increasingly dependent on her. From a couple of things that've been said, it seems like she even injects him with his insulin."

"And meanwhile," O'Brien picked up, "Nina is around less and less. She passes through her own kitchen like a stranger. People sound almost surprised to see her there. And embarrassed. Everyone seems ill at ease."

"Okay," said Mouw, "so we have a nice little soap opera shaping up. But what we're supposed to be monitoring is criminal activity. I'm not sure I see how it connects."

"The way it connects," said Andy Kurins, "is that it shows how out of touch Paul is getting. Look, whether he knows it or not, he's already got a morale problem on his hands. Dellacroce's people are operating almost like a separate family, plus he's got the drug thing making everybody nervous. Now he's making it worse by forcing even the loyal guys to deal with this woman they can't stand."

"You know for a fact they don't like her?"

"No," Kurins conceded. "But I sense it. I mean, no one sits down at the man's table and says, 'Sorry, Paul, I can't stand your girlfriend.' But what happens, especially in the morning, is that guests arrive when Paul is still upstairs. So Gloria shows them in, and right away she's yammering, chattering, trying to be cute.

Most of the guys barely answer her. It's like, as far as they're concerned, she's still the maid, and you don't go out of your way to be charming to the help. Some of the things she says, you can almost hear them rolling their eyes."

"It's like she's the Yoko Ono of the Mob," said Joe O'Brien. "The bandleader thinks he's found the love of his life, the other guys think he's lost his mind. He think she's exotic, they think she's wildly inappropriate. He thinks he's been set free, they think he's making a total ass of himself. Plus, give these guys some credit—they're loyal, and they've known Nina for twenty, thirty years."

"You wait and see," said Andy Kurins. "He's following that metal dick of his into a cold and lonely place."

CHAPTER 43

GARBAGE in Nassau County. Road building in New Jersey. Pornography in Times Square.

The longshoremen's union. The painters' union. Ten different locals of the laborers' union. The mason tenders' union.

The supermarket business. Wholesale meat. Demolition. Cement.

Trucking. Linens. Liquor.

Nightclubs. Restaurants. Video arcades.

Stock frauds on initial public offerings. Fraudulent bankrupting of Mob-controlled firms.

Threats. Extortion. Bribery. Murder.

As the Castellano surveillance wore on, a truly impressive range of topics was overheard at Big Paul's table, and even partway through the monitoring, it had already become clear that no one could possibly keep close track of it all. Law enforcement couldn't—it would take dozens of people several months to cross-reference all the tapes, and even then there would be voices never identified, allusions never figured out. For that matter, it seemed unlikely that Castellano himself had anything but the loosest understanding of certain aspects of his empire. The machine was simply too big, with too many moving parts. No written records were kept, of course, and new pieces were being added to the enterprise all the time.

Castellano's *capos* came to the Staten Island White House with the oddest schemes, often on behalf of associates who were not themselves initiated mobsters. One man proposed, through Joe Armone, that the Godfather become a partner in a massive olive oil–importing plan, a veritable tidal wave of extra-virgin. "This sounds legit," Castellano told him. "Why are you coming to me?"

Another visitor, who apparently had never heard of the Securities and Exchange Commission, wanted to print up stock certificates and sell them on the street.

Not all the new ideas were from crackpot outsiders who tried to gain a brief audience with the Pope on the strength of a good word from the cousin of a nephew of a friend. Some of Castellano's longest-standing advisers still came to him with fresh opportunities for making dubious dollars.

Joe Armone, through a young West Coast relative of his, had met a man named Danny Sims, "a black guy who's like a talent scout, who says this thing called 'promotional work' is easier and better money than selling drugs. Companies pay like fifty, a hundred thousand just for pushing a record." And even though, as Armone conceded, "the record business is not what it once was," there were still "big numbers if you can get your own man in to exercise some control." So the Gambino family, without the bothersome necessity of a board of directors meeting or a business plan or a market test, blithely entered into the payola racket. All it took was a lift of Big Paul's eyebrow to add another cog to the conglomerate, another count to the eventual indictments.

If the range of Castellano's business ventures provided vivid evidence of his economic reach and power, his responses to favors asked of him showed how that power intersected with the spheres of other crime families. Big Paul was the king of mobsters, but it would be a mistake to imagine that his hegemony was total. He had his turf, and one of the ways he protected it was by respecting the turf of others. At times this territorial maneuvering called for a kind of gruff diplomacy worthy of a gutter Machiavelli.

In the spring of 1983, for example, Sardi's Restaurant, the theater district landmark, had a problem. It seemed that public taste was changing, and a place no longer qualified as classy just because it had a battalion of mustachioed and tuxedoed captains who sneered imperiously at out-of-towners while ushering them to tables near the kitchen and sticking out their oily hands for tips. Strange to say, people were now paying at least a little attention to the food. But Sardi's, meanwhile, had over a hundred thousand dollars' worth of sneering captains on its annual payroll, and according to the restaurant's contract with Local 6 of the Hotel Employees and Restaurant Employees International Union, said captains could not be fired. So a payoff was arranged to a Local 6 official named Jackie DeRoss—a man controlled by Castellano—who was thought to have the power to void the agreement.

It turned out not to be so simple. There was another local involved, one which had closer ties to the parent union, which in turn had crime family attachments of its own. So Jackie DeRoss could not deliver what he'd promised, and when he complained to Castellano about the embarrassment this was causing him, Big Paul gave him the following explanation:

"Ya gotta understand. It's a situation where you had the locals and somebody else had the international. This is what I'm trying to tell ya. You know, I gotta, I gotta watch. See, I don't like to fuck around where other people are doing what they have a right to do. And no one fucks around with what I own. This is my local, and I don't want anybody to touch it. The international, that's outa my hands."

The Sardi's affair could not have ended more happily: Jackie DeRoss was convicted of racketeering, and the sneering captains all got fired anyway.

But the results of certain other union shenanigans discussed at Big Paul's table were both less felicitous and less clear. Not infrequently, it seemed, someone got dead around union election time, when control was up for grabs and long-nurtured relationships were in jeopardy. In a conversation regarding Local 32A of the laborers' union, an unidentified male offered the confident opinion that "the man got shot by someone who has but one objective." Who was the victim, and what, precisely, was the objective? No one knows. But *capo* Jimmy Failla did reveal, in connection with this bit of violence, a sensitivity to the importance of public relations: "It puts you in a bad, you know, a little bit of a bad light."

Aside from the frustrating array of criminal matters that never quite came into focus for law enforcement, there was another category of goings-on that Castellano only half revealed even to his own intimates. Big Paul was a man in whom caution and tact were at war with insecurity and braggadocio. He had a constant need to remind himself how important he was, but he hadn't risen to the top of the Mob pyramid by being a loudmouth. Sometimes he met himself halfway by boasting about his legitimate-world contacts without naming names.

"Then there's this third party involved," he said on one occasion, in a discussion about the construction business. "He happens to be a politician, a big politician. We're gonna have lunch together . . . no, uh, dinner together next week. Now already this is something of, like, a problem. I hate to go anyplace. I hate to go out. I hate going because what happens is that there's always eyes. You wait. They'll criticize me for being seen with him. They'll criticize him for being seen with me. Pain in the ass. I mean, what kinda fucking world is it, where two people can't sit down and break bread together?"

One answer to the question of what kind of world it was, is that it was a world of murder contracts in which it cost between fifty and a hundred thousand dollars to have somebody killed. At least, that was the impression derived from this statement of Tommy Gambino to his uncle Paul.

"They wanted eight grand. . . . Now what do you do? I say to Pete, fifty to a hundred thousand instead to get him killed . . . Hey, that's too much money, what are you doing? I said to Arnold, let's give him fifty, I'll get Pete, and Paul has to agree, okay? But I'll let you know, but keep your mouth shut. Don't say anything . . . because it's my ass if [inaudible] Tommy said hundred thousand to kill a guy from Paul. . . . It may sink us all . . . Whether it's ready or not, it's coming down . . . now play with it. That's the end of his problem."

CHAPTER 44

LISTEN, MILLIE,' I say to her, 'they can't fire you. It's civil service.' 'But Joe,' she says to me, 'eleven years with a judge. All that time I have in.' 'Millie,' I say, 'I understand. But there's no risk. It's civil service. Ask Big Gus.' "

"Big Gus? Ha," squawked Tommy Bilotti. "Big Gus is a fucking idiot."

"Am I saying he isn't? But he's her son-in-law. She listens to him."

"Then we all got trouble," said Paul Castellano. There was a dutiful round of laughter.

"No," said Joe Butch Corrao, "I'll tell you who has trouble. Alphonse Persico. That's who has trouble. That's what we were talking about. Millie says to me, she says, 'Jeez, it's a shame. Because I did see an indictment just the other day. A superseded sealed indictment,' she says."

"What's 'superseded' mean?" asked Bilotti.

"It means worse than it was before," said Castellano.

" 'Yeah,' she says," Corrao resumed. " 'Alphonse Persico. That poor boy has got some problems.' "

"What kinda problems?" asked Big Paul.

"Well, that's the thing," said Corrao. "She clammed up. Every time I go through this with her, it's the same thing all over again. Like pulling teeth. She says a little, she stops. She wants to help, she's scared. She don't make a move without she talks to her daughter, which means the advice is coming from Big Gus."

"And Big Gus is a douche bag," said Bilotti.

"So there it is," Corrao concluded.

"It wouldn't hurt to do a favor for the Snake," said Castellano.

"Never hurts," echoed his bodyguard and driver.

Andy Kurins and Joe O'Brien sat in the attic on Richmond Road and played their well-practiced game of connect-the-dots. Certain links were easy. "The Snake" was Carmine Persico, boss of the Colombo family. He hated the nickname, and allowed only one person to use it to his face. That was his girlfriend, whose moniker was even dopier: Tootsa.

Alphonse was his son, one of those wayward types who make parents wonder where they went wrong. Alphonse was always testing the boundaries. He refused to stay within the range of appropriate activities for his age and standing, like they weren't good enough for him. Loan-sharking, extortion, skimming the trades—he could have made a damn good living, and also safe-guarded his future. But no, he had to go his own way. The only problem was that he went into bigger things than he could handle, and did so with flaky associates. He tried to muscle in on hotels and casinos where he was clearly outmuscled. His pals were coke freaks and junkies—one of them had recently been found dead in his bed at the age of twenty-four—and there was a presumption, never proved, that Persico himself was a hophead. Being his father's son, he was well insulated and given a good deal of slack by senior hoods whose toes he stepped on. But his colleagues were bad news. They had no character, no moxie. They got pinched for something, and right away they sang. They didn't even wait to be offered a deal by the prosecutors; they proposed the deal themselves. *Hey, how would you like a shot at somebody named Persico?* Young Alphonse was screwed.

As for Big Gus, that had to be Augustus Sclafani, a Gambino soldier and cousin of Corrao's, a towering, spluttering, sloppy man who could best be thought of as two hundred and sixty pounds of noise and ineptitude.

And since Sclafani had only one mother-in-law, "Millie" had to be Mildred Russo, a deputy clerk in the United States District Court for the Southern District of New York. Russo, along with several other government employees with access to sensitive documents, had been under observation for some time. Here was the taxpayers' money at work, helping criminals go free.

Joe O'Brien and Andy Kurins looked at each other and made

221

sour faces. They reserved a special contempt for those who violated a public trust, who made a mockery of the idea of government service. They also knew how difficult it would be to persuade
a jury of Millie Russo's guilt. She was a tiny, blue-haired lady with
soft eyes and a widow's peak surmounting her handsome forehead. She looked like such a perfect Italian grandmother that you
could have stuck her portrait on a label for tomato paste. A criminal? A Mafia associate? Someone who cost the government hundreds of thousands of dollars and helped mobsters stay on the
streets where they could break knees, torch buildings, and murder
people? Impossible. The lawyer would do the antidefamation
dance. He'd whine about the incredible strain poor Millie was
subjected to because of her understandably conflicting loyalties.
He'd make the prosecution look heartless, petty, ridiculous.

Millie would take the witness stand and cry. She'd end up
holding the jurors' hearts firmly in her Kleenex, along with the
tears.

No, this was one the government would lose. Unless, maybe,
Grandma Millie could be caught red-handed. Unless a case could
be presented to the prosecutors sealed, wrapped, and tied up with
a bow.

CHAPTER 45

COME HERE, GLORIA. Sit down. Let me tell you something."

It was ten o'clock on a May morning—quite early for Paul Castellano to be downstairs. Joe O'Brien and Andy Kurins could picture him sitting in his favorite chair in his red satin bathrobe, letting his feet flop out of his soft slippers while he sipped the first coffee of the day. Probably he was unshaven, gray stubble spiking out from his sallow face. The liverish sacs under his eyes would be swollen with sleep. Maybe his thigh still stung from the morning's shot of insulin.

"Gloria, listen. The main thing in this world is ya gotta survive."

There was no response other than the clatter of dishes and the running of water. The maid had apparently declined her boss's invitation to sit with him at table.

"You do what you gotta do for me, I do what I gotta do for you. Right?"

Again there was no reply.

"You understand what I'm saying to you, Gloria?"

A strange, pinched, almost whining note had entered the Godfather's voice, a hint almost of pleading. It seemed to the listening agents that some perverse and upside-down ritual of power was being played out at the Castellano table. The master says *Sit here, be my equal.* The servant says *No thanks—my advantage lies in remaining apparently inferior.* The master says *Let's talk as man and woman.* The servant says *No, I will keep a seemingly respectful silence, which is my way of withholding what you need.*

"If you want me to do you a favor," he wheedled on, "if you

want me to be nice to you, then you have to make sure you are nice to me."

When Gloria Olarte finally spoke, her voice was measured and cold, her words chopped into little packets by the noise from the household chores she would not stop doing. "Leesten, Meester Paul . . . you talk to your keeds, hokay? . . . You talk to your wife . . . then you let me know. Then we talk, Meester Paul. . . . The other day, you know, I wait. I theenk maybe you have an answer for me. I wait till eleben o'clock. . . . Gloria she get tired of waiting."

"So who's stopping you?" said the Godfather. He said it with a flash of anger, but there was no real force behind it; it was one of those wide punches thrown off-balance. The maid hit back with silence, and got the better of the exchange.

"Don't make a mistake, Gloria," Castellano resumed. "Okay, it isn't perfect like it is. I grant you that. But think what you have. You know Waldbaum's, Gloria? The supermarkets? I'm almost the boss of Waldbaum's now. They pay me. You know why? Because of my influence. When I sit down, I talk to a man, 'Oh, Paul,' they say, 'how ya feel? How's everything?' And I say to them, 'Look, now I want you to be nice to my boys. And I want my boys to be nice to you. When they don't do that, you come see me. I'll straighten it out. 'Cause, listen, while I'm alive this is my business.' 'Paul,' they say, 'don't worry. We have got a lot of respect for you. When we need help, we'll come to you.'

"So they come, Gloria," the Godfather continued. "Waldbaum's, they come. The unions, they come. Frank Perdue, the big chicken man, he comes. I don't care who he is. If the President of the United States, if he's smart, if he needed help, he'd come. I could do a favor, some favor for him."

"Meester Paul is just like the President," said the maid. Did Kurins and O'Brien detect a hint of sarcasm in her voice? The Godfather apparently did not.

"No," he said. Having received his stroke, he sounded more benign, almost modest. "I'm not like the President. The President is a big man. I'm not like him. But everybody can do somebody a little favor. That's what I'm telling you, Gloria. You understand?"

"Yes, Gloria understand."

"So come here, baby."

Through the surveillance microphone there came a moist noise that sounded suspiciously like a kiss. Was the tiff over, or had the maid simply decided that she'd pressed her advantage as far as she could right then? The kiss was followed by a breathy whimper that sounded more than a little like a groan.

"Not under the skirt, Meester Paul. Meesus Nina . . ."

"Just a little feel, Gloria. With my coffee. That's better, isn't it?"

The maid was silent, whether luxuriating or being stoic it was impossible to judge. The Godfather, his hand presumably remaining up his servant's leg, now chatted amiably, a tone of satyrish teasing in his voice.

"That fat man with the beard," he said, referring to God knows who, "he kissed you."

"He never kiss me before," she said. "I surprised."

"And Mr. Julie, he flirts with you."

She giggled. "No, he's only being nice."

"Well, don't you be too nice to him."

"No," said the maid, her voice oddly transfigured. "I not nice to anybody but Meester Paul."

"See, he's Jewish," said Castellano, his words falling into a peculiarly percussive cadence. "He's Jewish. Jews are very, very funny people. They make you fuck their wives, and make believe they don't know nothing. They don't have strong minds. You understand what I'm saying, Gloria?"

"No," she said, "Gloria doesn't understand."

"Doesn't matter," said the Godfather.

"Doesn't matter," said his maid.

CHAPTER 46

IT WAS NOT UNTIL JUNE that the FBI got the opportunity to listen in on a meeting between Paul Castellano and the Gambino family *consigliere*, Joe N. Gallo. For several reasons, it was hoped that this conversation would be a particularly fertile one. Gallo was logical and relatively articulate. As family counselor, his specific roles were to advise the Boss on delicate matters and to act as ambassador to the other families. Gallo had not visited the Hill in several months; presumably there was a backlog of business to discuss.

Moreover, at that juncture Gallo's own standing within the Gambino organization was a bit shaky. As Tommy Gambino had suggested, the *consigliere*'s blithe stance toward the Greater Blouse, Skirt, and Undergarment Association had to some degree damaged family interests in the garment district. More important, Gallo, without authorization, had been indulging himself in some free-lance bribery that wasn't working out. Law enforcement knew about his activity; if Castellano knew of it as well, Joe Gallo would have some serious explaining to do.

Given the presumed agenda, then, it was a little surprising when the opening focus of the sit-down turned out to be literary criticism.

"I tried to take ten minutes of that fucking book," said Paul Castellano. "I thought it would be interesting, you know, what with knowing a lot of the people. But fuck, I can't read that shit."

"It makes you wonder," said Joe N. Gallo. "Is this son of a bitch senile, or is he a fucking nut?"

"Well, what I think," said a third voice, "what I figure, is it was some kind of deal, instead of going to jail." This third voice was identified by Andy Kurins as belonging to Gallo's driver,

Frankie "the Hat" Di Stefano. Unlike other balding mobsters, who ran to Joseph Paris Hairpieces for their gleaming toups, Di Stefano had made peace with his vanity years before by keeping his fedora on at all times. He was not a big man, but was known to be handy with his fists and his feet. He often carried a Little League bat up his sleeve, and no one ever told him to remove the chapeau.

"What the fuck," said Gallo. "This is a new kind of plea bargain, or what? Go to the slammer or write your memoirs and make your friends look lousy?"

"The memory," said Big Paul. "That's what gets me. The fucking guy acts like he remembers every word ever said to him since 1927."

By this point, it was clear that the volume under review was the just-published autobiography of Joe Bonanno, *A Man of Honor.* The Mafia—or at least that select group of Mafiosi who can read—likes to read about itself. The illiterates wait for the movie. Either way, mobsters look to the media for a sense of their own history. The Tradition, the Code—it is not too much of an exaggeration to say that these things have now been given over to the keeping of editors and screenwriters, who feed them back to a new generation of thugs with no real sense of the past, no real sense of the Old Country—just a crew of mutts who happen to have Italian surnames and would like to feel that they are part of something slightly less mean and sordid than their own criminal impulses.

"But that's the remarkable thing about these cocksuckers, Paul," said Gallo. "Maybe they can't read and write, but they remember. It's like they have another sense. It's unbelievable. You know this guy, what the hell's his name? Joe, Joe Soderik—something like that. Can't read. Can't write. But he can sing you an entire opera, word for word. All the parts. Fucking soprano shit. He sings it through his nose. Sounds like a real faggot. But what I'm saying is, his memory is unbelievable. There's a word for that—when a guy is a moron about almost everything and a genius at one thing. I can't think of it."

Joe Gallo finished his ramble and there was a silence at the Castellano table. Agents Kurins and O'Brien knew by now that such stillnesses were rare; maybe mobsters didn't speak well, but they were seldom at a loss for a curse, an opinion, a piece of news. When they fell silent, it was for a purpose.

"Hat," said the Godfather, "do me a favor. Go pick some daffodils."

There was the scrape of a chair, then another silence. A long one.

"Joe, you fucked up bad on this Iannuzzi thing."

"I know, Paul," said the *consigliere,* sounding not at all surprised at the raising of the subject. "I'm sorry." Andy Kurins could picture the old man sitting there, his neat hands splayed out on the table, his forehead turning rabbit pink.

"Well, how the fuck did it happen?"

"I was set up. I was suckered. I was handed some wrong advice, and I took it. Tommy A. tells me Joe Dogs has a line into the prison guys. He tells me he already got a guy moved for Carmine Persico. It's on the record that the guy was moved. And why shouldn't I believe Tommy A.? I'm his *gumbah*. He says, 'Use me.' He's doing me a solid. He don't know Iannuzzi's turned. He don't know Iannuzzi's fucking all of us."

"And I gotta hear about it from Piney?" said the Godfather. "That ain't right, Joe. You know that ain't right."

"Listen, Paul, I know. You want me to mop the floor with my tongue, I'll do it. I know and I'm sorry."

"Why didn't you come to me?" asked Castellano, in a voice that seemed to convey less anger than hurt feelings. "Why didn't you ask?"

Oddly, Joe Gallo, the transgressor, now sounded like the angrier of the two men. "Because what if you said no? I've never disobeyed you, Paul. Not once. I've served well. I'm proud of that. But here, Paul, if I asked you and you said no, it's too risky, don't do it, I would have said fuck you, this is my son.

"This keeps me awake nights," the *consigliere* continued. "Him up there with a bunch of niggers. He ain't got no friends up there, he ain't protected. You know, you figure, your kid goes to the can, okay, that's the breaks. But not like this. Not some state jail full of fucking animals. It's a wrong thing."

"Joe, hey," said Castellano. "I'm a father. You think I don't understand that?"

But Gallo was not to be deflected. "And who the fuck is Piney to be running to you with this?"

"Don't blame him," said the Godfather, with the regal finality he could sometimes muster. "He did right. He's not looking to make trouble. Tommy A. came clean with him, because Tommy A. is in the deepest shit of all. Besides, it woulda come out anyway. You know that."

"So what now?" asked Gallo.

"What now," said Castellano. "To tell you the truth, I don't know what now. Agro is fucked, that's for sure. How big a problem he is for the rest of us remains to be seen."

"Iannuzzi's the problem," said the *consigliere*.

"Iannuzzi's in the loving hands of the feds," said the Godfather. "Who's gonna take the contract? You?"

Again there was a silence, but now it seemed to the listening agents that it was the befuddled quiet of two old men who were powerless to act.

"It's all turning to shit, isn't it?" said Joe Gallo.

The Godfather said nothing.

"I mean," the counselor went on, "you spend your life working on this thing, this thing of ours. You think you're doing right. Then something happens, something goes off track, you get old, it don't look like it used to look. Disappointed. You end up disappointed. And the bitch of it is, you can't put your finger on what went wrong. You're doing good, you're doing good, you're doing good. But somehow, the way it all adds up, you ain't done shit. It all ends up small. It all ends up sour."

"Speak for yourself," said Big Paul Castellano.

CHAPTER 47

LEMME ASK you something," said Bruce Mouw, swiveling in his desk chair and looking through the dirty sixth-floor windows to an almost clear June sky. "The bug's been in, what, ten weeks, eleven weeks? How many times have we intercepted Neil Dellacroce?"

"We haven't," said Joe O'Brien.

"Well, doesn't that strike you as peculiar?" asked Mouw. "I mean, the *capos* check in once a week or so. The bagmen and the hangers-on find plenty of excuses to drop by. Bilotti practically lives there. And the underboss, whose house is only half a mile away, doesn't pay respects once in almost three months?"

"Neil runs his own show," said Andy Kurins. "Has since Carlo Gambino died."

"Granted," said Mouw. "But what I'm wondering is where's the line between two guys operating independently, but with a sense of order, and two guys operating against each other."

"That's been a thin line ever since Paul took over," said O'Brien.

"Fair enough," the supervisor said. "But my point is that the line seems to be getting thinner all the time, and I'm not sure it hasn't already been crossed."

He reached into a desk drawer and produced a stack of documents, flagged here and there with bits of yellow paper. The documents were transcripts of conversations among Gambino family members—conversations intercepted on bugs and wiretaps other than the one in Castellano's home. They told a tale that in some ways ran parallel to, and in other ways was on a collision course with, the story unfolding at the Godfather's table. Just as, in the case of individual conversations, the agents had to play connect-the-dots to make a picture, so they had to consider the pictures emerging from various surveillances to cast the image of the Gambino organization into three dimensions.

"Here's Angelo Ruggiero talking to Pete Tambone," said Mouw. " 'That fuck, that motherfucker, he ruined you.' Nice way to talk about your Boss, huh?"

"That's how Angelo talks about everybody," said Joe O'Brien.

"Besides, that's the heroin business," said Andy Kurins. "That's been a problem in the family for years."

"Right," said Mouw. "But it used to be the *only* problem. It used to be, the rules were clear: You wanted to work with Paul, you stayed out of drugs, or you kept it very low-key. End of story. Now, it's like they're using the drug thing as an excuse for hating him. It's hard to tell what they're really mad about, and what they're just using as justification for being mad.

"Listen. Here's Ruggiero again, this time with Gene Gotti, talking about the split from labor payoffs. Ruggiero is talking about picking up some cash, and Gotti says, 'The fucking Bosses can count on the unions like the fucking sun coming up in the morning, and meanwhile all the men are starving.' This has nothing to do with drugs. Now they're just saying he's cheap. You see what I'm getting at? They're just out to find fault. They're testing each other—and testing themselves, like kids do—to see how far they'll go in being critical of him."

"I don't know," Kurins said. "I mean, these are just a few guys who've hated him all along. The people *we* hear—we get an altogether different view of it. Everybody laughs at his jokes, they practically kiss his feet. It's all 'How ya feelin', Paul?' 'Ya look terrific, Paul.' There's a lot of respect and a lot of goodwill. There's more than that. There's . . . there's affection, for God's sake."

"Lemme ask you this," said Mouw, biting down on the stem of his pipe and offering his men a thoughtful wince. "Can you imagine John Gotti having a big decision-making job under Paul Castellano?"

"Yeah," said Joe O'Brien. "Like I can imagine Jesse Jackson having a Cabinet post under Ronald Reagan."

"Oil and water," added Andy Kurins. "Gotti is street. Gotti is flash. Gotti is publicity. Gotti is everything Castellano doesn't want."

"Well," said Mouw, "we got intercepts talking about Gotti for 'an administrative position.' Dellacroce wants him to have it. Which is not surprising. He's a logical successor to Dellacroce. But there's some surprising people supposedly on board. Paul's friend Frankie De Cicco says Gotti should have a bigger job. Joe Gallo has said he'd support the idea."

"They're just feeling the wind," said Kurins. Though he could not have justified the emotion, he felt oddly pained at the possibility that Big Paul was perhaps being slighted in old loyalties. "It's just talk."

"That's right," Mouw said. "It's just talk. What the hell else you get on wiretaps? But I'll tell you guys something: I think you're wrong if you imagine there's two camps, it's carved in stone, and it's a stable situation. Maybe it's stable for now, okay. But the balance can't last forever. The personalities are too strong and there's too much money up for grabs. There's gotta be movement in some direction. Paul's gotta either kick some butt or smooth some feathers, or there's gonna be more defections. You got tapes of a soldier named Robert Di Bernardo, right?"

Kurins and O'Brien nodded. Di Bernardo, known to his friends as D.B., was a fairly regular visitor to the White House. He was one of the charming ones, with real hair. He brought pastries. He kidded with Gloria. He was a good earner, the Gambinos' main man in the porno business. With Paul he was never anything but cordial and respectful.

"Well," said Mouw, "I got tapes of him, too. I got tapes of him supporting Gotti. And I got tapes of him complaining about Paul." Mouw riffled through to another of his flagged sheets of transcript. " 'He uses me. He makes me look bad. *Look at D.B. He makes his money in pornography.* Like he's some kinda high-and-mighty. Mr. fucking Clean. Does it stop him taking his cut? Sorry, Paul, you don't wanna touch those dollars—there's pussy on 'em. Ha! He'll take 'em anyway. He wants it both ways. Get paid. Act clean. My ass.' "

232

Kurins and O'Brien looked through the grimy, streaky window to the even filthier piles of brick and glass across Queens Boulevard. They were troubled, and they felt a little sheepish for being so. They had come to feel a perverse proprietary bond with Paul Castellano. He was their prey, their quarry, and they regarded him with the murderous respect that the fisherman feels for the trout. They did not want anybody else harassing him or muddying his pool. They preferred to think of him as serene and secure behind his rock, vulnerable to no snares but theirs.

Bruce Mouw, a law enforcement officer for fifteen years, didn't need to be told what they were feeling. "Listen," he said, "all I'm saying is, let's hang on to some perspective here. Let's not kid ourselves that we are the only problem Castellano has. Because, guys, with all due respect, I wouldn't bet my last dollar that we are even the biggest problem Castellano has."

CHAPTER 48

M

Y PANTS, NINA. Sometimes I see 'em sittin' there three days in a row. What's the story? I ain't got that many clothes. It's asking too much, you should take 'em to the cleaners like you're supposed to?"

"I'll tell the maid to do it," said Nina Castellano.

"Since when is it the maid's job to take stuff to the cleaners? No, Nina, you do that. You don't have to tell nothin' to the maid. I'm askin' you."

"Three days?" said the wife. "You're saying they're there three days?"

"Right," said the Godfather. "And I don't have that many clothes, don't you understand?"

"So *you* take them. Pick them up off the floor and take them."

"Listen, Nina, what I do . . . I do what I have to do for myself. I do it. And I don't wanna involve . . . I don't wanna make things worse, what with you bringing my daughter here, and the kids, and everything's a show. Everything's like a goddamn fishbowl. I don't wanna make it worse."

"I'm not saying make it worse. I'm saying pick up your pants. I'm saying make it clear what you want from who, Paul. You don't make it clear. Maybe Tommy can read your mind. I can't. That's why there's no supper."

"I want some peace in my own house, woman. I don't like anybody running my house, see? I don't like this, all of a sudden, your kids are here, they're staying over, everything's all rear-ranged . . ."

"Since when don't you want your own children under your roof?"

234

"My life changes, Nina. It changes. You don't seem to get that."

"Why, Paul? Why does it change?"

"None of your business, why it changes. It changes because it changes. Bring me some aspirin."

"The maid can bring you aspirin, dear."

CHAPTER 49

IN MAFIA FAMILIES, as in other business organizations, there is an ebb and flow in the careers of executives. People's stock moves up or down in accordance with what the firm—and the Boss—needs at a given point in time. At certain junctures, flamboyance is called for; other times a quiet steadiness wins promotions. Sometimes sheer energy carries the day; other times finesse prevails. The Chief, in finding favor with certain subordinates rather than others, does not simply choose among individuals but sets a certain tone.

In June 1983, the tone that Paul Castellano seemed to be striving for was one of calm. Paul's situation in those days was deeply paradoxical. Outwardly, the Gambino organization was in terrific shape. It was flush with cash and invested with an impressively diversified portfolio of scams. Its preeminence among New York's five crime families was ever more apparent. As far as staying a step ahead of law enforcement was concerned, Castellano had good reason to feel smug; FBI harassment of family members had eased off since the heyday of the RH factor, and while Big Paul continued to be concerned about the ongoing visual surveillance of his house, as well as paranoid about the prospect of his phone being tapped, it never seemed to dawn on him, even as the remotest possibility, that his innermost sanctum might be bugged. Presumably, he imagined that the feds—who had ebbs and flows of their own, after all—had backed off for a while.

At the same time, the man had plenty to feel harried about. His home life was a mess. His health was more and more of a problem; the tapes featured almost daily references to headaches, indigestion, high blood pressure, occasional spells of lightheadedness. His confidence in Joe Gallo had been damaged by the *consigliere*'s ill-advised bribe scheme on behalf of his son. And maybe—though it is impossible to say with certainty—he was beginning to sense how deep were the divisions within his own ranks.

In any case, what he seemed to want was solidity and reliability. Tommy Bilotti provided some of that, and the two men apparently drew even closer through the spring of '83. But there was something too passive and not intelligent enough about Bilotti's brand of loyalty. It was a comfort, sure, but never totally satisfying. There was no real interchange. Talking to Bilotti was like talking to the dog, and Castellano needed more than that. He needed someone with whom he could talk about the why and the how, the then and the now, someone with whom he could gruffly philosophize, someone who spoke softly and didn't jangle his increasingly tender nerves.

That someone turned out to be Joe "Piney" Armone, Paul's nearest counterpart in age and wisdom. With Piney, the Godfather didn't just give orders; he thought out loud. At times, he almost seemed to be using the courtly old *capo* to review his whole management approach.

On one occasion, for example, the two elders, in the course of discussing family business, digressed onto the subtle strategic question of when, and when not, to have people rubbed out.

"Look," said the Godfather, "when we sit down to clip a guy, we have to remember what's at stake here. There's some hazard. Guys forget that. They get a guy behind in his vig payments, they get a hard-on about it, right away they wanna whack him. Why? Just because they're pissed off, they're aggravated. But what I say is, 'Hey, you're making a living with this guy. He gets you aggravated, and right away you wanna use the hammer? How do you get your fucking money *then*?' "

"It's means and ends," Joe Armone said softly. "The idea is to collect. But you know, Paul, I think some guys just take so much pleasure from breaking heads that they'd almost rather not get paid."

"Yeah, yeah," the Godfather agreed. "We got some guys like that. Dick-fists, I call 'em. I'm always sayin' to 'em, 'Just to take a guy out, that ain't the point.' Because I'll tell ya, Piney, anytime I can remember that we knocked guys out, it cost us. It's like there's a tax on it or some shit. Somebody gets arrested. Or there's a fuckup, which means we gotta clip *another* guy, maybe a guy we don't wanna lose."

"Of course," Joe Armone interjected quietly, "if there's a pattern . . ."

"If there's a pattern," Big Paul picked up, "the guy is dead. If he's fucking us, he's dead. But let's be honest, Joe. Of all the people we do business with, how many of them are so fucking stupid that they would knowingly try to fuck us? All right, now and then there's a guy who has delusions. A lunatic. He thinks he's protected. He thinks he's got a whole union or a big politician protecting him, something like that. But usually it's just sad-ass guys who make mistakes. They can't stop gambling. They think they got a brilliant business idea that turns out to be a dog. They're not trying to rob us, they're just assholes, they're pathetic. Now here, we got a judgment call. Do we let these sorry bastards ride? Hey, they knew the rules. It's not like we got a Jew lawyer springing fine print on 'em. Is there any chance we're gonna get satisfaction? Or are they gonna be a permanent liability? If it's permanent, it can't stay permanent for long."

"Or then again," said Piney, "you can end up with some complicated situation like this thing with Mikey, where the question isn't how much does this guy owe but who does he owe it to?"

Sitting in the Richmond Road dormer, Joe O'Brien put down his Styrofoam cup of coffee and scrawled on his yellow pad: "Pappadio?" Andy Kurins scrawled back: "Probably."

Mikey Pappadio was a Lucchese soldier who operated mainly in the garment district. His specialty was making extortionate loans, which he then parlayed into equity shares of various businesses. But Mikey was a short-term investor. He wanted his profit yesterday. So he pressured his "partners" to "bust out" their businesses—that is, to strip the assets and declare fraudulent bankruptcies. If that seemed like too slow and unwieldy a procedure, there was always arson.

"The guy's into Mikey for fifty grand or so," Joe Armone

continued, "and he can't pay. The company just isn't producing the cash. So one day the factory catches fire. But the guy ain't too smart about how he does it, and he ends up in the can. One year, I think. Plus he don't get the money. So Mikey is stuck.

"Well, now the guy is out again, and he wants to go back in business. But now he's partners with Ruggiero and Gotti, and he don't say nothing about the old deal with Mikey Pappadio. His attitude toward Mikey is, 'Hey, I took the fall, I went in the can, I don't owe you nothing.' Well, Mikey wants to get paid. He threatens the guy. And the guy—he has *guyones*, ya gotta say that for him—tells Mikey, 'I'm with Angelo and Johnny now—you sure you wanna fuck with me?' And Mikey, he don't know what to do. He's got a beef, but if he leans too hard on the guy, then Ruggiero and Gotti got a beef. He goes from being right to being wrong."

"Yup," said the Godfather, with a weariness he didn't try to hide. "Sometimes the toughest thing of all is doing business with our own friends."

"Gets complicated," said Armone.

"Complicated? It gets fucking impossible. Ya can't do business with friends of ours from other families, unless you clear it. Now, okay, in principle, that's a good rule. Otherwise, you got guys running all over the place like chickens with their heads cut off, you got no discipline, everybody's grabbing, it's mayhem. But in practice? Shit. You got a guy, say Joe Blow. He's with you. But he's got a cousin or a brother-in-law, say, who's with the Snake. And he likes those guys. Now, let's face it, Joe, it's human nature. You can tell guys what the rules are, but you can't tell 'em who to like. And eventually they're gonna do things with their friends. So say Joe Blow's a good earner. You know he's bending the rules, but what're ya gonna do? You gonna spank the guy for making money? Then one day there's a beef. Ya gotta sit down. Who do you back? D'ya back Joe Blow, just because he's your guy? D'ya sell him out because he wasn't going by the book? Plus, it's embarrassing. It makes you look bad, like you weren't enough in control. Does the guy get clipped for making you look bad?"

"Jurisdiction," said Joe Armone, as soothingly as if the word were a tranquilizer. "It's a question of jurisdiction."

But the intended palliative had just the opposite effect on Paul Castellano, sending him off on another complaint. "Jurisdiction. You know what jurisdiction means? Jurisdiction is a half-ass word for power. You have power, you do what the hell you want to do, and that's the end of it. You have jurisdiction, everything's a god-damn discussion. Pain in the ass.

"Lemme tell you something, Piney," the Godfather went on. "That's why I value Funzie Mosca. Okay, the guy ain't a world-beater. But he's a fucking genius on jurisdiction. He could sit on the Supreme fucking Court. I mean, he knows exactly where the lines are drawn. Four stories up, that's done by machine—that's Two eighty-two, call Bobby Sasso. Five stories and higher, that's by hand—ya need a different union. This bid over here, it's Biff's turn—leave it alone. That job over there, that's Julie Miron's people—let him pick up the dough. This other site, it's over the city line into Yonkers—pay this guy. The man has the whole thing mapped out in his head."

"Makes life easier," said Armone.

"It does," said Castellano. "Otherwise, it's like you're sup-posed to call the shots, you're supposed to do good, but like you're in a goddamn straitjacket. So whaddya do? You don't want trou-ble, you can sit tight. You don't say nothin', you don't do nothin'. But ya can't live in this world doin' nothin'. Am I right?"

"You're right, Paul, you're right."

"You only live once, Piney. Am I right? You don't get to do everything. No one does. Me, I got no regrets. The only thing I wish, I wish I had more education, I wish I was more, ya know, educated. But I say that now. At the time, what I wanted was the streets, so I took 'em. I always felt, if there's something you want to do, do it now. Don't fuck around waiting. Am I right?"

"Yeah, Paul, you're right."

"But at the same time, let's not kid ourselves. This life of ours, this is a wonderful life. If you can get through life like this and get away with it, hey, that's great. But it's very, very unpredictable. There's so many ways you can screw it up. So you gotta think, ya gotta be patient. A lotta guys, they're yanking their zipper before their dick is put away, then they wonder why they get snagged.

And they don't know when to zipper their fucking mouth shut, either. I tell 'em: 'You listen, you learn. You talk, you teach.' Am I right, Piney?"

"Yeah, Paul, you're right."

"Because there's just so many fucking things that can blow up on you."

"Yeah, Paul, there are."

"There's so many fucking ways they can get you."

CHAPTER 50

T HAT FUCKIN' JOE O'BRIEN," piped Tommy Bilotti, in
that braying clarinet voice of his. "He knows he's a ball-buster. He
knows just how to break your balls."

"Give 'im that," said Joe Butch Corrao. "The cocksucker
knows how to get under your skin."

"You know why he can do it?" Bilotti went on. "Because he
doesn't mind looking like an asshole. Other guys figure, hey, I
can't do that, I'll look like a douche bag. O'Brien, he don't care."

"He *likes* looking like a douche bag," said Corrao.

At the Richmond Road plant, Joe O'Brien looked at Andy
Kurins and scribbled on his yellow pad: "No I don't."

"I gotta tell ya what this fuckin' jerk-off does the other day,"
says Bilotti. "He's cruisin' by my house, snoopin' around, but I
ain't there. I got my brother watchin' the place for me. So O'Brien
comes cruisin' along, and he's in this car, it ain't the piece a shit he
usually drives, it's got Jersey plates. And my brother, he don't
really know O'Brien. Anyway, it just so happens that the Brownies
or Girl Scouts or some shit are runnin' this charity thing, they're
washin' cars on the block. So O'Brien figures he'll be smart, he'll
get his car washed, he'll get to talk to the neighbors—like what're
they gonna tell him, right?

"So anyway," the Wig continued, "these little girls are washin'
his car, and this lady next door looks out the window and thinks,
hey, wait a second—this guy comes all the way from Jersey just to
have little girls wash his car? I think we got a pervert on our hands.
So she calls my brother. He comes out of the house. He's yelling,
'You're lookin' up their skirts, ya fuckin' pervert, ya Puerto Rican.
Get your car washed in Jersey, ya sick fuck! You wanna Simoniz?
Here's some Vaseline—Simoniz your dick, jerk-off!'

"So O'Brien, real calm like, says, 'You must be Tommy's

brother.' But my brother, he ain't the type to go around tellin' people his name. He just says, 'Tommy who?' And O'Brien just says, 'I'm Joe O'Brien.' And my brother, ya know, he knows the name, but in the heat of the moment it don't register, and he says, 'I don't give a fuck if you're Frank Sinatra. You're a sick bastard, and I want you outa here.' "

Joe Butch Corrao laughed. Paul Castellano laughed. Then Gloria Olarte broke in on the conversation. She came in ahead of the beat, like a child eager to horn in on the dimly grasped merriment of the grown-ups.

"Meester Joe O'Brien, he come to my house," she said.

"He what?" said the Godfather. He wasn't laughing now. Neither was O'Brien.

"My seester's house. In Queens. He come there to talk to Gloria."

"Son of a bitch," said Bilotti.

"Shut up, Tommy," said Castellano. "When, Gloria? When did he do this?"

The maid hesitated. It seemed to the monitoring agents that she was realizing she had made a mistake, that her attempt at joining in the boys' levity had fallen exceptionally flat. Now she chose her words carefully. "Oh, eet was in the winter. Three, four months ago. He finds me on my day off. But I no tell heem nothing, Meester Paul."

"What did he want to know?" the Godfather insisted.

"He ask me what you talk about, what I hear. I tell heem I only work, I don't hear nothing."

"Why didn't you tell me before?"

"I no want to make trouble."

"For who, Gloria?" said the Godfather, in a sharp tone the agents had not heard him use with his mistress before. "Who didn't you want to make trouble for?"

"For nobody," she said, a pout in her voice. "Not for Gloria. Not for Meester Paul. Not for Meester Joe."

"Who gives a fuck if it's trouble for Mister Joe?" said Bilotti.

"Tommy, goddamnit, sit still. I don't like it, Gloria, that you didn't tell me this. I don't like it at all."

There was a silence as the sting of the scolding sank in. Kurins and O'Brien imagined it as one of those moments when no one could meet anyone else's eyes. Gloria, probably standing as she served the men, would be looking down at her cracked shoes. Bilotti, smarting from his own reproach, would be wearing the lovelorn expression of a rebuked hound. Joe Butch, steering clear of trouble, might perhaps take out his pocket clipper and do a ream job on an immaculately manicured nail. And Paul Castellano, regal but not at peace in his red satin bathrobe, would glare around the table, his risen blood pressure making splotches on his wattled neck, labored breath whistling slightly through the coarse hairs of his nose.

"I tell you why I no tell you before," said Gloria Olarte, her voice a mixture of defiance and affronted virtue. "I no tell you because I no like to see you get so mad. Because Meester Joe, he bother me a lot. He go to see my family in Bogotá."

"Colombia?" said Bilotti.

"*Sí*. Yes. He make me have beeg fight with my father."

In the Richmond Road dormer, Kurins and O'Brien looked at each other and crinkled their eyebrows. Joe O'Brien had never been to Colombia in his life. He'd never met or spoken with Gloria Olarte's parents. True, he had arranged for a Bogotá-based FBI agent to pay a visit to the Olarte family. Was the maid confused, or was she making trouble?

"What did he say to your father?" asked Joe Butch Corrao.

"He say, 'Your daughter, Gloria, she working for berry bad man, and eef she no help us, we can make beeg trouble for her and for you.' "

"He was trying to scare him," said Bilotti.

"Yes, he trying to make him scare. And so my father, he berry angry with me. He call my seester Nellie. He say, 'Gloria, she do bad things in America. She make shames on the family.' And I have to call him back and say, 'No, Papi, Gloria she work for berry good man. Meester Paul, he berry kind, berry generous. You no believe Meester Joe O'Brien. He just trying to make you scare.' "

"But Gloria," said Castellano, his voice seeming to hover between anger and an almost whining desire to be reconciled with his sweetheart, "you should have told me this right when it happened. Why didn't you tell me?"

"You promise you no be mad, Meester Paul?" She said it coyly but with utter confidence. The maid was back in control.

"I'm mad already," said the Godfather, but he didn't really sound it anymore. "So tell me."

"Meester Joe," said Gloria Olarte, "I no theenk he really mean to make trouble. He has nice smile. I like heem. He berry handsome man."

Oh Christ, thought O'Brien. *This I don't need.*

"Handsome?" said Bilotti. "That fucking fish? He looks like a pimple on my ass."

"No, Meester Tommy. Excuse me, but you are wrong. He berry handsome. He handsome like Meester Joe Butch. But Meester Joe O'Brien, he have blue eyes and that mustache—like, it would tickle, you know, anywhere he keess. I theenk maybe he even more sexy."

"You stay away from him, Gloria," said the Godfather. He said it not in the measured tone he used when discussing tactics for evading law enforcement but in the gravelly rumble of the jealous male.

"Gloria stay away. Hokay. But eef Meester Joe comes finding me . . ."

"We could fix it so he doesn't," piped Bilotti.

"Easy, Tommy," said Joe Butch softly. "Some things ya don't say."

There was a silence at the Castellano table. It used to be remarked of Carlo Gambino that he seldom if ever had to order a man killed. So articulate were his expressions, so attentive his minions, that he could sign a death warrant with a lift of an eyebrow, execute someone with a slight frown.

"I sure don't like the guy," Joe Butch resumed.

"I think that goes for all of us," said Big Paul Castellano.

"You worried, Joe?" asked Andy Kurins, when the recording equipment had been switched off.

It was a hard question for O'Brien to answer. Only a jackass would deny that there was an element of atmospheric, ongoing fear in working the turf of organized crime. That fear was part of what kept the juices flowing, kept the concentration honed. Beyond a certain threshold, however, the anxiety became destructive; there was nothing to be gained by lingering on it. "That woman is confused," he said.

"I don't think Castellano would go after an agent," Kurins said. "Remember his attitude on the Pistone contract."

"I remember what he said. I'm reserving judgment on whether he meant it."

"Pistone is still around."

"That's a point," said O'Brien. He tried to analyze the situation as though the veiled threat had been made against somebody else. "But of course, the Pistone thing was official business. This craziness with the girlfriend is more of an emotional matter."

"Yeah," Kurins agreed. "If he thinks she's got the hots for you, I guess that qualifies as emotional. But really, Joe, I don't see what he's got to be jealous about."

"Thanks."

"I mean, he's rich, he's powerful, he's the top guy. And you . . ."

"Me what?" said O'Brien.

"Well, you're just you."

"Maybe that's exactly it. Okay, he's got all the trophies. But how does he really know what she thinks of him, once you get past the money and the big house and all that respect bullshit? He's not a dumb guy. Maybe he knows he's not that big a bargain."

"I don't know," said Kurins. "Most guys don't know that about themselves."

"He's almost seventy years old. He's got all kinds of diseases. He's got a dead dick that he's gotta crank-start like a Model T. If you were him and had a thirty-year-old hot tamale for a girlfriend, you don't think you'd be jealous?"

"Not to the point of killing people about it," said Andy Kurins. "Ah shit, Joe, sorry. I guess I shouldn't've said that."

CHAPTER 51

IN THE JULY 25, 1983, issue of *New York* magazine, there was an article, written by organized crime reporter Jerry Capeci, entitled "Frank Perdue Meets the Godfather."

It was one of those articles that make no one happy. For the chicken king, the piece called into question the old maxim that there's no such thing as bad publicity. True, Capeci went out of his way to stress that there was nothing illegal about Perdue sitting down with Big Paul Castellano at a Manhattan restaurant called Paul and Jimmy's. There was nothing unlawful about his seeking out the most powerful Mafioso in America—a man widely known to "own" various unions—to discuss his labor problems. Nor was there anything beyond the pale in Perdue complaining to the Godfather about the treatment of his birds by several New York supermarket chains, notwithstanding that a board member of one of those chains was also a Gambino family *capo*. Perdue, the article stressed, was not a mobster or a criminal, just a cautionary example of how fine, upstanding American businessmen were sometimes funneled into whirlpools of unsanitary contacts. Yet, as in Antony's famous speech over the body of Caesar, the more Capeci insisted that Perdue had done nothing wrong, the sleazier old Frank appeared.

If the article must have sent Perdue's PR staff scurrying into meetings on damage control, it didn't create joy at the Brooklyn headquarters of Dial Poultry, either. Again, Capeci reported that Dial was a legitimate meat and poultry distributor, that it belonged to a respected industry association, and that its proprietors, Joseph Castellano, then forty-five, and Paul Castellano, Jr., then forty-three, had never been convicted of unlawful activity. In a lovely bit of understatement, however, the article also pointed out that "law-enforcement officials believe, based on taped conversations, that Dial has links to organized crime."

One of those "taped conversations" had taken place at Paul Castellano's table on May 31. On that occasion, Paul junior—who apparently had already been contacted by someone at the magazine—told his father that "they wanna write an article on who controls the poultry business in New York. They're saying that you control the business. . . . You must have thirty guys. . . . Dial is only one of them."

Tommy Gambino, visiting at the time to discuss business of his own regarding the Greater Blouse, Skirt, and Undergarment Association, had complained that the press can "distort anything they want."

"Actually, it really hurts business," the Godfather had conceded.

Then Paul junior had made an oblique but poignant comment about the difficulty of carrying the Castellano name. "But, you know, we could take it a step further. But what about the children? If you stay in the business, you know, it's a commitment. What [unintelligible] is saying to them about poultry [unintelligible] . . . do with me? . . . You know, afraid I'm gonna put it on record. . . . No matter who we are, we're a part of it."

"Well," the Godfather had said, "it's just a matter of backing them off on the same thing. They don't expect an admission, you know. . . . They do stuff which really sometimes ya shouldn't let 'em get away with it. A lotta times ya think about it, ya say, 'Forget about it.' "

But Big Paul apparently did not forget about it, because on the day the article appeared, he was sitting in his favorite chair, reading parts of it aloud to his maid and mistress.

"Look what it says here, Gloria. 'Frank Perdue Meets the Godfather.' "

"Who's the Godfather, you?" asked Gloria Olarte.

"Yeah," said Castellano, "yeah. Here it is: 'Why would Frank Perdue want to talk to this quiet, graying Staten Island man?' Why? Why? Because Frank Perdue told the FBI I'm the Godfather."

Then, weirdly, Big Paul slipped into the pidgin English he often used when alone with Gloria. "This man, he ask me for a favor and I say I can't do. I show you. Here: 'Mr. Castellano said he was not able to [help], and the matter was dropped.' That's the Perdue spokesman talking. And oh, look at this. That fuckin' Joe O'Brien, he's someplace here. Wait'll I see Joe O'Brien here, son of a bitch. Yeah, here: 'FBI agent Joseph O'Brien, whose office is on the sixth floor of the building that houses the Perdue Chicken Restaurant'—do you believe it, Gloria?—'stopped in to talk to Frank Perdue about his meetings with Big Paul Castellano. O'Brien and his supervisor, Bruce Mouw, said they could not comment.' Course they wouldn't. Assholes.

"Now listen to this," the Godfather went on. "It say here Perdue conducted his own private investigation. Okay? He investigate us. And listen: 'According to one official, [he] found that Big Paul had a reputation for being honorable in his dealings.' You hear, Gloria? I got a reputation. Everybody say that Paul very fair man. I'm fair to you, too."

But at this point, to the considerable surprise of the agents monitoring the conversation from the Richmond Road plant, the maid seized the initiative and steered the talk onto a tangent of her own.

"No, Meester Paul," she said, "you not always fair to Gloria. You can be berry honorable in beezness, yes, weeth people outside. Even weeth me you are, usually. Yes. But weeth Meesus Nina, everything you say about Meesus Nina, I don't believe you."

"You don't believe it's because I'm honorable that I act like that?"

The maid said nothing.

"Wait, wait a minute, Gloria. Please. You don't believe it's because I'm honorable I don't throw her out, I don't insist?"

"No. I don't theenk so."

"You think an honorable person would do that, Gloria? Throw a woman out on the street?"

"I don't say I want her to go away," said the maid. "I don't say that."

"Oh yes, you are saying that, Gloria."

"No, I don't. But I don't believe you. Don't you theenk I'm sure that in thees life you love Meesus Nina more than anything else before?"

"Gloria," said the Godfather, "I don't make sacrifice for her. I make sacrifice for you. You see, Gloria, what I do now is very, very hard for me to do. You ever see me beg her? You ever see me beg Mrs. Nina to stay here? Mrs. Nina, please stay with me? The truth, Gloria—did you ever see that? No. All you see is *get out, get out,* right? Then she say she's gonna change, she's gonna be good, and she comes back in. Then she do again, and I say get out. Right? I no change my opinion, Gloria."

The maid said nothing.

"If I wasn't fair to you," the Godfather resumed, "and you say to me, 'I'm gonna go away,' I say, 'Oh thank God, I get rid of that pain in the ass.' But no, Gloria, I say to myself, 'Now wait a minute, that pain in the ass is the girl I love, and if she go away she's gonna hurt herself. I can't make her do that.' "

The maid did not respond. In her white room at the Colombian institution, she had cultivated a vast capacity for quiet. So Big Paul Castellano rambled on. In his voice was a kind of masked panic, as though he felt something might fall through a moment's silence as through a deep gash in the earth and, with a sickening finality, flutter downward, out of sight.

"Gloria, Gloria, what you have to be jealous from? I want to be with you forever. Not ever for you, Gloria—I can't live that long—but ever for me. Please, Gloria, don't you understand that? You know who's talking to you now? Your father. Your mother."

"I know," said the maid.

"Don't ever say you don't believe me, baby. Don't ever say that."

"Why am I gonna do?" said Gloria Olarte. Then she whimpered, once, like a cat. It was not a wholesome sound.

"Gloria, come on, baby. My God, I can't see you like this. I can't see you act like this, you know that. Come on, baby, what could we do for you?"

"Nothing. Nothing."

"Come on, baby, don't tell me nothing. Come on, Gloria, turn around. You break my heart, baby, you know that?"

There was no answer, and now the Godfather's tone was a clenched and queasy blend of scolding, pleading, and fear.

"Try to stop now, Gloria. Come on, try to stop. Don't talk yourself into getting sick now. See how nervous you are. You're all stiff, Gloria. Don't hurt yourself, baby. Come on, Gloria, don't go crazy on me now.

"You know when you go crazy, baby? Paul, he tell you when it's good to go crazy. When that salami go up your stomach, right in your stomach. Yes, that's good crazy, isn't it, Gloria? Come on, baby, come back. Look at me and smile. Hey, come back. Give me a kiss. Yeah, that's better, baby.

"Big smile. Come on, Gloria, a kiss. Yeah, baby, those eyes. I no lie to you, baby. Oh Gloria, you make me too happy."

CHAPTER 52

S O HOW YA FEELIN', PAUL?" asked the subtle and deferential Funzie Mosca.

"Lousy," said the Godfather. "I had this splitting headache for like four days now. Sinuses, I guess. Humidity. I stay in the air-conditioning, but it don't get better."

"Sometimes the AC makes it worse," said the bagman. "Me, I got bronchitis. I got this stuff . . ."

"Phlegm," interjected the porno specialist Robert Di Bernardo. "I get it a lot. Makes ya hafta clam."

"Yeah, phlegm. Just layin' on my lungs. Makes me understand what Joe Gallo's chest must feel like when his angina kicks in."

"Nah," squeaked Tommy Bilotti. "Angina's different. When my ulcer was bleeding, I talked to this guy in the next room. He just had a heart attack, still had all these tubes and shit. Said angina grabs your heart like a cold hand squeezing your balls."

"Piney's limp is getting worse," put in D.B. "Ya know, sometimes I think it's the climate. I don't think this is a healthy climate here."

"Cousin a mine moved to Arizona for the climate," said Funzie Mosca.

"How's he like it?" asked the Godfather.

"He died. Caught cancer."

"Ya don't catch cancer," said D.B.

"He did," Funzie insisted. "His girlfriend had it."

"She die too?" asked Bilotti.

"No, she got better. Strange, ain't it? 'Scuse me, I gotta go outside and spit."

It was the last week of July 1983, and New York was in the middle of a heat wave. Asphalt streets were melting; people were passing out on the number 7 train. Manhattanites were fighting over taxis; in the Bronx there were stabbings over parking spaces. At Sheepshead Bay people ate festering seafood and had to have their stomachs pumped. Inevitably, there was talk of blackouts, race riots, looting.

At the summit of Todt Hill, Big Paul Castellano was comfortably insulated from all of that. He had his problems, sure, but he was a man at the top of his profession, at the top of the city, at the top of his world. What breezes there were in that muggy July cooled the heights of his privileged precinct before dropping dead in the cluttered canyons lower down. The ugly sounds of sirens rarely carried so high up, and were barely heard above the surprising city music of tree toads and crickets. As for street crime, it was virtually nonexistent in neighborhoods where Mob-controlled private security guards packed snub-nosed .38s. No, in the Godfather's enclave of seven-figure houses and chauffeur-driven cars, the only annoyances that could not be filtered out were stubborn summer colds and the sniffles that went with the onset of allergy season.

This is not to say that Big Paul and his associates were disengaged from the more general life of the city. On the contrary, the Gambino family was even at that moment discussing ways of becoming still more actively and profitably involved in one of New York's keystone industries.

"So where it stands," Funzie Mosca was saying, "is that we were the low bidder."

"Yeah," said the Godfather, "but it was, ya know, like a modified bid."

"Well, yeah," said Mosca. "A little bit modified, yeah."

"It's always fucking modified," Tommy Bilotti horned in. "It's modified to the point where you can't make no fucking money on it."

"That's exactly what I been trying to tell you," said D.B. "It's the same thing that come up with Cody about price-fixing on the highway bids. It's gettin' to be all confrontations now. Everything's an argument. Like on the Queens College job. Fifteen thousand yards. But it's a Queens job, not a Manhattan job. And Cody says, 'Hey, don't worry, everybody's lookin' at the job, but you got the job.' "

"So far, so good," said Castellano.

"So far, so good," echoed D.B. "Right. But here's where it ain't so good. Time passes. Cody's indicted. Technically, he ain't in charge no more. Bobby Sasso's in charge. But what all this really means is that Cody's in charge when he wants to be, and when he don't want to be, he shrugs his shoulders and says, 'Hey, I'm indicted, what the fuck can I do?'

"So now it's time to stop promising and start delivering," D.B. continued, "and now we're hearing a different story. Cody says, 'Well, Jeez, there's this Sunshine contractor we gotta think about. We gotta give the work through Biff. We gotta throw something to Richy Naclerio, and he says he's more comfortable with Buster than with Bobby.' And the worst of it is that he's saying all this *in front of* Bobby, like Bobby was the fucking maid or something."

"D.B., hey," said the Godfather.

"Jesus, Paul. Sorry. But you know what I'm sayin'. It coulda been handled much more discreetly, instead of all this bickering, all this nickel-diming."

"It's like they're killing the chicken that laid the golden egg," piped up Tommy Bilotti.

"Goose," said Funzie Mosca. "The goose that laid the golden egg."

"Who gives a fuck?" said Bilotti. "You know what I'm sayin'."

"Yeah," Mosca said. "It's like, some jobs ya don't even wanna bid. By the time you finish schmearing everybody that needs schmearing, you might as well stay home and scratch your ass, for all the money you're gonna make. Like Hunnert Thirty-fifth Street. They come to Al Chattin, they say, 'Al, do us a favor, we need a bid.' So he gives 'em a bid. They say, 'Al, do us a favor, cut the price on the concrete.' So now he's gotta ask me. I tell him no: 'We don't cut no price. We cut the price today, it's the same price tomorrow. Forget it.' So now I'm the heavy. They come to me and say, 'We're gonna get hurt with this bid.' 'So get hurt,' I tell 'em. 'You'll make it back on the next one.'

"Except they don't wanna wait," Mosca continued. "So next thing I know, we get Tony Grace subcontracting the foundation. 'Why the fuck we need a sub on this?' I ask. 'He needs the work,' they say. Then all of a sudden we got two more unions involved. Why? Well, the Colombos get a piece, so Vic Orena's putting some guys in. Then all of a sudden Matty's a partner. Why? Because he's with Carmine. So my question is this: How many fucking ways can we slice it up before it ain't worth having?"

Sweating and itchy in the Richmond Road dormer, Joe O'Brien and Andy Kurins hunkered down and tried to follow the threads of this web of names. In the age of RICO, the golden word for law enforcement is "conspiracy," and the prosecutorial weapon of choice is the link. Perhaps the image is not so romantic as that of the smoking gun; in practice, however, the link is what gets results, and the naming of names in the same sentence is the first step in establishing the pattern of collusive criminal enterprise. Here was a mother lode of acknowledged associations, suggested conspiracies.

"It's gettin' aggravating," Funzie Mosca resumed.

"Exasperating is what it's getting," said D.B. "I mean, I thought we had some pretty clear-cut rules here. Like, two points for the Club. That was solid. Now on this last job, they're takin' two and a half, even three points. That ain't right. The Club is gettin' grabby, like they're forgetting who needs who."

"I'd like to see the Club stand on their own," said Tommy Bilotti. "They'd fall right on their ass."

"Okay, okay," said the Godfather. "There's a lot of things here that's very, very important. It's a pain in the ass, I'll tell ya the truth. I don't know what to tell ya."

A wavering leader opens the door to advice, and advice accepted is not infrequently advice regretted.

"Well, listen, Paul," said Funzie Mosca, "it's your show, but if you ask me, I'd say that sooner or later there's got to be a sit-down on this. Otherwise, it's just gonna get more and more out of hand."

"I'm with Funzie," said D.B., a little too quickly, as if maybe they'd rehearsed. "It's gotta be ironed out at the top. With Chin.

With Tony. With Snake. With Scopo. Otherwise, what you're gonna have is grab, grab, grab, till it all goes down the drain."

"It's gonna be like throwing the baby out with the bathtub," said Tommy Bilotti.

"The bathwater," said Funzie. "Not the bathtub."

"Ah, fuck it," said Bilotti. Then, as ever, he exulted in his doglike loyalty by urging the master to exercise his majesty. "You're the only guy that can do it, Paul. You're the only one who can take charge and hammer this thing back into shape."

Castellano hesitated. It would be unthinkable to hold such a high-level, interfamily sit-down at his own house, and he hated going out. It meant giving up the red satin bathrobe. It meant putting aside the soft slippers, moving away from the security of the well-stocked medicine chest. It meant descending from the safe heights of Todt Hill to the lower streets where things sometimes went wrong.

"I don't know," said the Godfather. "Those big meetings, they're a pain in the ass to pull together. The planning. The security. Ya gotta worry about whose toes you're stepping on if they ain't included. And let's face it, anytime you bring that many of our friends together, there's a little bit of risk involved."

At the Richmond Road plant, Joe O'Brien and Andy Kurins hugged the headphones to their sweaty ears and tried not to whoop. What was being discussed at Big Paul Castellano's blond wood table was nothing short of a conclave of the Mafia Commission. And as for the Godfather's assertion that such a meeting entailed a bit of risk, that would turn out to be the most exquisite piece of understatement in the entire audio surveillance.

PART 4

CHAPTER 53

D URING THE FIRST WEEK of August 1983, odd and
distressing noises began to issue forth from the Castellano bug.

Conversations were overwhelmed by screeches like cats in
heat, pops like the uncorking of champagne, beeps and hoots like
the sound track from an old submarine movie. There were times
when the mike went silent altogether, then came alive with an
ear-shattering burst of static. At moments, the sound through the
monitoring headsets was as crisp and clear as it had been back in
March, only to degenerate into a vague rumble of rasps and grunts.
Then, on the afternoon of August 4, as Tommy Bilotti was advo-
cating getting tough with the Chinese, the mechanism barked out
a final tortured farting squawk, and went irredeemably dead. At
the Richmond Road plant, the reel-to-reel recorder obliviously
kept turning, marking only an archival silence.

No one knows or ever will know why the apparatus failed.
Perhaps a transformer shorted out and the delicate transmitter
fried. Maybe the lamp got kicked, thrown during a domestic
squabble, or knocked over by one of the Dobermans. In any event,
the FBI surveillance was at least temporarily out of business, and
this called for a sit-down in Bruce Mouw's office.

"Do we go back in?" the supervisor asked.

"Can we?" asked Andy Kurins.

"I'd need advice from Washington on that," said Mouw.
"Probably not on the same affidavit."

Joe O'Brien looked out the window, and groaned. It was one
thing to spend months drafting a document in support of what was
then essentially a fantasy. It was another to sit down at the type-
writer and do the same damn thing again.

"But I'm not sure we want to," Mouw resumed.

The remark took Kurins and O'Brien a little bit by surprise. The Castellano surveillance had been an open-ended affair. There was no set date for terminating it, and as it happened, the end had been both unforeseeable and disturbingly abrupt. For the monitoring agents the sudden end to the eavesdropping left an uncomfortable vacuum, as if, say, baseball season had been instantly called off. The Richmond Road plant had become a sort of second home to them, a clubhouse. They loved the place and they hated it. On the one hand, the cramped dormer represented an enforced absence from wives and families; being there entailed many long hours of boredom and created an antsiness like that of a child confined to his room. On the other, that narrow apartment above a doctor's office had been the scene of one of American law enforcement's most intimate triumphs, the bugging of the Godfather. That was a hard thing to give up.

"It's not like we've gotten everything there is to get," protested Andy Kurins.

"No," agreed Mouw. "But face it—we could listen in for twenty years and not get everything there is. Especially since there's new stuff all the time."

"But even with the old stuff, there's so many things we sort of half know about," said Joe O'Brien.

"This business with the leaked indictments," Kurins said.

"The Underpants Association."

"The prison bribes."

"Whether Nina gets kicked out."

"Okay, okay," said Mouw. "But we've got to think in terms of costs and benefits. It might take months to get another shot at getting in the house. We'd have to reassemble the whole team. It's very expensive and it takes a lot of time."

"No offense, Bruce," said O'Brien, "but you sound like an administrator."

"What can I say? I *am* an administrator. But hey, I can remember a time when you guys were pretty handy at getting information without it being spoon-fed to you through a microphone."

"All right," O'Brien said, "you got me back. So what do we do?"

"I'm not sure," said Mouw. "I just don't know that redoing

the bug is the best way to go. We have plenty of stuff to follow up on. We've got more leverage than ever with our informants. Maybe it's time to get back in the street. Lemme make some calls, and let's all sleep on it."

But the phone calls were *pro forma,* and the sleeping on it was really just part of the process of letting go. For all practical purposes, the bugging of Big Paul Castellano's Todt Hill mansion was already slipping into the past.

Under cover of night, an FBI technical team visited the Richmond Road plant and collected the tape recorders, sound meters, and headsets. Kurins and O'Brien gathered up their clean shirts and changes of socks and underwear, and cleared out the detritus of a stakeout—the Styrofoam coffee cups and sugar-smeared Danish wrappers, the cans of tuna fish and jars of olives, the yard-sale plates and silverware they'd stocked to make the place look lived in, in case anyone came snooping. Mr. Joseph O'Brien/Greenberg, the blue-eyed Jewish lawyer from Syracuse, drafted a formal note to the landlord, politely asking for the return of his thousand-dollar security deposit.

Without doubt it was a melancholy business, this abandoning of the plant. The agents found themselves mooning around, slightly ill at ease with the hours they had to fill. Strangely, they missed hearing the Godfather's voice, that clenched rasp that was sometimes magisterial, sometimes lewd, at moments surprisingly full of need. They missed the parade of foul-mouthed *capo*s and eccentrics, the jerky cadences of Mafia speech. They even missed the bizarre pronouncements of Gloria Olarte. A great deal of vicarious intrigue had vanished from their lives, and they felt the dim depression of soap opera addicts whose favorite program has been canceled.

It was Tommy Agro who pulled them out of their short-lived doldrum.

The violent little lunatic simply could not help doing unwitting favors for the FBI. On August 8, a warrant was issued in Florida for Tommy A.'s arrest, and the loan shark and enforcer took it on the lam. He was now a federal fugitive, and the need to bring him to justice provided focus for the frazzled members of the Gambino squad. The briefly stymied team was up and running.

CHAPTER 54

"**T**OMMY AGRO is a no-good, has-been, cocksucking piece of shit. What else would you like to know?"

At Sperrazza's Luncheonette, on the corner of Crescent and Broadway in Astoria, Joe N. Gallo toyed with his espresso spoon and largely avoided Andy Kurins's eyes. The feisty old *consigliere* did not seem to be having one of his better days. His color was off, a tinge of yellow lurking beneath the hypertensive pink. He was irritable to the point of crankiness.

"Well," said Kurins, "I'd like to know where he is."

"I don't know where he is, I don't care where he is, and to tell you the truth, just hearing his name gives me a pain in my chest."

"I thought you guys were friends."

"Don't start with the bullshit, Andy."

"I didn't think I was."

"Listen," said Gallo. "Once upon a time I slightly knew this asshole. He was a sick fuck, but he seemed to mean well. But the bottom line is that he has made a royal shit-pile out of every single thing he's ever touched in his life. I haven't had anything to do with him for a long time, and I never will again."

He called out for a glass of water and, not without a certain theatricality, tossed back an angina pill.

Everyone who lives long enough gets old, but everybody ages differently. For some people aging happens in a gradual smooth curve; there's a graceful roundness, a beauty, to it. But Joe Gallo, over the past few months, seemed to have aged in a quantum tumble that left him all burrs and jagged edges. It was like an adolescent growth spurt in reverse; it happened so fast that his coordination and social skills had not had time to adapt to the changed conditions. His charm was all but gone. The perverse, ferocious logic seemed to have drained out of his defiance, leaving him merely bitter. His paranoia was no longer balanced by a vulpine joy in his own craftiness; now he just seemed put upon, fearful, ready to hate.

"Agro isn't going down alone, Joe," Kurins said.

"So now you're threatening me?" said the *consigliere*. "That's what you're doing?"

But the truth was that, at that moment, Andy Kurins was not exactly sure what he was doing. The surveillance at Big Paul's table had changed everything. All the rules and all the strategies needed reinventing. The FBI, in one obsessively concentrated stint, had gone from knowing far too little about the workings of the Gambino organization, to knowing almost too much. The knowledge, however valuable, was in some senses unwieldy. The investigating agents had to find ways to use what they had learned, without creating too much speculation as to how they had learned it.

The Castellano bugging was still a secret, and sound law enforcement practice demanded it remain that way. It was stupid to let people know what you had on them any sooner than the law required. There were too many tracks that could possibly be covered, too many corroborating players who could possibly be disappeared before cases came to trial. Discretion was paramount.

"I'm not threatening anything, Joe," said Kurins. "I'm putting you on notice."

"Notice of what?" the *consigliere* asked sourly.

"Nothing you don't already know about."

"Well, then that doesn't help me much, does it?"

"I'm not here to help you."

"Okay, Andy, fair enough. You're putting me on notice. Well, I'm putting *you* on notice. If you ever come here to arrest me, don't bring a cop car. Bring a fucking ambulance. Because I promise you, I'll keel over on the spot. And it'll be on your head, Andy."

"Who said anything about arresting you? I'm here to talk about a fugitive named Tommy Agro."

"Let's not start in with that gutter scum again, okay?"

"He may be gutter," said Kurins, "but he reaches high."

263

"Yeah? How high does the little bastard reach?"

That was precisely the question that Andy Kurins wanted Joe Gallo to think about, preferably late at night, when those with clearer consciences were sleeping soundly; there was no way Kurins was going to answer it.

"Joe," he said instead, "I want you to know I pay close attention when you talk to me. Half a year or so ago, you told me I should never offer you a deal. So okay, no deals. But Joe, you got a lot of guys under you, and a few guys above you. You're like the pivot in a cockeyed seesaw. Pivots have leverage, Joe. Think about it."

"I'm tired of thinking," said the *consigliere*. "I'm tired of everything."

CHAPTER 55

J OE O'BRIEN had given considerable thought to the question of getting back in touch with Gloria Olarte. He sat in his cubicle above Queens Boulevard and marshaled the arguments pro and con.

Now that the audio surveillance was over, the maid might prove to be the FBI's most fertile source of information as to the Godfather's activities and frame of mind. With the exception of Paul Castellano himself, Gloria was the only person who would be aware of virtually every visitor, privy to nearly every conversation. Given her need to vaunt her own importance, she might say more than she should. For that matter, given that Gloria seemed wholeheartedly loyal to no one but herself, there was always the chance she might wittingly turn against her employer and lover.

Those were some of the reasons for pursuing her. Opposed to them was only one inconvenient fact. There remained the slim but unignorable chance that contact with Paul Castellano's mistress could get Joe O'Brien killed.

Sitting there, looking through the dirty window, O'Brien wondered without malice whether the maid realized what a dangerous game she was playing with Paul Castellano's emotions. She knew just how to push his buttons—give her that. She smelled his insecurities as easily as a mosquito figures out where the skin is thinnest, the warm blood closest to the surface. She could make him furiously jealous with a syllable, an instant's glance bestowed on someone else. But okay, Castellano was not such a buffoon as to declare war on the FBI because his mistress seemed to like the color of a certain agent's eyes. Then again, Gloria was probably not aware of the time-honored Mob tradition of trigger-happy underlings making points with the Boss by taking it upon themselves to remove irritants from his life.

Then *again,* the most potentially damaging things Gloria had ever said with regard to Joe O'Brien had been total fabrications anyway. If the maid lied whenever it suited her purposes or simply struck her fancy, what was to be gained by steering clear of her? She would say whatever she felt like saying, and whatever would happen would happen.

So, on a muggy Wednesday in mid-August, O'Brien took his post against a dented orange wire trash can on Corona Boulevard, waiting for Gloria to pay her weekly visit to sister Nellie. He sipped iced tea and read the *Times,* watching the birdcage stairway every time a train roared in on the trestles and disgorged its freight of sweating passengers.

In expecting the maid to arrive by public transportation, however, the agent seriously underestimated the degree to which the dirt-poor girl from Bogotá had absorbed the American concept of upward mobility. Gloria no longer traveled by train, and while O'Brien had his eyes glued to the exit of the BMT, the maid came roaring down Corona Boulevard in her red Datsun 280, which she expertly parked in a bus stop.

Swinging her legs smartly out of the low-slung car, she walked to the curb in tight-fitting designer jeans, a leather purse slung over one shoulder, a Bloomingdale's shopping bag dangling from the other hand. It seemed, however, that there was a certain price to be paid for Gloria's newfound prosperity: she was getting chubby. Gone was the waiflike silhouette that O'Brien recalled from his first encounter with the maid, nearly two years earlier; gone, too, were the hollow cheeks that lent depth and poignancy to the alert brown eyes. Now Gloria's thickening torso was perched atop a high, round butt, and she had the beginnings of a double chin. And it must be said that there was something pasted-on, something unconvincing, about the tokens of her affluence. It would not be exactly fair to say she looked cheap; but she looked like someone's mistress, and she looked like she was strutting down Corona Boulevard in front of people she no longer considered quite her equals.

"Hello, Gloria."

"Meester Joe!" she said, with what passed for genuine delight. She put her shopping bag down and extended her arms toward the agent, as if to hug him. O'Brien forestalled the gesture with a handshake. "I no see you such a long time."

"Been busy. You look well, Gloria."

"I am well." She said it emphatically, even boastingly, as if her being well represented some great victory. "I berry well."

"And how about Mr. Paul," asked O'Brien. "Is he well?"

The maid pouted, whether in real sympathy or in pique at being distracted from her own buoyant spirits, it was difficult to tell. "No, Meester Paul he not so well. I berry worry for heem sometimes."

"Why, Gloria? What's wrong?"

The maid put on one of her coy, retreating looks, a tactic that had been more winsome before her face got pudgy. "I no should talk. He no like for Gloria to talk to you, Meester Joe."

O'Brien measured the moment. He did not believe that Castellano's mistress would clam up now; she was having too good a time showing off. So he dealt with her as one would with a cat. Make demands, it runs away; ignore it, and it rubs against your leg. "Then don't," he said.

Gloria looked down at the sidewalk in a momentary sulk. But she rallied quickly. "You buy Gloria *café con leche,* like before?"

"Sure."

The Cuban luncheonette had an enormous 1950s console air conditioner that sounded like an airplane and blew out lukewarm gusts which were then laced with grease from the deep fat fryers and endlessly recirculated by an oscillating fan. Smells of frying onions weighted the air; a neon sign for Miller High Life quivered above the espresso machine. Paul Castellano's mistress daintily ripped open three packets of Sweet 'n Low and watched the crystals dissolve in the froth of steamed milk.

"So, Gloria," said O'Brien, courting her again, "why do you worry about Mr. Paul?"

The maid stirred her coffee, sipped it, stalled. "I worry he keel heemself one day," she said at last.

For this the agent was not ready. Suicide was for victims, not predators; the mobster's credo featured murderousness toward others but extreme care and even a certain preening tenderness toward oneself. Besides, O'Brien had a tough time imagining that a man as proud as Paul Castellano would ever capitulate to his problems by cashing in his chips. "I wouldn't worry, Gloria. He's not the type."

"No, Meester Joe, I no theenk you understand. I no mean he keel heemself on purpose. I mean he do it by accident, weeth the needles."

"The insulin?"

"*Sí*. Yes. Ees easy to make a bad meestake with the needle, and eef you make a bad meestake, you die."

"But he's been injecting himself for years," said Joe O'Brien. "Why would he make a mistake now?"

"He gets worse. Berry weak sometimes. Deezzy. And usually Gloria geeve him the insulin. Meester Paul's doctor, Dr. Hoffman, he show me how to do it. He say to me, 'Gloria, now remember thees, ees berry important. When you put the insulin een the syringe, always do like thees.' " She gestured as if plunging a bit of fluid through the needle. " 'Always make a leetle squirt come out. Because, remember, Gloria, eef there ees a leetle air, just a leetle bubble, eet gets into a vein, and goes around, and when eet hits the heart, she stops.' So I say, 'Hokay, Dr. Hoffman, I always be berry sure there ees no air.' "

"But if you do the needles—"

"But wait, Meester Joe. Thees ees what I'm telling you. The other morning, Gloria she ees downstairs, making the coffee for Meester Tommy. We wait for Meester Paul. And Meester Paul he no come down. We wait. And after a long time I get to worry. So I go upstairs. 'Meester Paul,' I call, 'Meester Paul. You come down now?' But there ees no answer.

"So I go into his room, and Meester Paul he ees laying on the bed, but his legs are hanging off. His robe ees all twisted and his color ees all gray, like someone dead. His eyes roll back, only the white part ees showing. I run to him. 'Meester Paul, Meester Paul.' He say, 'Ah, Gloria, leetle Gloria.' He say eet berry strange, like groaning, like drunk. I say, 'Meester Paul, what ees wrong?' He

268

say, berry soft, 'I don't know. I had my shot, I should feel better by now.' And then, on the bed, I see the syringe, and the syringe she ees dry. He must be berry deezzy, berry confuse, he forget to put in the insulin. He shoot in all air. If he hit a vein like that, already he is dead.

"So now Gloria ees berry afraid. Fast like I can, I make a new needle, I shoot it in. But my hands shake. I cry. I berry afraid that Meester Paul die, that I lose Meester Paul. I say, 'Meester Paul, Meester Paul, you no take care of yourself anymore. Only Gloria she take care of you. Only Gloria take care.'

"And Meester Paul, *gracias a Dios,* he come back berry fast. Once he have the insulin, he come back berry fast. He turn his head side to side, like he just wake up. And he say, 'Yes, Gloria, only you take care of me. No one else.' And I say, 'Promeese, Meester Paul. Promeese that you no geeve yourself the shots anymore, only Gloria geeve you the shots.' But he will not make thees promise. He says, 'No, thees I cannot say.' So now, ebery day, Gloria has to worry."

Joe O'Brien breathed deeply of the stale and oily air, and sipped his cooling coffee. Gloria Olarte's monologue had sent his mind spinning into a murky whirlpool. He thought, for some reason, about the concept of punishment. If Paul Castellano was an evil man, a man who had ordered people killed and perhaps, in earlier years, had killed a few himself, did it matter whether his punishment came in the form of a long jail sentence or ten cc's of air that short-circuited his heart? He was chastened either way. But punishment really wasn't the point, was it? The point was to get to the bottom of something, to get some questions answered, some rules affirmed. That was justice, human style. But then, too, there was the weird mute justice that seemed to be exacted by the universe—a justice, for instance, that sucked the potency out of a man as powerful as Paul Castellano, that took this man who controlled the lives of so many and put him in thrall to a fanatically possessive mistress who wanted sole and exclusive control over whether he lived or died.

"Of course he wouldn't promise that," the agent said.

"Gloria no understand," she said, but in spite of herself she flashed a vixenish little smile that suggested she understood just fine.

"And where was Mrs. Nina while all of this was going on?"

Gloria shrugged, then waved a hand dismissively. "Meesus Nina, she don't do nothing for heem anymore. She no cook. She no chop."

"But Gloria," said Joe O'Brien, "she's still the wife. If he's really that sick . . ."

"Meesus Nina, she wasn't even home," said Paul Castellano's maid and mistress. Then her face went through a remarkable transformation. The look of concern vanished all but instantly and was replaced by a look of scheming triumph. The look was not girlish and not innocent. It was the carnivorous expression of Gloria against the world, Gloria the nation of one. "You want I tell you a secret, Meester Joe?"

"Tell me what you want to."

"Meesus Nina, the reason she ees not there—she ees looking for apartment. Yes, Meester Joe—pretty soon she move out. The beeg house—pretty soon it ees for Meester Paul and Gloria. Pretty soon Meester Paul and Gloria, we live there all alone."

CHAPTER 56

N EIL DELLACROCE has cancer," said Bruce Mouw.

"How bad?" asked Andy Kurins.

The supervisor shrugged, bit down on his pipe stem, winced. "It'll kill him, but who knows when. He could hang on for years."

"I wonder who makes more money off these guys," said Joe O'Brien, "the lawyers or the doctors?"

Mouw chose not to follow up this line of speculation, and returned instead to his own. "It's less a question of when he dies than of how long he can hold the reins, and who takes over next."

"Who'll it be?" asked Kurins.

"Can't be anybody good," Mouw said. "It's like, on that side of the family, there's a thirty-year gap in age and judgment. Say Paul Castellano drops dead tomorrow. He's got Joe Gallo. He's got Joe Armone. Guys who basically have the same philosophy. If nothing else, we could pretty much count on things continuing as usual. If Dellacroce goes . . ."

"There goes the balance," Kurins put in.

"There goes your peacemaker," said Mouw.

"Peacemaker?" repeated O'Brien. He pictured Aniello Dellacroce with his punched-in nose, boxer's ears, fat cigar, and breathy, commanding voice. "We're not talking Gandhi here."

"No," said Mouw, "but sick old men don't stage coups. If Dellacroce was going to make a move, he would have done it seven years ago. Now that he doesn't have the will to do it anymore, he can make virtue out of it by saying that's what old Carlo wanted. You think the next guy gives a crap what old Carlo wanted? To the next guy, Carlo Gambino is just a name, like Al Capone."

It was late October 1983. Beyond the sooty windows of the FBI office on Queens Boulevard, the air of New York seemed to be

271

visibly thinning out. There was less humidity to hold the brown tinge of diesel fumes and the orange glints of runaway neon. The gingko leaves had turned their unanimous yellow, and the sycamores were going quietly brown, seeming relieved at the notion of dying for the winter.

For the agents of the Gambino squad, it was a time of consolidation. Transcripts were being made of the Castellano tapes, and the process was almost inconceivably tedious. Secretaries— fine typists, so-so spellers—struggled bravely to eke out phonetic first drafts of the gruff and garbled speech; this took approximately fifteen hours for each hour of tape. Typically, however, these first versions were all but incomprehensible. Multisyllable names were botched. It was nearly impossible to tell the order in which things were said, since, as at many family tables, everyone seemed to talk at once in Big Paul's home. Then, too, Mob slang and Mob profanity were largely beyond the ken of the well-bred members of the typing pool.

So Kurins and O'Brien had to go over every page of the gibberish, figuring out, for example, that what was sometimes transcribed as "millions on" and other times as "melon sun" was actually a Sicilian mispronunciation of the Italian word *melanzana,* which means "eggplant," which is Mafia parlance for a black person. More crucial, where names were named, the agents had to compare the transcript with the original tape, to make absolutely sure the individuals were clearly and correctly identified.

In these instances, there were two different standards of certainty that had to be considered. Functional certainty was perfectly adequate for the Bureau's investigative purposes. But then there was *legal* certainty. Would a jury, unaccustomed to the profound imperfection of surveillance tapes, conclude beyond a reasonable doubt that Funzie Mosca, for example, was really saying, "I gotta ask Chin"? What if it sounded a little like "I gotta ask Jim"? It was by no means unprecedented for a major organized crime trial to hinge on the acuity of the jurors' ears.

So the agents had to check. Then the transcripts had to be revised. Then they had to be rechecked. Then they were vetted by counsel. Then they were sent back for polishing. It was beyond boring. It kept the agents chained to their desks for much of the fall. It threw them into uncontrollable fits of yawning. And it fostered in them a great desire to talk about something else, anything else.

"I have an idea about these leaked indictments," said Andy Kurins.

"I'm listening," Bruce Mouw replied.

"Well, we're pretty certain the leak is Millie Russo."

"Right."

"And we're pretty sure the conduit is Joe Butch Corrao."

"Right."

"So how about we dummy up an indictment against Joe Butch, route it through Millie, and see what happens?"

Mouw winced. "Guys," he said, "we can't just go around printing up fake indictments."

"Probable cause," chimed in Joe O'Brien. Ever since the preparation of the Title III affidavit, this had been a favorite phrase of his, a magic incantation that, quite literally, opened doors. "We've got very probable cause that Millie Russo and Joe Butch Corrao are conspiring to obstruct justice. I think it's a good idea."

"You would," Mouw said, and then fell silent, apparently hoping that this unorthodox notion, like a bad smell, might dissipate without the need of further comment.

"So can we do it?" Kurins pressed.

The supervisor sighed, looked out the window, frowned. "Tell you what. You guys draft a letter asking for permission. Make it good. If Justice goes along with it, okay by me."

"Do we get a break from the transcripts?"

"No," said Mouw. "You don't."

CHAPTER 57

I'LL TELL YOU the God's honest truth . . ."

This was a standard Mob opening, and what it usually meant
was that what followed would be a bald and blatant lie, a false-
hood so flaming that it carried with it an implicit insult to the
intelligence of the listener, an absurdity so patently inane as to
overstep the bounds of mere dishonesty and partake of the surreal.
But when Joe Armone said it, Andy Kurins was inclined to believe
him. Old Piney seemed to be one of the few mobsters left who
preferred the time-honored stance of silence to the more modern
technique of the wacko fib. If there was something Piney didn't
want to talk about, he'd say so. If he talked, you could trust what
he said.

"The God's honest truth," the gray-haired *capo* continued,
"is that I'm very disappointed in Tommy Agro. I thought he had
more class. I thought he had more nerve. But I don't know where
he is."

"Makes it awkward," said Kurins. "As long as he's at large,
we've got no choice but to stick close to people who know him.
Like yourself. Joe Gallo. Paul Castellano. It's a bother for everyone."

"You gotta do what you gotta do," said Piney. "I understand
that. Tommy A. should have understood it too. But he's being
selfish. A bigger man would have faced the music."

It was a white-skied afternoon with the electric smell of snow
in the air. December 1983. The two men were talking at one of
Armone's favorite haunts, a restaurant called Lanza's, which was
now emptying from the late-lunch crowd, smears of oil and wine
left behind on checkered tablecloths.

Lanza's was a dowdy old establishment located on First Avenue at Tenth Street. Lower First Avenue, in former times a Mob stronghold, wasn't even an Italian neighborhood anymore. There was Lanza's, sure, with its red sauce that would hold a spoon erect, its sinus-clearing garlic bread. There was De Robertis's *pasticceria,* with its tile mosaic walls and octagon floors; there was Veniero's bakery with its ricotta cheesecake spiked with rum. But other than that, the neighborhood had gone polyglot. For the whole-grains set, there was Pete's Spice, a store that sold weird foods that gave you gas. The old Sicilian groceries were all run by Koreans, and the tenement apartments housed hordes of Puerto Ricans, Haitians, and Senegalese. Punks walked around with blue mohawks, and cuff links punched through their snotty noses. Of the European ethnics, only the Ukrainians remained. They still stuffed their cabbages and ate their gunboat pirogi, prevailing on the streets by sheer breadth of shoulder and hardness of head. Amid this unquiet diversity, the Mob seemed like just one more cultural sliver, and a nearsighted old Mafioso like Piney seemed more a historic relic than an active criminal. You couldn't even call him a dinosaur, because dinosaurs were big, and Piney was getting more stooped and shriveled every day. His limp had gotten so bad that he walked almost sideways, like a crab.

"I hear Nina Castellano's moved out," said Kurins.

Armone looked at him through the thick glasses that smeared his eyes. It seemed to the agent that Piney was riffling through the unwritten pages of his code, trying to determine if it would be a violation to say anything about his Boss's private life. "It's a sad thing," he offered.

"And an unusual one. I mean, an actual separation."

"Yes, it's unusual," Armone conceded. He sighed; then he steamed his glasses with his breath and wiped them on a napkin. "Would you join me in an anisette, Andy?"

The waiter brought two pony glasses and left the bottle on the table.

"*Salud,*" said the courtly Mafioso.

"*Salud,*" said the FBI agent.

"You're married, aren't you, Andy?" Armone asked a moment later.

The agent said he was.

"Do you love your wife?"

The agent said he did.

"Me too," said Armone. "My wife, I mean. And I consider myself a lucky man. I think a man is lucky if he doesn't stop loving his wife. The heartache he avoids. The anguish he doesn't have to go through."

"You think Paul Castellano is going through anguish?"

"Of course," said the courtly Armone. "Of course he is. But don't ask me more about him. I'm talking only for myself now. I think it's a blessing for life to stay simple. You stop loving your wife, life isn't simple anymore. It's a great misfortune."

"But if it happens—" said Andy Kurins.

"If it happens," Piney interrupted, "then you've got to deal with it in a way that fits in with the rest of what you feel is right. Say you believe in loyalty. Say you believe in the sanctity of a promise. Well, there are promises, and there is loyalty. Maybe the love is gone, but the rest remains. So what do you do?"

He drained his anisette; the last drop of the thick liqueur oozed slowly back toward the bottom of the glass. He poured out another round.

"You know what's wrong with the world today, Andy? People aren't true to any one philosophy. They pick and choose among all different ones. They choose loyalty when it suits them. They choose independence when it suits them. They choose tradition when it suits them. They choose change when it suits them. They do exactly as they please, and they can always find a way to justify what they're doing. They can make it seem like, no matter what, they're being true to some morality or other. But you can't just pick little pieces of the package, Andy. You go with the whole program, or it doesn't mean a thing.

"Like this business with Tommy Agro," the old *capo* continued. "Supposedly he's got this certain set of rules, this code of honor. He lives by it until there's a crunch, then what happens? Uh-oh, the rules just changed. Now it's survival, the law of the jungle, saving his own skin. Well, okay, that sounds fine too. Only, what happened to the first code? He hasn't just left it behind, he's damaged it. That's what people don't realize. You take this pick-and-choose attitude, you drain the life out of your own beliefs. After a while, what's left?"

Andy Kurins sipped his anisette and absently ran his hand over the threadbare tablecloth. "But isn't Paul Castellano doing the same thing?" he said.

Piney didn't answer, and Kurins realized he wouldn't answer in a million years. Once he declined to discuss something, that was it. But the agent continued anyway. "I mean, he lives by this tradition, he profits from it. And part of the tradition is that you stay with your wife. You do what you want outside, but the home is the home. So that part of it gets inconvenient for him, so he cuts it out. But, like you say, he's amputating something from the code, he's weakening it. He's doing damage just like Tommy A. is doing damage."

Armone stayed silent. He looked at his empty glass and pointedly did not refill it, signaling in a firm yet courtly way that the interview was over.

Outside, it had started to snow, a drizzly snow so light it barely dampened the sidewalk. Paul Castellano had committed a serious violation of Mob protocol, there was no denying it. And it seemed to Andy Kurins that Joe Armone, who never conveyed more than he wanted to, had a purpose in putting him in mind of it. There would be consequences. Those few mobsters who took the code of honor anything like as seriously as Piney did would be genuinely offended. As for the rest, the cynical ones who didn't particularly care about the rules but could wield them as pitilessly as lawyers, they could use Big Paul's domestic transgressions as evidence that he was no longer fit to lead. For those inclined to turn against him, here was one more excuse for doing so.

CHAPTER 58

NINETEEN EIGHTY-FOUR dawned as a fine and terrible year for Big Paul Castellano.

He had seized his freedom, or at least that aspect of it that consisted in having the run of his own house with his maid and mistress. He lolled in his red satin robe, presumably still talking pidgin English to Gloria, savoring her expanding flesh in the somewhat peculiar fashion allowed by his penile prosthesis. No longer did the lovers have to steal moments together like furtive adolescents. No longer did the Godfather have to descend the social ladder to the servants' quarters to take his pleasure. They had all seventeen rooms to romp around in.

It seemed to be a honeymoon of sorts—either that, or a cross between a fantasy of the perfect retirement and a vision of Islamic heaven, complete with rugs, olive oil, and an endless supply of figs and pomegranates, compliments of the Top Tomato fruit market. Life's needs just appeared at the door of the Todt Hill mansion, and Castellano went out even less than he had before. Dial Poultry vans brought Oven Stuffer roasters, Tommy Bilotti brought news.

It was luxurious, it appeared serene. But there was another side to it. Paul Castellano was losing touch. At the age of sixty-nine, he seemed to be discovering the satisfactions of living in the moment. No doubt that was nice. But it seemed to come at the cost of tending to his destiny, and in an outfit like the Mob, if a leader doesn't tend to his destiny, others will tend to it for him.

As 1984 was beginning, Big Paul's power was still intact, virtually undiminished, but the prestige that underlay the power was beginning to erode. The erosion started slowly, and would snowball over time. Several things gave evidence of this.

During the months of eavesdropping at the Godfather's table, it had become abundantly clear that *capos*, soldiers, and hangers-on sometimes concocted very tenuous pretexts for gaining an audience. They came when there was pressing business, sure, but they came, as well, to flatter Castellano by asking his advice, to beg small favors that were almost beneath the Boss's notice, to bask in his reflected glory. The underlings, it seemed, got a lot of mileage from being able to say things like *Yeah, I saw our Uncle the other day,* or, *Well, I was up at the Hill, and the Pope, he says . . .*

Now, as routine visual surveillances confirmed, they seemed to come less. It was possible, of course, that Big Paul, newly protective of his domestic bliss, discouraged visitors. But it was also plausible that something in the air made it less desirable to be thought of as one of Castellano's boys, less career-enhancing to be among his inner circle. Certain once-frequent visitors were becoming scarce. Robert Di Bernardo—where was he in the early days of 1984? Jimmy Failla—was he all of a sudden tied up elsewhere?

Not that the drop-off in White House visitors was precipitous or all-embracing. Some people actually visited more often—but here, too, there was a troubling inference to be drawn. The frequent visitors, all in all, were not the guys who oversaw the uncontested Gambino family rackets but the ones who guarded the organization's flanks. Like Funzie Mosca, for example, interfamily bagman and Solomonic whiz on questions of jurisdiction. Why would Funzie be visiting so often, unless other players were making bold to muscle in on Castellano's interests in construction? Ambassadors are not quite so busy when relations are stable, when spheres of influence are clearly defined.

There was one final strand of evidence indicating that all was not well with Paul Castellano's regime, and that was the growing chattiness of certain FBI informants. Since 1980, a number of individuals had been furnishing information about Big Paul and his cadre. For obvious reasons, the identities of those people and their precise standing within the Gambino organization cannot be revealed here. Suffice it to say that there is an ebb and flow in the activities of informants.

It is a common misperception that a source "turns" once and for all, and is thereafter a steady and reliable source of useful news.

CHAPTER 59

B ULLSHIT," was all O'Brien could think of to say.

It was late February, and Bruce Mouw had just clued him in. A multiagency task force comprising city, state, and federal investigators was planning to indict Paul Castellano in connection with the activities of a dead Gambino soldier named Roy DeMeo.

DeMeo had been a shadowy power in the family until he was found frozen stiff as a TV dinner in the trunk of his car in January 1983. He had five bullet holes in his otherwise neat suit, and his corpse was crowned with a chandelier, the symbolism of which has yet to be unraveled. Before getting whacked, DeMeo had commanded a ragtag team of dirtbags who liked to think of themselves as the modern-day equivalent of Murder, Incorporated, but had nothing like the brutal courage and sanguinary vision of the original; they were just casual killers, with a reported thirty-seven hits to their collective credit.

When DeMeo and crew weren't erasing people, they were stealing cars. Some of the vehicles ended up in New Jersey chop shops, and others—in a scheme far too sophisticated for the Neanderthal DeMeo to have conceived—sprouted new ID numbers and made it all the way to Kuwait. DeMeo's *capo*, Nino Gaggi, was almost certainly involved in the caper; in all, twenty-one conspirators would be indicted. But the question was how far up the Gambino family hierarchy the trail of evidence would lead, or could be stretched.

"Look," O'Brien said when he'd collected himself, "this is a nothing case as far as Castellano goes. They wanna lock up some hit men and car thieves, fine. But as far as Castellano is concerned, DeMeo was an outlaw. He was scum. How many times was DeMeo spotted visiting the Hill? Maybe twice. How many times is this car business mentioned in the tapes? Zero. Where is Nino Gaggi's reputation in the family? In the toilet."

"Okay," said Mouw. "But shipping cars to the Middle East? This takes some brains. Who masterminded that?"

"That's a fair question," O'Brien conceded. "I don't know. But look, Roy DeMeo was exactly the kind of old-style gutter thug that Castellano did his damnedest to avoid. I would bet you that Paul didn't deal with him, except maybe to have him clipped. And if he did, he was performing a public service."

The supervisor bit down on his pipe and winced. "Joe, around here, we don't think of clipping guys as a public service."

"No," said the agent. "We're much too principled for that. Except when someone sees a chance to get himself on the six o'clock news. Then it all sort of goes out the window, doesn't it? Bruce, listen, this is exactly the kind of case that makes the government look bad. It's all hearsay from guys who are known crooks and killers, who are trying to save their own butts by delivering a guy eight levels up, who they've never met in their lives. It's garbage."

"It's RICO," said Mouw. "They just have to establish the pattern."

"I don't care if it's RICO. It's still overreaching. DeMeo was *supposedly* a member of an entity called the Gambino LCN crime family, and since Paul Castellano is *allegedly* the Boss of the *purported* criminal enterprise, it's Paul Castellano's fault that DeMeo stole cars and killed people? Come on. Juries draw the line at that. The bad guys end up with the sympathy, and we end up looking dumb."

Bruce Mouw made his fingers into a steeple and blew a little air through them. "Joe, I don't want to sit here and argue with you. The bottom line is, it's not our call to make. It's outside our jurisdiction."

"Jesus, Bruce. That sounds like something Funzie Mosca would say."

"He's got his politics to deal with, we've got ours. What can I tell you? But listen, I'm supposed to give you a message. The task force would like you to get involved."

In spite of himself, Joe O'Brien laughed. It was a clipped, bitter laugh that bounced around the office and came back sounding ugly in his own ears. "Are you ordering me to do it?"

"No," said Mouw. "It's up to you."

"Then I won't."

The supervisor was not the slightest bit surprised. In fact he did not quite manage to conceal a grudging smile. "Do you want me to give them a reason?"

O'Brien glanced through the dirty windows at the brown air of Queens. "Yeah," he said, "you can give them a reason. You can tell them that the first time I met Paul Castellano—I mean *met*, face-to-face, which these media hounds have never done—we had a little talk about what was fair and what was garbage, and I made a promise that I wouldn't frame him."

"Come on, Joe," Mouw interrupted, "we all know the man's a criminal."

"Well, I'm not," said O'Brien. "And I made a promise. This case is a frame job, and I'm not gonna be a part of it."

Mouw winced. "They're going to get there first, Joe. You're aware of that?"

"If they do, they do. But we're gonna come in solid. We're gonna go step by step, guy by guy, and by the time we get to Paul, the walls are already gonna be built around him."

CHAPTER 60

CONVICTING Joe Butch Corrao might have been difficult, but contriving a plausible indictment against him was easy.

The man was, among other things, a loan shark. His Mulberry Street restaurant, Café Biondo, functioned also as a small private bank. There was no vault, so large amounts of cash were kept in the ice cream freezer. Fifties and hundreds mostly, they were stacked in brown bags and bedded down among the five-gallon drums of pistachio and nougat *gelato;* they steamed with cold when taken out for counting. Deposits and withdrawals were sometimes made right at the espresso bar, as if it were a teller's window. The handsome Joe Butch was one of New York's most charming if least forgiving lenders.

This much had been known by the FBI for some time, but no actual prosecutions had yet been planned. The problem, as usual, was finding witnesses who were willing to testify about the extortionate interest, the bodily threats, the occasional beatings, slicings, or breakings of knees.

That was the beauty of the sting operation now unfolding around the court-authorized fake indictment. The victim-public did not have to get involved at all. It was a closed-loop operation, as intimate a procedure as catching fish. The only cooperation required was that of the fish themselves.

As there are many, many crimes committed in the Southern District of New York, there are many, many indictments processed through the offices of the federal court. The indictments, neatly typed on letter-size paper, are circulated in manila envelopes, which find their way through the maze of offices of prosecutors and judges, around the gray metal desks of clerks and secretaries, into the privileged files of grand juries and, later, the vast archives of the public record. There is a pleasing orderliness to the progress of these documents. They pick up stamps and seals to prove where they have been; they are marked with codes and caveats that spell out where they must not go.

The shylocking and extortion indictment against one Joseph Corrao was, in format and packaging, just like all the others— except that its manila envelope was marked with a faint red line that ran along its border. This innocuous marking allowed Joe O'Brien and Andy Kurins, who were hanging around the court offices on the pretext of doing routine legal research, to trace the document as it made its inexorable way toward the desk of Millie Russo.

It was a slightly dizzying process, this zeroing in on one small object out of all the tens of thousands of bits of paper being shuffled around that day. The red-marked envelope issued forth from judge's chambers, stalled in a clerk's out basket, resumed its journey in the hand of a gofer with a Band-Aid on his index finger. As O'Brien pored through a library-style drawer of index cards, and Kurins peered over the top of a computer terminal, the bogus document rounded a water cooler, was tattooed once more by a manager, and landed, at last, in front of the suspected Mafia mole.

She read it, looking for all the world like the perfect civil servant, the dear sweet grandma nearing retirement, benevolent enough to have her picture on the tomato paste can. Her face showed not the slightest discomfiture as she slipped the indictment into a drawer.

Nor did anything appear untoward when, some ten minutes later, Millie rolled her desk chair backward and leaned over. Perhaps she was adjusting a shoe. Maybe she'd dropped a pencil. But when she straightened up, the manila envelope was nestled inside a large brown folder. Millie took the folder and her purse, and walked, a little stiffly it seemed, through the maze of cabinets and the clatter of printers, to the Xerox room, after which she visited the ladies' room. Then she returned to her desk and waited for the workday to end.

Previous observations had shown that Mildred Russo generally left the office between 5:03 and 5:04. On this day she left at

4:57, heading off the rush through the marble lobby and out the revolving doors onto Centre Street. To the agents who trailed her across the small park and up toward Mulberry, it seemed that she was walking faster than usual. She did not stop for groceries, but went straight to her apartment at 20 Mulberry Street.

Now, the FBI had placed what is known as a pen-register on Millie's phone. This is not a tap—no conversations can be intercepted—but the device records the destination and duration of all outgoing calls. So it could be determined that, as soon as she got home, Millie dialed her daughter Patricia, the wife of Gambino soldier Big Gus Sclafani. She called several times in quick succession, for an average duration of seven seconds; presumably, Patricia's line was busy, and the somewhat feverish Millie was dialing again and again. Finally she got through, and there was a conversation lasting six minutes.

Across the street, sitting in a beat-up government Plymouth, Joe O'Brien and Andy Kurins waited.

Less than twenty minutes later, a plum-colored Cadillac pulled up in front of Millie Russo's tenement. In the backseat was Big Gus, all two hundred and sixty spluttering, sloppy pounds of him. Driving the car was a wiseguy named Danny Delilio, who was less than a nobody, since even the guy he chauffeured was a nobody. Big Gus poured himself out of the car and lumbered up the stone steps of his mother-in-law's stoop. Five minutes later, he emerged from the building, holding in his fat hand a scroll of papers he had rolled up the way kids do when they're playing telescope.

There now ensued one of the shortest, queerest, and most pointless car chases in the history of American law enforcement. Café Biondo was four and a half blocks, straight up Mulberry Street, from Millie Russo's apartment. Most people would have just walked there. But Big Gus? No chance. Maybe he was winded from climbing the stairs to Millie's. Maybe he just wanted to play the big cheese. In any case, he had to arrive in the Cadoo.

But if Gus was determined to play the moment to the hilt, then Danny Delilio was not about to be outdone. At this point, he had no reason to believe he was being tailed. Still, Mafia drivers never went anyplace in a straight line; everybody knew that. Nor did they allow themselves to be hamstrung by speed limits, stop signs, or red lights; this was a point of pride. So Delilio floored the Caddy, screeched west on Broome Street, and, just on general principles, started tearing toward the Holland Tunnel.

"What the hell?" said Joe O'Brien, and nosed the government Plymouth after them.

At West Broadway, Delilio veered north again, scattering tourists who had come to gawk at the SoHo galleries, giving the Jersey drivers one more reason to swear they would never again bring the car into New York. Half a block behind, still trying to avoid detection, O'Brien eased the Plymouth through the backwash of waving fists and quailing compacts. At Houston Street, the Mob chauffeur ran a light, turned east again, and crushed a rat; Andy Kurins frowned at its extruded guts glistening under a streetlamp.

At Wooster Street, a narrow lane of warehouses and lofts, Delilio hung a breakneck right and headed back exactly where he'd started. The Cadillac bounced crazily over the gray cobblestones, skinny cats crouched under the fenders of parked Step-Vans.

Then the FBI agents heard a siren.

The New York City cops were closing in on them. O'Brien had two choices: pull over like a good scout, or forget stealth, keep chasing Sclafani, and effectively recruit the NYPD into the chase. But of course, the idea wasn't to catch Big Gus, just to watch him. Besides, Bruce Mouw would wince if O'Brien ran somebody over. The city might get testy about federal agents tearing up the streets. Not without regret, O'Brien stopped the Plymouth in front of a store with big salamis hanging in the window. The Cadillac kept right on going.

A big blue uniform with brass buttons filled the driver's-side window. "You been drinking, fella?" asked the officer. His hand was on his gun.

O'Brien badged him. "On the job," he said.

"Jeez, sorry. Anything we can do?"

"You've already done it."

Thus ended the car chase, a grand total of two blocks from where it had begun.

But there was still the surveillance to be conducted, though by now even a low-rent driver like Delilio would have realized he was being followed. And in fact, when the agents again sighted the plum-colored Cadillac, it was parked in a closed gas station on Delancey Street.

Big Gus was apparently trying to figure out what to do next, and this, for him, was a hugely laborious chore. He could follow instructions okay, if they were simple and explained to him several times, but his sluggish mind changed directions about as easily as a brontosaurus in a bog. The agents parked across the street and watched. Sclafani, in turn, watched them. He got out of the car, as if the cold evening air might give him an idea; he leaned his enormous behind against the vehicle, and it heeled like a sailboat in a gale. Then he walked to a pay phone and made a call. Then he returned to the Cadillac, and off they went again.

This time their pace was leisurely. Delilio headed east and got on the FDR Drive. O'Brien and Kurins followed all the way to Harlem, across 125th Street, and down the West Side Highway. In half an hour they were back in Little Italy, having burned a lot of gas going nowhere.

Big Gus got out at the corner of Division and Monroe, and he was smiling. The smile was not attractive, as Big Gus had one of those flubbery faces with too much skin on it. The heavy folds left gaps at the corners of his mouth, through which he was in constant danger of slobbering. Still, it was intriguing to see Gus happy, and Andy Kurins decided to bid him good evening through the passenger-side window of the Plymouth.

"D'ya know me?" Sclafani demanded.

"Not without your American Express card," said Kurins.

"Then why ya been followin' me all night?"

"We haven't," Kurins lied, and Big Gus answered the fib with a look of consummate smugness. He thought he'd outsmarted the feds, and for him the notion of outsmarting anyone carried with it the exhilaration of novelty.

And it was true that, by Sclafani's reckoning, he *had* put one over on the agents. He thought Joe Butch Corrao was actually being indicted. He thought the handsome *capo* might be arrested any moment. He thought that by telling his boss he was about to be pinched, then running the Plymouth all over town, he'd done Joe Butch the enormous favor of giving him time to bolt.

He had no way of knowing that all the while, another agent had been sitting at Café Biondo, waiting to see if Joe Butch took the bait. The agent's name was Marilyn Lucht. She was dressed in the ultraconservative manner of the financial district, and she was staked out with a double cappuccino, a *New York Times*, a *Wall Street Journal*, and a red pencil, as if she was looking at the want ads.

At 6:22 P.M.—just the time Big Gus was making his call from the closed gas station—she heard the phone ring at the café. While she could not hear the ensuing conversation, she was able to observe a dramatic change in the expression and demeanor of the suave proprietor. He seemed agitated. He stopped table-hopping and grabbed his leather jacket. He reached into the ice cream freezer and removed a brown paper bag. Then he abruptly left and hailed a taxi. As the FBI would later learn, he headed to the Marine Air Terminal, near LaGuardia, and chartered himself a private jet to Florida.

He had become a fugitive from an indictment that never was.

The bogus document had reached Millie Russo's desk at 3:09 that afternoon; by 6:30 the government had an airtight case for theft of information and obstruction of justice. It happened so fast that Agents Kurins and O'Brien did not immediately realize what the caper represented: it was, as regards the Gambino crime family, the first job they had actually finished.

Of all the balls they'd thrown into the air since the seemingly ancient days of 1980, this was the first to plunk back down into their itching hands. Even before her arrest, Millie Russo would be barred from ever again handling sensitive papers concerning organized crime. Joe Butch would stay underground for three months; it was almost as good as having him in jail even before he went to trial.

The payoff for the work, the waiting, the nights away from home—the payoff was just beginning to roll in, and Kurins and O'Brien savored it.

CHAPTER 61

THEY DID NOT savor it for long, however, because on March 30, 1984, Big Paul Castellano was arrested by members of the multiagency task force, and Agents Kurins and O'Brien were subjected to the professional indignity of watching the event on television.

This, in a way, was fitting, as the task force's case played better on the tube and in the tabloids than it would in the courtroom. In those days, certain flamboyant figures were building big, if fragile, reputations as crime busters. They understood the American fascination with the Mafia, and the political mileage to be gained from setting up shop as the Mob's most vigilant and fearless enemies. They had a flair for drama, and they knew how thin the line was between news and show business. They didn't make a move without providing photo opportunities and holding press conferences. It was the age of the Yuppie, after all, the heyday of personal aggrandizement on the job, and prosecutors were apparently not immune to the virus. They were using their clout to become celebrities.

But celebrity prosecutors need celebrity criminals, and in this Big Paul had never cooperated. By 1984, he had headed up the Gambino family for eight years, yet the overwhelming majority of the public didn't even know his name, let alone what he looked like. So the task force decided to raise his profile, whether he liked it or not.

Now, when a person is arrested on federal charges, the usual procedure is to bring him to FBI headquarters, at 26 Federal Plaza, for fingerprinting, after which he is transported by car to the Manhattan Correctional Center, some three blocks away, where he is held pending a bail hearing. When Paul Castellano was brought in, however, the car in which he was to be driven to the MCC mysteriously disappeared, and so he was *walked* through the plaza in broad daylight.

The photographers loved it. They shoved their Nikons and Leicas in the Godfather's face, turned on their motor-drives and snapped the increasingly abashed expression of the tall, unbent, but rather ashen old man. Videotape cameras rolled, hand-held microphones were wielded like obscene lollipops. It was a cruel and decadent spectacle, reminiscent of a captive being paraded through the streets of imperial Rome—and of course, it rather obscured the fact that Castellano had been merely accused, and not convicted, of wrongdoing.

At his bail hearing, Big Paul calmly signed a two-million-dollar bond, putting up his Todt Hill mansion as collateral. Then he was allowed to go home. The show was over for that day.

By dinnertime, he had changed back into his red satin robe, had his shot of insulin, and was trying to figure out exactly what had happened. As he would later tell Andy Kurins and Joe O'Brien, he was somewhat baffled, somewhat angry, and not especially concerned. Roy DeMeo? Stolen cars? The hell with it—he was out on bail on what he considered a nuisance case. He'd seen colleagues go through it plenty of times; he knew the drill. Your blood pressure went way up, then gradually came down during the year or eighteen months before you actually went to trial. In the meantime, life and business continued. True, you couldn't travel; well, he wasn't planning on going anywhere anyway. Your lawyers got richer; well, that's what lawyers did. Paul was too tired to lose sleep over it, and he was racked out in his ice-blue silk pajamas before the eleven o'clock news came on.

As for the celebrity prosecutors, however, they wouldn't have missed the nighttime wrap-up for the world. No doubt they toasted themselves with champagne, or at least imported beer. One suspects, in fact, that they delegated friends and relatives to tune their VCRs to every single channel, accumulating a video archive of peak moments from their glorious careers.

CHAPTER 62

MEANWHILE, the grubby work of nailing Castellano right and proper continued at its less dramatic and less telegenic pace.

Fat stacks of transcripts were reviewed, revised, retyped. Ongoing researches were made into the Greater Blouse, Skirt, and Undergarment Association; the Key and Waldbaum's supermarket chains; the unions. None of this was flashy, only necessary. Without the weight and bulk of all the background information, there would be nothing to prop up the headlines. The big stories would blow down like false-front movie sets at the first gusts from the powerful lungs of defense attorneys. Then, too, without the knowledge that could be accumulated only fact by fact, detail by detail, there was always the danger that the big break, when it finally came, would be unrecognized.

During the late morning of May 15, 1984, Joe O'Brien was sitting at his desk, proofreading yet another pile of finally polished Castellano transcripts, when his telephone rang.

In this there was nothing unusual or momentous; the steely sound was as ever. Yet O'Brien would always recall that the phone rang once, twice, and was just starting on its third cycle when he picked it up; the first ping of the clapper was still hanging in the air. He would remember all this because the phone call brought one of the most valuable tips the FBI has ever received from an informant.

The caller, in the dozens of documents in which he has been cited, has never been referred to as anything but "G." All that can be said about him is that he was (or is) an initiated member of the Gambino family, that he was (or is) in good standing, and that at no point have his La Cosa Nostra brethren seemed to be aware of his divided loyalties. One can only speculate as to whether G. was protecting himself from prosecution, acting out of secret spite, or in the grip of some excruciating and pathological ambivalence.

"O'Brien," he said, "I got somethin' for ya."

"Yeah?" said the agent, with the studied blandness he used with informants. It didn't do to sound too interested. If sources got the feeling they could jerk you around, they'd jerk you to the ends of the earth.

"Something big."

"Good," said O'Brien, freighting the word with skepticism.

"You're gonna owe me."

"Maybe."

Silence on the line. If G. was waiting for O'Brien to beg for the information, he'd have to wait a long time.

"How'd ya like to see a Commission meeting?"

Now, there are times when the body reacts faster than the mind, and the first response to this utterly unexpected question was that the sparse brown hairs stood up on the backs of Joe O'Brien's hands. It was not difficult to sum up the entire history of FBI surveillance of Mafia Commission meetings: there had never been one. There had been attempts, of course, and they'd always failed. Someone spotted someone, and the whole clambake was called off. Or knowledge of the meeting came in too late—in some cases, fifteen years too late, when someone in his dotage decided to reminisce. The closest that law enforcement had ever come to observing a meeting of the Mob's board of directors was at Apalachin—and that was surveillance after the fact, done with the most rudimentary knowledge base, and besides, it was twenty-seven years earlier.

"Nah," said O'Brien. "I don't think I want to."

He was ninety-eight percent persuaded that G. was either misinformed, lying, or perhaps being set up to be unmasked and rubbed out by his friends; this last would be a misfortune all around, as G. had always been reliable in the past. But leaks just didn't happen when it came to Commission meetings. If street thugs were too suspicious to use their own telephones, if *capos* spoke in code even in the presumed privacy of their homes and social clubs, then a Mob summit partook of a paranoia that was almost sublime—especially since, under RICO, a single documented meeting with proof that criminal activity was on the agenda would go a long way toward sinking the entire enterprise.

"Don't be a schmuck, O'Brien," G. taunted. "It's a once-in-a-lifetime opportunity."

"Yeah," said the agent. "At the most."

He'd been burned before, albeit indirectly, when it came to purported Commission meetings. Just a year ago, he'd been blamed for the aborting of a conclave in Manhattan—a conclave that the New York State Organized Crime Task Force was set to cover. The meeting was to be held at a pizza-making equipment store called Bari, near Houston Street, in early June 1983.

But it never happened, and on the fourteenth of that month, a taped conversation between Lucchese family Boss Anthony "Tony Ducks" Corallo and his driver, Sal Avellino, revealed that the meeting was scrapped when "Agent Joe O'Brien" was seen in the area. In fact, O'Brien had been nowhere near the site, but such was Mob circumspection in these matters that some tall guy with a tie on was enough to trigger the alarm.

What made matters far worse was that the OCTF brass—who had been poised for glory, of course—did not seem to believe that O'Brien had not in some way subverted them; they were still pissed off at him, which, at this point, was just fine with O'Brien. But the incident had done nothing good for interagency relations. (Nor were feelings assuaged by the bit of comic relief also contained in the Corallo-Avellino intercept: When the meeting was called off, those already present decided to leave by the undignified portal of the men's room window. Genovese Boss Fat Tony Salerno could not wriggle his ample belly past the frame, and had to be yanked through by several colleagues.)

Another snafu, real or imagined, O'Brien did not need. He wanted some supporting facts. "What's the meeting about?" he asked.

"I'm supposed to do your fucking job for you, or what?" said G.

"Yeah. You are. What's it about?"

"How should I know?"

"You know there's a meeting, you know why. Otherwise . . ."

"Construction," G. said.

The word sliced straight through Joe O'Brien's skepticism. He knew that the construction business was where the stresses were in recent dealings among the New York families—and this was turning out to be the great bonus value of the Castellano tapes. Not only were they superb as evidence, they were perhaps of even greater worth in providing context and corroboration. Except for the tapes, who would have known the rules of the concrete-contracting Club or the nuances of interfamily jurisdiction, who would have known the details of Funzie Mosca's many errands, or his opinion that the time for a sit-down was coming due?

"It's your ass if you're giving me garbage," said O'Brien.

"I'm not giving you garbage," said G. "I'm giving you diamonds and rubies."

"When and where?"

"Thirty-four Cameron Avenue, Staten Island. One P.M. Today. Don't expect limos on the street. They'll be switching cars at different places and arriving separately from all directions. No one's gonna park near the house. So long, O'Brien."

The agent dialed Andy Kurins's beeper. Kurins called back in forty-five seconds.

"Where are you?"

"In a bar. Manhattan Cafe on First Avenue."

"A little early, isn't it?"

"I'm sipping a Virgin Mary and being lied to by Tommy Agro's former wife and current girlfriend."

"How'd you get them together?"

"Getting them apart would be the trick. It's the same person. You remember LuAnn Yaden? Half Puerto Rican, half Chinese? Was a bunny at the Playboy Club back when Tommy and the Hat were handling shakedowns over there? She tends bar here now."

O'Brien didn't answer, and Kurins had the distinct impression he'd stopped listening. This miffed Kurins, who had been feeling he was in the midst of a pretty good day's work. He'd learned that Tommy A. had contacted LuAnn Yaden just before he'd bolted. He had reason to suspect she'd helped him flee, and that she'd seen him since. God knows why, the mixed-race beauty with the mole on her upper lip still seemed to care for the deranged and brutal little maniac.

"You got your camera gear with you?" asked O'Brien.

"In the car," said Kurins, a little testily. "But Joe, I'm onto something here."

"Can you meet on Staten Island in half an hour? In front of the plant, for old times' sake?"

"Can you tell me what's going on?"

"Only a Commission meeting."

"Jesus Christ."

"He won't be there," said O'Brien. "But everyone else will be. Including the Pope."

CHAPTER 63

AT 12:15, Andy Kurins was parked in front of the former monitoring station on Richmond Road, trying to be inconspicuous, when a cruddy-looking van pulled up next to him.

Dented and dusty, with sagging fenders and a pitted windshield, the van looked like one of those uninsured deathtraps in which aging hippies still listened to Moody Blues tapes and with ever-diminishing frequency got lucky with lank-haired women who didn't shave under the arms. As for the driver, he seemed to have gone into a coma at Altamont and to have only just woken up. His head was wrapped in a paisley scarf tied off at the nape of the neck. He wore dark glasses of an opacity usually reserved for the legally blind, and a single gold-hoop earring. His denim shirt was torn at the shoulder and had albino places as though from spilled bleach.

"Yo, man," he said, "got a cigarette?"

Kurins did not want to be bothered. "No, fella, sorry."

"Wanna buy some meth?" asked the other, lifting his glasses.

"Cut it out, Joe."

"Get in," said O'Brien. "And bring the long lens."

The two agents drove to the parking lot of the Country Club Diner and plotted tactics. Cameron Avenue, they knew, was in a working-class residential neighborhood called South Beach, an area of brick and clapboard bungalows and small front yards planted with azaleas. Some quick research had shown that number 34 was owned by a couple named Dewey and Angelina Gheraldi. He was a longshoreman; she was a paraprofessional with the Board of Education and, more to the point, a first cousin of Tommy Bilotti. A Gheraldi son, Richard, drove a truck for Scara-Mix, the cement company run by Paul Castellano's youngest boy,

Phil. It all seemed cozily inbred and totally in keeping with standard Mob practice in the selection of safe houses: find trusted relatives without criminal records, slip them some cash, and tell them to stay away from their homes for a number of hours so that a business meeting could be held in privacy.

Around this business meeting, security would be tight—that much was certain. Mob sentinels would be sweeping the neighborhood, ready to abort the session at the first sign of anything suspicious.

Accordingly, Kurins and O'Brien decided to stay clear of the vicinity until one-thirty. Let everyone arrive, they reasoned. Let the conclave begin. That way, even if the surveillance was detected and the Commission members bolted, it could be documented that they had in fact convened. At the worst, it would be Apalachin all over again, this time with the nation's most feared gangsters running away across petunia beds and banks of rhododendron, clambering over pine-post fences and backyard swing sets, holing up at last in some abandoned swim club, gardener's shed, or public golf course.

"We need some plastic or cardboard or something to block off the back of the van," Kurins said.

"No shortage of garbage on Staten Island," said O'Brien. "Let's find ourselves a dump."

By 1:29, they had customized their vehicle with a sheet of black vinyl and a box from an Amana refrigerator, and were cruising through South Beach. Cameron Avenue was a narrow street ending at a T-intersection, and number 34 turned out to be a forlorn little one-story dwelling with scallop-bottomed window shades and a tiny yard dominated by a single spruce tree that seemed to be wishing it had been planted somewhere else.

There was no indication whatsoever that anyone was in the house.

The agents drove past once, then circled the block. They parked about a hundred yards up the street, the rear of the van facing the presumed summit, offering a clean sight line to the curb. Then they slipped past the black vinyl curtain into the cramped and dusty back of the truck, and they waited.

And they waited.

An hour later, there still had not been the slightest clue that there was so much as a gin rummy game, let alone a Commission meeting, going on at number 34.

"You know," said Joe O'Brien, "we're really gonna feel like horses' asses if we spend the whole day looking at an empty house."

"What's this *we* shit?" said Andy Kurins. "It was your idea."

O'Brien frowned, and scrabbled for a new position for his long legs. The metal floor of the truck had squeezed shut all his arteries, and his feet were asleep up to the buttocks. "I feel like a goddamn astronaut," he said.

By 3:15, half a dozen neighborhood kids had come shambling home from school, but there was still no evidence of life in the modest house with the lonely spruce. At 3:30, Kurins experienced a sensation that links cops to criminals, public servants to public enemies, and in fact connects the entire human family. "I gotta pee like a racehorse."

"A real man holds his urine," counseled O'Brien.

By now it was four o'clock. Shadows were lengthening, the hazy sunlight was taking on the orange cast of late afternoon. And finally there was a hint that something, after all, was up: Gambino *capo* Frankie De Cicco, behind the wheel of a maroon Chrysler that had been spotted on occasion at Paul Castellano's Todt Hill mansion, came driving down Cameron Avenue, seemed to slow down in front of number 34, then continued on. A short time later, more compelling evidence offered itself. Salvatore Barbato, the licensed private investigator who ran the quasi-legitimate Community Security Service when he wasn't running errands for Big Paul, pulled up in his gray Buick, jogged into the house, then exited again within three minutes.

"They're there," said Joe O'Brien, forgetting about his cramped legs. "They're in there."

Andy Kurins fondled his camera and checked the light meter. As the sun lowered and the haze got denser it was beginning to seem that the success of the surveillance would hinge on the sensitivity of the film. "They better not stay too much longer."

They didn't. The infamous procession began, in fact, at 4:39, when Funzie Mosca, dressed neatly in a brown business suit, came down the walkway of number 34, dashed across Cameron Avenue, and disappeared down a side street. Kurins captured him for posterity with a 300mm lens.

At 4:40, Fat Tony Salerno—his crumpled fedora crammed haphazardly onto his head, a big cigar protruding from his bulldog mouth, his trademark cane carried jauntily in his right hand—stepped onto the sidewalk. Genovese soldier Carmine Dellacava followed, a respectful step behind. Within a few seconds, Funzie Mosca returned in a red Oldsmobile, Dellacava opened the passenger-side door for his boss, and the three men departed.

At 4:41, acting Colombo family Boss Gennaro "Gerry Lang" Langella emerged, wearing a gray blazer with the open-necked shirt that distinguished him from the older generation of Mob bigs, who prided themselves on perfect Windsor knots in their shimmering silk ties. Gerry Lang was sporty; Gerry Lang had flair. He was followed by Colombo soldier Ralph Scopo, one of the Mafia's main union contacts.

"It's amazing," whispered Andy Kurins from behind his camera. "They're just coming out family by family."

It was true that there was a wonderful orderliness, an elegance even, about how the meeting broke up. A Boss, an aide-de-camp; a Boss, an aide-de-camp. It was like some formal dance, and it occurred to Joe O'Brien that this old sense of fittingness was no small part of the reason the Mafia had held on to its mystique these many years. Here they were, these mobsters, reduced to meeting in a dowdy little house in a frumpy little neighborhood, beset, archaic, at times almost comically inept; yet they also had this courtliness about them, this decorum it was all but impossible not to admire.

Then again, they also had Tommy Bilotti, who now stepped onto the sidewalk wearing a loud sport jacket in a windowpane plaid—a jacket that belonged at the racetrack, if anywhere. As if by synchronization of watches, Frankie De Cicco at that instant made another loop down Cameron Avenue, and Bilotti hopped into the passenger seat of the Chrysler.

At 4:44, Castellano's darling returned, driving his Boss's powder-blue Cadillac. He parked in front of number 34, took a quick look up and down the street, and went back inside. At 4:47, Frankie De Cicco swept through yet again and parked.

At 4:53, the parade of the families continued, with Lucchese underboss Salvatore "Tom Mix" Santoro strutting out ahead of *capo* Aniello Migliore, both men being chauffeured away by De Cicco.

Now, by 1984, the Bonanno crime family was in such disarray that it no longer held a seat on the Commission. That meant that only one Mob leader was presumably still inside: Paul Castellano, the Pope, the *capo di tutti capi*. With the sure instincts of the star of the show who saves his own curtain call for last, and makes the audience wait an extra beat for his appearance, Big Paul stepped forward at 4:55.

He was wearing a gray jacket and black slacks, and he was in no hurry at all. He looked around at the trees, the telephone wires, as if he were savoring the novelty of being outside. He puffed on a cigar and seemed to be sniffing at the air. He smiled. Apparently the sit-down had gone well. Tommy Bilotti, edgy and vigilant as ever, was casting nervous glances in all directions as he held the car door open for his Boss. But Castellano declined to rush, refused to stoop to furtiveness. He flicked ash on the sidewalk; he cast a final backward look at the now-empty house. At the moment he slipped into the Caddy, there seemed something very regal about the man, and something very doomed.

CHAPTER 64

THE SUPERVISOR sat at his desk, surrounded by the Mafia Commission. "Guys, this is really good."

Coming from the laconic Bruce Mouw, the comment was like a "Hallelujah Chorus" of unmitigated praise.

Blown up life-size, Andy Kurins's photographs were very grainy and a little blurry at the edges, yet they had about them a great vitality and presence. Fat Tony was thumbtacked to a high bookshelf and dangled down almost to the floor; his stomach seemed to be billowing in the slight breeze that came in through the sixth-floor windows. The cockiness of Gerry Lang's walk could be felt in the way he was almost skipping off the curb. And Paul Castellano, even standing alone on the sidewalk, still seemed somehow to be presiding, controlling things with the tiny gestures and changes of expression he had learned so well from Cousin Carlo.

"Juries eat up this show-and-tell stuff," Mouw continued. "It's exactly what we need."

Kurins and O'Brien just sat there, basking in the approval, drinking in the photos as if they were much-loved family portraits. O'Brien couldn't help gloating a little. "Paul must really be worried about that other case if he's out running Commission meetings."

"Now, now," said the supervisor. "Be nice."

"Why?" asked O'Brien.

"Because . . ." Mouw began. "Because . . . Shit, I don't know why." He gestured around the office at Santoro, Dellacava, Bilotti. "But don't get smug if this is all you accomplished yesterday."

"It isn't," said Andy Kurins. "We also found out that Tommy Agro is in Canada."

"You what?"

"Well, we *sort* of found out. You remember Agro's wife?"

"Monica?" said Mouw. "Is that her name? French woman, part Vietnamese or something?"

"Close," said Kurins. "Monique. French and Laotian. Is on the books as handling the liquor accounts for Regine's and Club A. But that's not the wife I mean. I mean the ex-wife, LuAnn Yaden."

"Part Puerto Rican, part Chinese," said Joe O'Brien. "He likes 'em exotic."

"That I can understand," said Mouw, with a wince. "But what's in it for them?"

Kurins shrugged. "Insanity has its appeal. Besides, LuAnn Yaden doesn't seem all that stable herself. Real waterworks. I got her talking about the old times with Tommy, the big fuss that people made over them at the clubs, and she started crying. I didn't realize how much makeup she wore till it started coming down like cake frosting. She's talking about what good times they had, her with the champagne, him with the pills, how she liked the royal treatment, how she wished she hadn't let him get away the first time.

" 'Whaddya mean, the first time?' I ask her. 'You mean there's a second time?'

"With this," Kurins continued, "she turns off the tears. Now she's leery. 'No,' she says. 'I just mean I had my chance with him, and it didn't work out.' I decide to gamble. 'Look, LuAnn, the government pays my salary. You think I'm working for Monique? It's nothing to me that you and Tommy are an item. You can get him back, more power to you.' "

"Lemme guess," cut in Bruce Mouw. "This gets her competitive juices flowing, and she can't help flashing a mean little other-woman smile."

"Close enough," said Kurins. "Actually, she starts crying again. In any case, it seemed to warrant some routine checking around. And guess what? Agro took it on the lam last August eighth. On August seventeenth, LuAnn Yaden crossed into Quebec Province from a little town called Trout River, New York. In the car with her was a man carrying ID as Paul Stanisci, Jr. Does that ring a bell? Well, it's a brother-in-law of Tommy Agro. So there

303

you have it. He's up north, and she's trying to win him back by being the rescuing angel."

"So," said Mouw, "we just watch her till she goes to visit."

"Easy," said Joe O'Brien. "Just follow the trail of runny mascara."

CHAPTER 65

THUS IT WAS that LuAnn Yaden came under FBI surveillance, and thus it was that Canadian authorities were recruited into the search for Tommy Agro, a.k.a. Paul Stanisci, Jr.

In New York, agents kept tabs on Yaden's work schedule at Manhattan Cafe, noting vacation periods or long weekends when she might head up north. Meanwhile, Canadian immigration had in its computers a standing request to report the entry of the half-Asian, half-Hispanic woman.

Several months passed. Then, on August 12, 1984, a half-Asian female crossed into Canada, by bus, at the small Quebec town of Blackpool. Her appearance in itself was not suspicious—although she was more heavily made up and more elaborately dressed than might be thought appropriate for a bus ride. She had straight black hair and dark almond eyes. She told immigration authorities that she was unmarried, yet she showed them documents that featured an Italian surname.

As this did not quite compute, the border guards asked for a closer look at the woman's personal effects, and discovered several other anomalies. She was carrying twenty thousand dollars in U.S. currency. She also had two passports and three driver's licenses, issued under a variety of names. While the mixed-race woman melted into a puddle of tears, her makeup running like batter, the Royal Canadian Mounted Police arrested her for giving false information.

But if the Mounties believed they were detaining LuAnn Yaden, they were wrong. They had arrested Monique Agro. The lawful wife was undone by her husband's extreme preference for a certain physical type.

Grace under pressure, it appears, was not Monique's strong

suit; neither was stealth. She lied abominably and folded almost immediately. Asked her intended address in Canada, she named the Mount Royal Hotel, in Montreal. In her possession, however, was a key to a room 307, to which, improbably, the mail tag had been left attached; the address was P.O. Box 243, Postal Station H, Montreal. Having effectively ruined what was left of her husband's life, Mrs. A. then accepted the Canadians' offer of voluntary deportation, and hightailed it to Paris—whether to escape the Mounties or the wrath of her spouse remains unclear.

The address corresponding to the post office box was number 1975 rue de Maisonneuve. When the police arrived there, no one was at home; from the manager of the property, they learned that the tenant in room 307 was an American named Paul Stans, who was identified from photographs as being Agro/Stanisci. The fugitive's belongings were still in the suite, though Agro himself had not been seen for several days.

He'd been out, as it happened, enlisting perhaps unwitting help in his flight. Tommy A. had always been a big tipper, popular in clubs and restaurants, and he'd been spreading a lot of cash around at a place called Café La Brise, whose proprietor was a man named Mohammed Mekki. Mekki, as a favor in return for Agro's generous and loyal custom, picked his things up for him in early September and moved them to a new address on Nuns' Island, Montreal. By that time, however, Agro seemed to be staying at the apartment of a new girlfriend, Ann Okcha, who just happened to be half-Japanese. To her, Tommy Agro/Paul Stanisci/ Paul Stans had introduced himself simply as Tony. Tony, the friend of Mohammed.

But for all the writhing and wriggling that Agro was doing to stay out of custody, his world was getting smaller and smaller, he had less and less room to maneuver. The Mounties caught up with him during the early evening of September 8, at a restaurant called Le Cabot.

Unfortunately for Tommy A., at the time of his apprehension he was in the manic phase of his loony cycle, the phase when, by his own description, he felt like "fucking Superman." This inaccurate self-image led him to imagine he could slug his way past the two enormous officers who had come to arrest him. He threw a straight left, a roundhouse right, and was just about to fly away, when he was seized by the elbows and, without great exertion on the part of the Mounties, pinioned to a table. He then proceeded to have a coughing fit and to spit some blood on a napkin.

In the photograph that accompanied the arrest report from Canada, the dapper Mr. A. did not look anything like his polished apple best. Furrows lined his forehead, there were bags under his eyes. Something had gone very wrong with his toupee. The rug had swiveled ninety degrees in the brief scuffle, and its lacquered pompadour now rose up from the little mobster's left ear; like a compass needle, the toup seemed to be waiting for the world to realign itself beneath it. Standing between the two giant Mounties with their waxed mustaches and chests like small buildings, Agro looked less like an adversary than a mascot, a miniature grotesque with some of the repellent cuteness of a troll.

The extradition formalities would take some time. There would be the usual protests and appeals. But Tommy Agro was coming home not in triumph but in handcuffs. His upcoming trials aside, America did not hold a lot of laughs for him anymore. He had alienated almost everyone by skipping out, and, except for LuAnn Yaden, he had no friends left either in New York or in Florida.

CHAPTER 66

WE GOT AGRO," said Andy Kurins. "I thought you might like to know."

"I should give a shit?" said Joe N. Gallo.

The old *consigliere* was leaning against a tan brick tenement on Crescent Street in Astoria, seeming to cower in the shade of a shoe store awning. Dressed in chino pants, a baggy brown shirt that was not tucked in, and his incongruous Nikes, he looked more than ever like a pensioner from the neighborhood, a quiet old man with neither the strength, the curiosity, nor the money to wander very far.

"Up in Canada," Kurins resumed. "Montreal."

"Andy," said Gallo, "I really don't care." He looked down at his sneakers, then up the street, indulging himself in the serene rudeness of ignoring the agent altogether.

In spite of himself, Kurins tried to court the old man, tried to coax him out of his snit as one would a cranky child. Gallo, in certain ways, was becoming a child. Where he used to debate, now he just griped; where he used to parry, now he just pouted. He gave in more and more to his own funks and irritations, and paid less and less attention to what anyone else was saying. The suave diplomat was, at this late stage, becoming a bit of a brat.

"Come on," said Kurins, "I'll buy you a coffee."

"No thank you."

"Well then, sit with me while I have one."

Gallo looked at him with narrowed eyes and broadened nostrils. "Andy, you don't seem to be catching on. I don't want to talk to you. I don't want to see you. I'm cutting you off."

At this, weirdly, Kurins felt a cold hollowness in his stomach that meant only one thing, and that was a sense of loss. He didn't want anything from Joe Gallo; there was no pressing professional reason for his visit. It was just that: a visit. "Joe, hey, we've always been able to talk to each other."

"Yeah," the old *consigliere* acknowledged, "we've had some good talks. But now I feel like I didn't really know who I was dealing with."

"I've always been straight with you."

"So you're fond of saying."

The white-haired man pulled his eyes away. Restraint calls for a certain kind of stamina, and passive aggression, like anything else, takes practice. It wasn't Joe Gallo's natural mode, and he seemed to be wrestling with his former joyous impulse to go on the attack. That impulse finally mastered him. "Then you pull some bullshit like this jerked-off case against Paul."

"That's not our case," said Andy Kurins.

Joe Gallo chose not to hear.

"You know what it's like, Andy? It's like you're in the twelfth round of a really good, clean, hard fight, and one guy comes out and hits the other in the balls. The fight is ruined. Everything that went before—the strategy, the respect, the waiting for the decision—it's all spoiled. It's like, why did you bother? Why did you show regard to this opponent, if the whole thing comes down to one low punch?"

"Joe, it's not our case."

"Lemme tell you something, Andy. Paul's gonna walk away from this with his head high, and the government is gonna look like a bunch of assholes. Mark my words, it's gonna be Three Stooges time. They're gonna put these lying pissants on the stand, these half-ass punks who would shit in their pants if Paul Castellano ever so much as looked at them, and the dumb fucks aren't even gonna be able to keep their bullshit straight. By the time you and O'Brien get up there to testify—"

"We're not gonna testify, Joe. Read my lips. It's not our case."

"Not our case. Not our case. Bullshit, it's not your case. I got a question for you, Andy. You got this law called RICO, right? This law basically says that if anyone, anywhere, gets caught doing

something wrong, then everybody's guilty. Up and down the line. So if this applies to us, why doesn't it apply to you? You're trying to get Paul Castellano for crimes committed by people he's never met in his life, and the case is being put together by guys you work with all the time, and then you have the balls to tell me it's not your case?"

"Joe, I'm sorry, but you just don't understand how it works."

"No," said Gallo, "I guess I don't. I guess it's just too subtle and fancy for a guy from Queens like me. But you know when I'll understand it? I'll understand it when the next batch of goody-goody prosecutors go into private practice. Then they'll explain it to me for three hundred bucks an hour. Then I'll understand why it's RICO for us and not for you.

"But in the meantime, Andy, do me a big fat favor and don't come around here anymore. You embarrass me. Come when it's time to arrest me, then tell me it's not your case. In the meantime, leave me the hell alone."

CHAPTER 67

THROUGH THE FALL and into the winter of 1984–85, a thrumming but unspoken excitement could be felt in the New York offices of the FBI, the chambers of the Organized Crime Task Force, and the downtown headquarters of the U.S. Attorney for the Southern District. Invisible galvanic currents connected these disparate and sometimes warring agencies; a new esprit cut across the traditional turf boundaries, as when the Army, Navy, and Marines put aside their usual competitiveness for an all-out assault on a strategic beachhead.

And in fact an all-out offensive is precisely what was in the works. Law enforcement was preparing the most sweeping, complex, and successful prosecution in the entire history of the fight against organized crime—the Commission case.

To be sure, some big egos were featured on the government team, and while they didn't shrink in the name of getting the job done, at least they seemed to mesh. Probably the biggest was that of U.S. Attorney Rudolph Giuliani, recently sent up from Washington, who coordinated the prosecution cadre. He was perfect for the job—an Italian-American with the righteous fire of a crusader and the publicity instincts of an impresario. A man of naked political ambitions, Giuliani seemed to see himself in the tradition of Thomas E. Dewey, that other Mob buster who had used his dragon-slayer reputation as a springboard to high elective office.

But while the purity of Giuliani's motives may be open to debate, his imagination and energy as a prosecutor are not. He was using RICO with unprecedented boldness and vision to dismantle the entire top echelon of the American Mafia. To accomplish this, he and his team had been assembling a grand mosaic of criminal

311

ties and associations that would define once and for all the leadership structure of La Cosa Nostra.

That mosaic was so vast and multifaceted that no one person could master it all; individual prosecutors schooled themselves as experts in *parts* of the case. In all, some thirty volumes of evidence would be assembled before a single word of testimony was spoken. Correlations would be drawn among scores of alleged and proven crimes. Cross-references would be made among multiple wiretaps and bugs—bugs planted in mobsters' cars, bugs worn by Mob informants, bugs placed in Mafia social clubs, and, most crucial of all, the bug placed in Paul Castellano's inner sanctum.

As Big Paul was at the apex of the Mafia pyramid, indisputably the most powerful member of the ruling board, so he was the fulcrum on which the entire Commission case seemed to turn. Intercepts of Paul talking with Funzie Mosca about the rigging of construction bids, with Tommy Gambino about how the families divvied up proceeds from the garment district, with Joe Armone about the restaurant unions or the entertainment business—these were compelling indications of the Mob's reach as an ongoing conspiracy. And in case there remained even the remotest doubt that the families acted in concert, there were Andy Kurins's epic photographs of the May 15 Cameron Avenue conclave, illustrating the Mafia quadrille as the conferring Bosses and their aides danced off two by two.

At the same time as the Gambino squad had, since 1980, been building its intelligence base with regard to that family, other FBI teams had been targeting the Luccheses, the Colombos, the Genoveses. Now it was time to pull all those far-flung researches together. No living New York Mob executive was beyond the reach of the Commission case. Even the venerable Joseph Bonanno, then eighty-two years old, living in Arizona, and about as retired as Bosses ever got without dying, was stung—he would do a year in jail for refusing to give videotaped grand jury testimony.

Considering the sheer scope of the Commission case, not the least remarkable thing about it was how long and how faultlessly it had been kept a secret. As 1985 began and the time for the handing down of the indictments grew nearer, the risk of leaks grew ever more severe. Hundreds of people were involved in preparing the case, and a fair proportion of those people had regular dealings with the press. Yet the business was handled with the clandestine finesse usually reserved for espionage matters. No one talked; no one goofed. Nothing was allowed to spoil the grand spectacle that was being planned: a great and all-inclusive roundup of Mob Bosses and their underbosses, nearly a score of simultaneous, surprise arrests made all over New York by almost fifty agents, while the television stations raced to dispatch their film crews and the newspapers stopped the presses to redesign their front pages.

February 25 was the date set for the blitz. As one New York paper termed it, it would be "the Mob's worst day ever." Fat Tony Salerno would be pulled in, as would the jaunty Gerry Lang. Tony Ducks Corallo, boss of the Luccheses, would be pinched, as would Colombo chieftain Carmine "the Snake" Persico. Scopo, Santoro, Gambino underboss and peacekeeper Aniello Dellacroce—they would all be herded in that evening. They'd be kept apart, prevented from talking to one another—though if they had been allowed to communicate, at least one topic of conversation would have been certain to come up: at the last moment, it had been leaked to the press that in 1983 the FBI, in a caper whose details could not be revealed, had bugged the residence of Big Paul Castellano.

This was what the tabloids called a shocker. It gave the media one more juicy fact to chew on, the mobsters one more thing to worry about. And it reconfirmed Big Paul's position at center stage, his status as the Boss of Bosses.

At 7:25 P.M. on February 25, traveling in convoy with two other agents in a following car, Joe O'Brien and Andy Kurins took what was, for them, the very familiar ride to the mansion on Todt Hill. But the resonance of this trip was different from what it had been on any of their many dozens of previous drive-bys. Now they were going to arrest Big Paul. Theirs would be the high honor and the ambivalent pleasure of bringing in America's most powerful mobster to be charged in the most significant Mafia prosecution ever.

CHAPTER 68

T HE CIRCULAR DRIVEWAY. The broad and gracious portico steps. The stately and imposing columns. All were as they had been on Joe O'Brien's very first visit to the Staten Island White House. The view down to the majestic Verrazano Bridge was as ever; the security cameras panned as they had always done. O'Brien rang the doorbell.

"Who is it?" The voice was unmistakably Castellano's, that breathy rumble that seemed to squeeze past a closed throat and grudgingly parted lips. He didn't sound as if he was expecting company.

"It's Joe O'Brien, Mr. Castellano. FBI. I have a warrant for your arrest."

"Ach," came the reply. The syllable seemed to hold only slight surprise and slight concern. Then there was a soft click as Big Paul broke the circuit of the intercom. O'Brien and Andy Kurins shuffled their feet and watched their breath steam in the pink glow of the Godfather's floodlights. The accompanying agents, posted as sentinels, lingered at the base of the portico stairs. Then the front door opened.

Paul Castellano appeared, his tall and rather hulking body filling most of the dim rectangle of yellow light. He was wearing gray slacks, a pale blue silk shirt, and his almost dainty slippers. His hair was neatly but not severely combed back, and he had on his lightly tinted aviator glasses. His voice was without anger. "May I ask what this is about?"

"RICO conspiracy," said O'Brien, showing the warrant. "A dozen or so of your colleagues are being arrested right now, sir."

"Really?" said the Godfather. "Right now?" He glanced out over the bay, as if he could picture his comrades being confronted all around the city. He seemed to take a connoisseur's interest in the neatness of what was, after all, law enforcement's version of a multiple hit. "Well, come in."

Silently, the Godfather led the agents through his vast entrance hall and down the long corridor, past the formal living room with its lamps like statues and the dining room like something off a cruise ship, to the kitchen. Gloria Olarte was there, her thickening body encased in designer jeans and a red cashmere sweater. With her was a distinguished-looking gentleman whom Castellano introduced as Dr. Richard Hoffman, his physician and friend.

It seemed they were just about to eat. The blond wood table at which Big Paul held his conferences was set with Lenox china and Waterford crystal, arrayed around an enormous platter full of rare roast beef, expertly sliced and oozing fatty blood. Near the head of the table, next to the high-backed chair in which the Godfather always sat, was the chrome gooseneck lamp with the dead microphone still secreted in its hollow base. The agents struggled not to look at it.

"Hello, Gloria," said O'Brien.

Castellano's maid and mistress did not answer. Her posture was rigid and her eyeballs were bulging.

"Be civil," Castellano coaxed her. "The man's only doing his job."

"Hees yob, hees yob," she hissed. "Hees yob ees only to make trouble for other people who they don't do nothing. I no like thees Meester Joe O'Brien."

Oddly, Castellano smiled. Perhaps he felt vindicated to hear his lover renounce her former fondness for the agent; perhaps that struck him as adequate compensation for the fact that he was at that moment being put out of business. He gave his massive head an indulgent shake, then absently glanced over at the roast beef. It was beautiful meat, sunburst red, and the former butcher regarded it as other men might a painting. "I'd like to change into a suit."

"That isn't necessary," said O'Brien.

"I know it isn't," Big Paul said. "But I'd feel more comfortable. I'm asking as a favor."

315

Kurins and O'Brien glanced at each other. Their instructions were to bring Castellano in as quickly and smoothly as possible— no fireworks, no delays. He was going to jail, not a party; there was no particular reason to allow him time to change. But Castellano himself was being a gentleman. With his doctor, by coincidence, right on hand, he had available to him the oldest dodge in the world—the feigned heart attack or angina, the writhing, dizziness, or passing out that would earn him a nice cushy trip to the hospital. Yet he stooped to none of that.

Then, too, greatness has its prerogatives, and, to the agents standing there in his kitchen, the impression was making itself irresistibly felt that there was a greatness about Paul Castellano. This was not, God knows, a moral judgment, nor did it have to do with the man's wealth or the grandeur of his home. No, it was less rational and more primal than any of that. It was something in his bearing, some aura of pained wisdom earned through the acceptance of large responsibility. He may not have been a good man—in many ways he was an appalling one—but he had shrunk from nothing, he'd seen it all, he'd taken monstrous vows and stuck to them. You couldn't say to this man, no, you can't change into a suit, go face your accusers in a sport shirt. Certain people it is just plain wrong to embarrass. Embarrassing them is an affront to everyone, because everyone, like it or not, has a stake in their dignity. The king is allowed the royal purple even at his beheading, after all.

So Paul Castellano was allowed to change his clothes. He went up to his bedroom, accompanied by Gloria and Dr. Hoffman.

Then the doorbell rang. Joe O'Brien said hello through the intercom.

"Joe," said one of the sentinels, "there are some people here. Relatives. They wanna come in."

"Who?"

"The daughter. The son-in-law. Their baby. And the wife."

"Oh shit," said O'Brien. He glanced at his watch. Big Paul had been upstairs barely over four minutes. He must have asked Gloria to call Connie, who lived just around the corner; Nina had probably been there visiting. "Let them in."

"You sure you wanna deal with it?" asked the other agent. "They're pretty upset."

"Like screaming?"

"More like zombies."

"It's their house. Let 'em in."

A moment later, Connie Castellano marched into the kitchen, trying, as always, to look feisty and, as always, falling short. Joe O'Brien could have sworn she was wearing the same leather pants and translucent white blouse as on the first evening they had met. "Where's my father?" she demanded.

"Upstairs, changing," said O'Brien. The daughter looked like she didn't believe him. Her eyes darted wildly around the room, as if her father had for some reason been stashed in the broom closet.

Nina followed, and she seemed to be sleepwalking. She cast a quick, appraising look at the set table and the other woman's roast beef. She moved near it and sniffed the air. "On mine," she said, apropos of nothing, "I put rosemary."

Joe Catalanotti, Connie's second husband, trailed the women. He was carrying his infant daughter, and seemed somehow to be hiding behind her. For him the present scene was a no-win situation. His wife would want him to beat his chest and make some noise; that's what husbands were for. But this would irritate the FBI, and, given Cat's station in life, there was little percentage in that. On the other hand, incurring his spouse's wrath by seeming wimpy was an unappealing prospect also, especially since, for Catalanotti's predecessor, marital discord had proved fatal. So he just acted totally absorbed in handling the kid.

Big Paul returned to the kitchen, wearing a midnight-blue suit and a red silk tie, flanked by Dr. Hoffman and Gloria—the maid, the mistress, the new lady of the house. He briefly greeted his family and kissed his granddaughter with a smacking sound.

There followed a scene of such consummate awkwardness as to live in memory with the sick vividness of a bout of poisoning. Gloria started to cry. But she didn't cry like normal people, for whom tears are a release of tension; she actually got more rigid as she sobbed, her wet face crazily immobile. Castellano embraced her as his daughter looked on in rage and disgust; Nina drifted even farther off behind her tranced and vacant eyes.

Then an unmistakable odor filled the room: the Castellano granddaughter had filled her diaper. Joe Catalanotti, still playing the model dad, gently placed the infant on the dinner table, among the Lenox and the Waterford, and proceeded to change the soiled Pamper. Halfway through the job, as if unconsciously, he reached toward the platter of roast beef, picked up a slice with his fingers, and ate it.

Gloria had stopped bawling for the moment, and now it was Nina's turn to break down. She cried softly, almost silently. Then she opened her arms and started running toward her estranged husband—running slowly, with small old woman's steps that seemed to advance her hardly at all.

The Godfather's face riffled through a number of expressions as the mother of his children inexorably approached. First he looked baffled, then nonplussed, then as close to panic as the agents ever saw him. At the last possible moment, with the sure instincts of a veteran quarterback, he feinted left, ducked right, and his wife, empty-armed, ran right past him. She ended up hugging Andy Kurins.

"I think it's time," said Joe O'Brien. Dr. Hoffman handed him a small paper bag containing insulin, syringes, and medical instructions.

The Godfather, resplendent now in his immaculately tailored mohair and silk, his supple loafers and gauzy socks, seemed almost relieved to be going. He led the procession to his own front door, and walked briskly down the portico steps to the government Plymouth.

CHAPTER 69

T HANKS FOR not handcuffing me in front of my family."

This was the first thing the Godfather said as the car door was closed behind him, and it took Kurins and O'Brien a little by surprise. They had decided with a shared glance to bend regulations and not subject Big Paul to the indignity of being manacled in his own house; they didn't think he'd notice the omission.

"I know the drill," Castellano went on. "You're supposed to cuff me. It was kind of you not to."

The agents found it difficult to respond to his gratitude, and the little two-car convoy set off in silence, the sentinels in the lead car, Andy Kurins driving the other, with Castellano and O'Brien sitting in the back. They wound down from the summit of Todt Hill, past the fences and confident houses of millionaires both legitimate and otherwise. The Godfather gave off a good smell of clove and peppermint.

At Richmond Road, the cars turned left, toward the Verrazano Bridge, and Andy Kurins put an all-news station on the radio. The speakers blared out a loud and obnoxious commercial for Crazy Eddie, the electronics dealer who claimed his prices were insane, and tried to prove the point by using a wacky announcer with the world's most irritating and maniacal voice.

"I'd like to kill that guy," said Castellano.

O'Brien couldn't help staring at him.

"Just a figure of speech," said the Godfather. "I mean, lots of people would."

Then the regular newscaster came on. *This just in,* he said. *At this moment, agents of the Federal Bureau of Investigation and the New York State Organized Crime Task Force are arresting the reputed leaders of all of New York's five Mafia families. According to*

U.S. Attorney Rudolph Giuliani, the arrests are part of the most far-reaching Mob investigation ever, an investigation aimed at convicting the entire Mafia leadership—the so-called Commission—under federal racketeering statutes. Tonight's arrests cap a four-year law enforcement effort, which, according to one highly placed source, included the 1983 bugging of the Staten Island home of Paul Castellano, alleged Boss of the Gambino family and de facto head of the Commission.

Andy Kurins watched the road.

Joe O'Brien looked straight ahead.

The Godfather leaned forward so as not to miss a word. Then he gave a little groan. "Is that true?" he asked. "Did you guys bug my house?"

No doubt he was using "you guys" generically. He could not have known that the agents in the car with him were the very ones who had planted the microphone. Still, it was not a comfortable moment.

"Yes, sir," said O'Brien. "I'm afraid it is."

"*Jesu Christo.* When? How'd ya do it?"

"I'm sorry, we can't tell you that."

"No," said the Godfather, "I suppose you can't."

His chin collapsed onto his chest, and he became totally subdued. But with Castellano, as the agents would realize during their strange and privileged time with him, it was hard to tell how much his behavior had to do with frame of mind and how much with blood sugar. His diabetes made him prey to wild swings of mood. Depression would suddenly sweep down on him like an inky cloud; then, just as suddenly, he might burst into ribald and sometimes bizarre humor. At moments he seemed so weary as to be used up, defeated, sinking; then he'd rebound as if buoyed by some saving but subversive knowledge that nothing mattered all that much, life was almost weightless, if you just stayed calm and held your breath you would bob back to the surface.

"I feel some indigestion coming on," Big Paul said softly. "D'ya think we could stop for some Tums. And some candy bars. I don't feel too good."

Andy Kurins sought out Joe O'Brien's eyes in the rearview

mirror. Stopping would be highly irregular and would pose a security risk. But the man was ill. Besides, Bruce Mouw would wince if his quarry was brought in in a diabetic coma. O'Brien nodded yes, and Kurins notified the other car on the two-way.

"Hershey bars okay?" Kurins asked, in the parking lot of a 7-Eleven.

"Snickers if they have 'em," said the Godfather.

They continued toward the bridge, and the smell of cheap chocolate in waxy wrappers made the journey seem like something out of childhood, a ride home from school. Castellano wolfed two candy bars, but seemed to take no pleasure from them; they were medicine. They brought him around incredibly fast. By midspan of the Verrazano, with the Manhattan skyline gleaming to the north, he was alert and chatty again.

"I love this bridge," he said. "It ruined Staten Island, but it's beautiful. I know a guy worked on it—he riveted his initials on the top of one of the stanchions. It's seven hundred feet up, something like that. I says to him, 'Who's ever gonna see your name up there?' He says, 'No one.' I start to ask him then why did he do it, but then I stop. I know the answer. That's what it's like for most people— somewhere they leave a tiny little mark, knowing that nobody knows or cares it's there. But they do it. That's how people are. If they believe in God, they think God sees it. They don't believe in God, they do it anyway. It's this thing about leaving some reminder you were there. You get to leave a bigger reminder, that's called being lucky. Or maybe unlucky. I go back and forth on that one."

The agents made no response, and the Godfather fell silent. But the sugar jolt had made him hyper, and in a moment he started in again.

"Bugging a man's house," he said. "I'm sorry, fellas, I know you got your job to do, but I don't think that's right. Place of business, okay. Social club, all right. But a man's home? It's personal. No one needs to know what a man says or does when he's home. I'm sure you know all sorts of things about me that no one really has the right to know."

"There's this thing called minimization," said Joe O'Brien. "We try not to listen to personal stuff."

The Godfather gave his big head an unpersuaded shake. If he had lived in biblical times and hadn't been a criminal, he would have made a great judge, the kind who just listened, watched, and decided. You couldn't fool him. "No," he said, "you're trying to spare my feelings. But I know you know. You know all about my marriage. You know all about Gloria and me. You know all about my health. You even know about my dick."

The agents were too abashed to speak. But Castellano went on, a note of goading defiance in his voice. To Kurins and O'Brien, it did not seem that the defiance was directed against them or even against the law; it seemed, rather, to be a wider rage against all the forces that scraped away at a man's dignity, that reduced him at last to something small, fragile, quailing, ridiculous. Strip me naked, the Godfather seemed to be daring, know the worst: you can't make me ashamed.

"Come on, boys," he goaded. "Don't be squeamish. The body is just the body." He gave a dismissive glance down at his lap. "It's a bitch, this diabetes. Before the operation, I could only get a sixty percent erection."

In spite of himself, Joe O'Brien wondered what that meant, exactly. Only sixty percent as big as before? Or did it have to do with the angle? Grotesque and unwelcome images cropped up in his mind, and he looked at the skyline to banish them.

But Big Paul, his mind at full gallop now, blitzed by his runaway sugar levels, was already onto something else. "Florida?" he said. "Was the bug planted while I was in Florida?"

"I'm sorry, Mr. Castellano," said O'Brien, "we're not allowed to talk about it."

"I *knew* there was something there," he said. "That's what gets me. I had the house swept twice. You probably know that. You probably know a lot of things. How bad does it look for me?"

"Very bad, sir."

Instantly, Castellano seemed depressed again. He leaned back against the vinyl upholstery and rubbed his eyes. He ate more Tums and stared sullenly out the window. Then, just as Andy Kurins was pulling into the Brooklyn-Battery Tunnel toward Manhattan, he started to laugh. The laugh began as a low rumble that just slightly shook his broad shoulders, then mounted to a sort of whinny that rocked his entire frame and stretched back his lips to reveal large and equine teeth. Tears sprang to his eyes, he sniffled, and he kept right on laughing.

"Can I ask what's funny?" said O'Brien.

"Fat Tony," guffawed the Godfather. Then he was convulsed again. "Are they bringing in Fat Tony?"

"Yes, sir, I believe they are."

Castellano gave a vigorous, flubbering snort. "Fat Tony's been living on his farm. He wears overalls and flannel shirts up there. Man of the soil. He's gonna look like such a horse's ass."

The courtyard of 26 Federal Plaza could be seen from a long way off. It was lit with the biting blue white of television lights and peppered with the little shocks of strobes. All the networks were there, the famous logos emblazoned on their trucks. Newspapermen scrawled in spiral notebooks, radio reporters talked confidentially into microphones. Paparazzi lined the sidewalks, their carnivorous Nikons hungry for the shot that might make *People* magazine. From the number of government vehicles parked at curbside, it seemed clear that most if not all of the other mobsters had already been brought in. The grand entrance of Paul Castellano, the Godfather whose house had been bugged, would be the climax of the media carnival.

The lead car of the Godfather's convoy nosed in toward the curb, and immediately the newshounds began to swarm. Cameras high, microphones held like truncheons, the journalists surged toward the vehicles, their faces thrust forward in the unnatural glow like something out of a nightmare. Paul Castellano now mastered his wildly pulsating moods and composed his face into a mask of utter neutrality. But his color was bad, and as he silently presented his wrists to be cuffed he could not quite hide the tremor in his hands. Strobe flashes were already knifing off the windshield. Reporters hung over the police barricades, shoving each other like drunks at a ball game.

Andy Kurins looked over his shoulder at Joe O'Brien. "These people are vultures. I say let's duck 'em."

"Do it," said O'Brien.

Kurins floored the Plymouth and screeched away from the curb. Looking back, O'Brien relished the fallen faces in the dimming floodlights, the microphones drooping like stalks in a drought.

They drove around to the dark side of the building, where a guarded ramp led down to the employees-only garage. There they ushered the Godfather into a back elevator, to bring him to the twenty-eighth floor for processing.

"So now I owe you two," said Paul Castellano, a man who saw the just tallying of favors as the very heart of right behavior.

"You owe us nothing," said Joe O'Brien. "But give me your wrists. I've got to cuff you before we go into the office."

CHAPTER 70

Y OUR WATCH. Your cash. Your tie tack."

Joe O'Brien handed the possessions back to Paul Castellano. It was late the next morning, February 26, 1985, at the interior gate of the Manhattan Correctional Center, where Big Paul had spent the night. He'd had his insulin, he'd managed to get some rest. He'd slept better, he said, knowing that his jewelry was in the safekeeping of the FBI. He didn't hold a high opinion of prison guards. "No better than Mexican customs men," he opined. "They see something they like, they take it. You protest, they laugh."

For Big Paul, as for the other Commission case defendants, this was to be a day of paperwork and technicalities, of shuttling back and forth between FBI headquarters and the courthouse, leading up to a bail hearing at three P.M. In between the bureaucratic steps, there would be pockets of dead time, and Kurins and O'Brien offered the Godfather a choice: he could stay in the cramped and bustling marshal's lockup, or he could hang around with them.

Castellano tugged at his perfectly knotted red silk tie and seemed to be considering. "Lemme ask you something," he said. "You guys hate me?"

Kurins and O'Brien hesitated, not because their answer was in doubt but because they were nonplussed to be asked the question. "No," O'Brien said, "we don't hate you."

"Good," said the Godfather. "I'm glad of that. So let's say we get to talking. The things I say—you gonna use them against me?"

"We can't promise that we won't," Andy Kurins said.

"No," said Castellano, "I guess you can't. So I gotta watch my ass. But you know, I'm so tired of doing that. The lousy health—that's where it comes from, I think. All that caution."

"You're entitled to call your lawyer," said O'Brien. "Get his advice if you want."

"Nah," said the Godfather. "The hell with it. My lawyer I can talk to anytime. For a fee. How often do I get to schmooze with the FBI? You got a quiet place we can smoke some cigars?"

With their docile prisoner properly shackled, the agents strolled through the long tunnel that connected the MCC with the courthouse, then wandered the corridors until they found a small empty office with a green metal desk, two yellow pine chairs, and a pair of smudged windows fronting on the grand staircase below. Once safely behind the frosted glass door, they removed the Godfather's handcuffs, and he produced three huge coronas from an inside pocket of his jacket.

"Partagas," intoned Kurins. Not what one usually smoked on a government salary.

Castellano gave a modest shrug. "A guy sends them to me. As a present." He leaned forward in his chair as O'Brien offered him a light. Then he laughed. "People send me the damnedest things. Sometimes people I don't even know. Gigantic crystal jars full of artichokes. This gold pinecone that it took me six months to figure out it was a cigarette lighter. And shoes. People know I like shoes. The thin leather, the workmanship. So they send me shoes, but they don't even know my size. I got a closetful that don't fit. I'm in a funny business."

The agents puffed on their cigars, wondering what exactly the Godfather would call the business he was in, if he chose to name it. But of course, he wouldn't go that far. He slightly misread the curiosity on their faces and veered off on another tack.

"Hey," he said, "I know you disapprove. That's why we're here, after all, isn't it? So the United States government can make the point that *we do not approve of how certain guineas make their living*. Okay. Fair enough. If I was the United States government, I wouldn't approve either. If I was the government, I'd put my ass in jail for a thousand years.

"But not because I'm *wrong*," he went on. "You see, that's the part I object to—this idea that the law is right and that's the end of the story. Come on. We're not children here. The law

326

is—how should I put it? A convenience. Or a convenience for some people, and an inconvenience for other people. Like, take the law that says you can't go into someone else's house. That's convenient for people who have houses. I have a house, so, hey, I like that law. The guy without a house—what's he think of it? *Stay out in the rain, schnook.* That's what that law means to him. Besides, the law can always change its mind. Like, the law can say you can't go into someone's house, unless it's Paul Castellano and you want to put a bug in it."

Andy Kurins flicked a glowing ash into a green metal trash can. "But you can't just have people obeying the laws that suit them," he said.

"Obviously," answered the Godfather. "But that's exactly what I'm saying. It's a practical question, nothing more. The government wants to put me away as a practical matter, hey, they can. They got the power. Me, I try not to kid myself. Some people think I'm a big man. Bullshit. What can I do? A few people, maybe I can get them jobs. They have some trouble, I can help their families. But look at this . . ." His expansive gesture took in the massive courthouse building, the huge marble steps and vast paved plaza beyond. "*This* is power. What's my little bit of influence compared to this? The government decides I'm too much trouble, they can crush me like a cockroach. I understand that. No hard feelings."

He drew deeply on his cigar and seemed, in fact, quite serene. He crossed his knees, then with unconscious fastidiousness smoothed the crease of his pants.

"Practicality," he resumed. "That's what it comes down to. I'm from Brooklyn. I grew up poor. Don't get me wrong—I'm not saying I was poor, so I didn't have to go by the rules. I hate that crybaby shit. I'm just saying I saw two choices. Practical choices. You do things one way, you got a certain set of chances. You do things the other way, you got a different set. Either way, there's pluses and minuses.

"Then, too, there's family obligations, traditions. The Castellano family was very close with the Gambino family—"

"We know that," interrupted Joe O'Brien. "In fact, we did a family tree for you that goes back five generations."

"Really?" said the Godfather. "I'd like to see that sometime." He seemed genuinely flattered, and so O'Brien didn't tell him that several of the interfamily unions legally qualified as incest, or that the inbred clans had given rise to a number of certifiable idiots.

"Well," Big Paul continued, "then you know. There are certain promises you make that are more sacred than anything that happens in a court of law, I don't care how many Bibles you put your hand on. Some of the promises, it's true, you make too young, before you really have an understanding of what they mean. But once you've made those first promises, other promises are called for. And the thing is, you can't deny the new ones without betraying the old ones. The promises get bigger, there are more people to be hurt and disappointed if you don't live up to them. Then, at some point, you're called upon to make a promise to a dying man."

"Cousin Carlo," said Andy Kurins.

For the first time since being taken into custody, the Godfather seemed close to taking offense. His eyes narrowed; he lowered the hand that held the smoked-down cigar. "Certain names," he said, "we don't use lightly."

He got up from his chair and went over to the window. The winter sun cast a feeble greenish light that threw pale shadows across the paving stones. "Isn't that Giuliani?"

The agents looked down, and sure enough, the prosecutor was standing at the base of the courthouse steps, smiling broadly and chatting affably with a gathering cluster of reporters. From above, his neatly parted hair could be seen to be thinning; his broad forehead, pointy chin, and glowing complexion made him look strangely like a walking light bulb.

"Well," said the Godfather, "if you've gotta get fucked, it may as well be by a *paisan*. Is anybody else getting hungry?"

Kurins and O'Brien realized quite suddenly that they were, and Kurins offered to fetch them some lunch from the employees' cafeteria.

Castellano groaned. "Cafeteria? That's like being in jail before you go to jail. I could really go for a good corned beef sandwich."

"From Second Avenue Deli?" asked O'Brien.

"Yeah," said the Godfather. "D'you know that's my favorite?"

"Mr. Castellano—"

"Paul," he corrected. "Enough of the mister."

"Paul," said O'Brien, strangely savoring the sound of the name, "we've been studying you for five years. You think we don't know whose corned beef you like?"

"It's the best," said the former butcher. "Lean but not too lean. Iridescent, like fish scales, the way it gets when it's cured just right. Served on that crusty rye bread with lots of caraway . . ."

Kurins and O'Brien caught each other's eyes. *Nah,* said Andy Kurins's expression. *No way,* said Joe O'Brien's gaze.

"It's only five of twelve," said the Godfather. "The bail hearing isn't till three. Of course, if you don't have the balls . . ."

CHAPTER 71

TAKING THE GODFATHER to a delicatessen—this was a truly absurd idea.

The man was a federal prisoner, the central target of a vastly complex and vastly expensive law enforcement dragnet. It had taken the government half a decade to get him into the courthouse building; now two FBI agents were going to blithely let him out again to get a sandwich? No, too much could go wrong. The hovering reporters might spot him and swarm, and Kurins and O'Brien would spend the next year writing memos to justify their actions. The government Plymouth might get sideswiped by a taxi on the way uptown. Big Paul might choke on a piece of gristle and drop dead at the lunch table; this would be awkward to explain. Then, too, for all his silk and mohair, for all the seeming calm of his conversation, the fact remained that the man could be not unjustly characterized as a desperado. The seriousness of the Commission indicment seemed to be getting through to him hour by hour; he must have felt cornered, and he was not accustomed to losing. His sense of right conduct notwithstanding, his mood swings made him unpredictable and his actions, like his conversation, were at moments bizarre. It was by no means out of the question that the Godfather had some escape plan in mind. No, taking him to a delicatessen was out of the question.

"We'll take the cuffs off when we get to the car," said Joe O'Brien.

"Good," said Castellano. "I'd have a tough time eating otherwise."

"Now we'll walk through the hallways like we own the place," said Andy Kurins.

"Is there any other way?" the Godfather asked.

With Castellano between them, the two agents, stone-faced, strolled through the busy courthouse corridors. Clerks seemed to be fighting the temptation to stare; secretaries whispered to each other behind their hands. A robed judge walked by, appearing not to have the faintest idea who the manacled fellow was. Avoiding the main bank of elevators, the threesome descended a dimly lit stairwell to the underground garage, encountering no one but a young paralegal who was blowing a chestful of marijuana out an airshaft window.

They got into the Plymouth, Kurins driving, O'Brien and the now unshackled Godfather again in back. At the head of the ramp, out in the greenish sunlight, the television crews had already parked their trucks. Spiked antennas poked at the sky; technicians milled, waiting for the action promised later that afternoon. Producers strolled around with clipboards; women reporters raised the collars of their furs and sipped tea from cardboard cups.

"Paul," said Joe O'Brien, "you might want to duck your head as we go by."

"I'm sorry," said the Godfather. "I don't do that."

But since the media people weren't expecting news, they didn't seem to notice that news was going by. The Plymouth wheeled onto Chambers Street and headed uptown at Centre.

"I'm starting to fade," Big Paul announced, as they crossed Canal Street. "Fucking blood sugar. The way it comes on, there's a moment you can notice it happening, the wooziness, the field of vision closes in. If you don't notice it right then, you lose track of what's going on. Then you got a problem."

He smiled, a far-off smile like you sometimes see on the faces of old immigrants when they talk about the Old Country—except that Paul was talking about the house from which he'd been exiled only since yesterday. "At home," he said, "I have this trail of food. Over here I have a bowl of raisins. Over there, a dish of almonds. Somewhere else, I got some pignolia cookies stashed. Gloria, she always makes sure the dishes are full. She checks. She says, 'Meester Paul, you almost finish all the feegs; Gloria, she get some more.' She takes good care of me, that girl."

Andy Kurins turned east on Houston Street and drove on in

embarrassed silence; Joe O'Brien looked pointedly out the window. Oddly, it did not make them particularly uneasy to be going out for lunch with a man who could sentence people to death with a lift of his eyebrow. They didn't avert their gazes from Big Paul because he bribed cops, corrupted politicians, made a travesty of labor unions, or stuck his meaty fingers in the city's food supply. But when he started gushing like a teenager about his girlfriend, they simply couldn't look him in the eye.

"I know you don't like her," he blurted out. "You think I don't know that? I mean, you'd like her fine if she was just the maid. You'd find her funny, gutsy, entertaining—just like I did. But then you'd draw the line, right? The hired help. The spick. My friends feel the same way. They wouldn't say it to me, of course, but I feel it. I don't really give a shit, but yeah, it disappoints me. Lack of imagination is what it is. They have this image of the mistress—piled-up hair, long nails, big boobs. I ask you: Does this have anything to do with what really happens between a man and a woman? No. It's just a certain style, it goes with the watch and the car."

Eager to cut short the Godfather's defense of his girlfriend, Andy Kurins slipped through an amber light at Second Avenue and Tenth Street, and parked in front of a fire hydrant alongside the deli's awning. Castellano pointed up at its peculiar lettering as they moved briskly across the sidewalk. "That sign always cracks me up," he said. "If you don't look closely, you'd really think it was Hebrew."

Inside the noisy restaurant, the harried-looking maître d' started to give them a perfunctory hello, then did a double take. His wide eyes made it clear that for Paul Castellano a lifetime of discretion and self-effacement had largely gone by the board in the past twenty-four hours; of all the things Big Paul was fated to lose, his cherished privacy was the first to go. Anyone who read a newspaper, watched television, or listened to the radio now knew that he was the Godfather and that he had been arrested. People who had never heard of him until yesterday now spoke of him familiarly, and as for those already acquainted with his name and face, if not his job title, he now appeared as someone larger than life and back from the dead. The maître d', in fact, bore the terrified expression of someone either looking at a ghost or expecting to be taken hostage.

"Mr. Castellano," he mumbled, "I thought you were—"

"I was," the Godfather cut in, forestalling any indiscreet remarks. "These are friends of mine, Max. Mr. Kurins and Mr. O'Brien."

The flustered little man smoothed down his hair and tried to recapture his composure. "Ah yes, I believe I've seen you gentlemen in here before."

"You have," said O'Brien. "But you've never talked to us."

Max blinked.

"Put us way in the back," Castellano ordered. "And forget that we were here."

He led them through the maze of close-packed tables. If Kurins and O'Brien had been worrying about Castellano being swarmed at the restaurant, they needn't have: at Second Avenue Deli, no one looked up from his food.

Seated, the Godfather dug into the stainless steel bucket of sours that was placed on the table between the napkin dispenser and the pot of mustard. "Dill pickles on an empty stomach," he said. "Best thing for my indigestion."

He polished off the gherkin, grabbed another, and continued. "Can you believe there are people who don't love to eat? I don't trust people like that. Something's missing in 'em. It's like they don't really love the world, they don't really feel that life is wonderful. Hello, Sadie."

The waitress had come over. She was around sixty, had blond hair like straw from too much bleaching, and she combed only the parts that she could see. Nor did she have the gift of quiet speech. "Mr. Castellano," she bellowed.

The Godfather put a finger to his lips, a gesture that even in this incongruous setting seemed to crystallize the Mafia dictum of *omertà:* silence. "Corned beef, Sadie. Rye. And a Cel-Ray."

"Three," said Joe O'Brien.

"That bug," said the Godfather, when the waitress had retreated. "I been thinking about it."

He wagged a finger at the agents. The prospect of food seemed to have perked him up, and his tone was probing, almost playful. But Big Paul had so many tones. With his subordinates, as the tapes amply displayed, he could be gruffer than gruff and cruder than crude, not just matching his boys' obscenities but topping them in profane ingenuity. With associates from the legitimate business world, he could mouth the expected executive platitudes that sounded solid and revealed nothing. With law enforcement, he was faultlessly polite, yet imbued his words with a certain edge that kept it clear where the lines were drawn. When he hoped to extract information, he might use the disarmingly direct question, or the slyly oblique one, or a kind of schoolyard humor.

"Yeah," he resumed. "I can't get that bug off my mind. And I think I finally figured out where you put it. I started feeling irritable, see? Little things, they bothered me. I got short-tempered, moody. Then I finally figured out why. You put the bug up my ass, didn't you? Yeah, you put that bug right up Big Paul's ass!"

The corned beef arrived, and Kurins and O'Brien hid behind the mountainous sandwiches. They were not about to get drawn into a discussion of where the surveillance microphone had or had not been placed. Undaunted, the Godfather switched gears and went on chatting.

"Jesus, that's good," he said, having removed a prodigious bite from his sandwich. "Exactly what I shouldn't be eating, but what the hell."

Then, much to the agents' chagrin, he brought the conversation back to his paramour. "It's amazing," he said, "how Gloria makes the stuff I'm supposed to eat taste like real food. She uses these Spanish herbs and spices—stuff I've never heard of."

Kurins and O'Brien silently munched their corned beef and sipped their Cel-Rays, yet their disapproval seemed to be loud in the Godfather's ears. Carefully, almost daintily, he put the rest of his sandwich back on his plate.

"Listen," he began, "there's something I'd like you guys to know. I don't know why I give a damn, but I do. I want you to know I was never a womanizer. The occasional encounter, okay, it happens. But I was never one to keep a mistress. I didn't need a young babe at my elbow like a lotta these guys. I was too busy, I didn't see the point. Besides—laugh if you want—I loved my wife. And my kids. And it seemed to me, you cheat, you're not just cheating on the woman, you're cheating on the whole family. That didn't seem right to me.

"All right, so now you say I'm an old fart, an old hypocrite, my body's all messed up, I've got this young girlfriend, and I've been a bastard to my poor dear wife. But it isn't quite that simple. I'm old, yeah. I'm sick. But desire remains. Maybe it would be better if it didn't, but it does. And what the hell is a man supposed to do when desire remains and he simply cannot bring himself to touch his wife ever again?

"You guys are young. I'm sure your wives are pretty, and I hope to God you enjoy each other. And I hope that what happened to me never happens to you. It happened in the morning. That's when it always happens, I think—never at night, but when you first crack an eye, you wanna look at the new day and see some hope. You wake up, you look over at your wife, who's still asleep. And you see an old lady. Gray hair. Papery skin. Loose flesh. You're still fond of her. In a way, maybe you even still love her. And you know she's no older or more beat-up than you are. But you also know in that moment you will never touch her again. You can't. Touching her would be like making love with death."

The Godfather wiped his lips on a paper napkin and pushed his plate away from him. Fastidiously, he smoothed his tie. Then, with a harshness that surprised the agents, he called for Sadie to clear away his half-eaten lunch.

"Didn't ya like it today?" she asked him.

CHAPTER 72

T HE RIDE BACK to the courthouse was a somber one.

Absently, Big Paul Castellano had offered his wrists to Joe O'Brien as soon as the three men climbed into the government Plymouth.

"I don't need to put them on till we get there," the agent had said.

"What's the difference?" said the Godfather. "Do it now."

He settled back in the seat and looked out the window with no great curiosity. Now and then he glanced down at his bound wrists as if they belonged to someone else.

"Weird, isn't it," he said at one point, "the things we do to each other?" He held his hands in the air. "I mean, who the fuck invented these things?"

In front of the courthouse steps, the bustle had increased dramatically. Word had gone out that the Mafia Commission would be coming down those broad stairs en masse after paying up their bail. This promised to be a scene that had everything: cowering criminals covering up their faces, scar-faced goons pushing women photographers aside, lawyers making elegantly snide remarks about government tactics. Without question, it would be the lead story on every metro edition of the evening news. Moreover, out-of-town reporters had now had time to jump in on the coverage. There were crews from Philadelphia, from Washington, from Boston. There were stringers on site from London and Paris, eager to reassure their European audiences that gangsterism was alive and well in the United States.

"Reporting live from the gates of hell," said Paul Castellano. He gave a bitter little laugh, and rattled his handcuffs, as if putting on an obliging show for the media. "Bottom feeders."

The agents whisked him unseen into the underground garage and upstairs to the marshal's holding pen. James LaRossa, Castellano's attorney, was waiting there, and he did not look happy. "Christ, Paul, where ya been?"

"Just hanging around with some old friends," said the Godfather.

LaRossa looked at the agents with the condescending sneer that is taught only at the better law schools. "If there's been any violation of my client's rights . . ."

"Save it, Jimmy," said Big Paul. "They've been fine."

The lawyer stopped talking but kept sneering; the sneer had a certain momentum to it. "Well, we should talk," he said to Castellano. "If you gentlemen would leave me alone with my client."

At five minutes before three, Paul Castellano, flanked by Special Agents Andris Kurins and Joseph F. O'Brien, entered a third-floor hearing room in the federal courthouse in Manhattan. The Honorable Michael Dolinger would be on the bench, and the church-like courtroom pews were filled with notables from the world of organized crime, their attorneys, and their families.

Tommy Bilotti was there, and he stared at the agents with all the friendliness of a mastiff whose place of honor at his master's side has been usurped. The loyal Nina Castellano attended, wearing a tasteful dark blue suit and hat; with her was her daughter, Connie, and her three sons, Joe, Phil, and Paul junior. The Godfather greeted them warmly but with restraint as he walked slowly down the center aisle toward the long and crowded double rank of defendants' tables. At the swinging gate that separated the spectators' area from that of the principals, Kurins and O'Brien passed the Godfather along to the marshals; they felt strangely like they were giving the bride away at a wedding.

Castellano took his place next to James LaRossa. Alongside him was Fat Tony Salerno, represented by the notorious Roy Cohn. Cohn was thin and yellow; no one yet knew he was dying of AIDS. The jaunty Gennaro Langella drummed his fingers on the table, while his mouthpiece, Frank Lopez, scribbled notes on a yellow pad. In all, nine men, the entire top echelon of the New York Mob, were coming up for bail.

There were no cameras allowed in the courtroom, but courthouse artists were sketching away, and Kurins and O'Brien looked over their shoulders to see what they made of Big Paul. They seemed to accent his broad and bridgeless Picasso nose, its aggressive line suggestive of something imperial, antique. Their drawings showed the massive head hanging forward, buzzardlike, from the strong but wattled neck, as if drooping under an extra burden of gravity that the Boss of Bosses had carried within himself for many years.

The hearing lasted two and a half hours and was deathly dull, a droning litany of technicalities, formulas, useless protests, and repeated results. But somehow the proceedings' very dullness served to persuade the Mafia Bosses of just how much trouble they were in. From the first, there was something implacably confident and glacially patient about the government's approach in the Commission case. Every word, every gesture, seemed to say, *We got ya, it's over, now it's just a matter of going through the steps.* By the end of that hearing, Fat Tony's loose jowls were ashen, and even Langella had lost some of his gleam. In all, the members of La Cosa Nostra's governing board looked as wrung out and depressed as if, at the end of a campaign filled with grandiose hopes and moments of triumph, they had just signed an armistice for the losing side.

The amounts set for bail were almost irrelevant, though they were the sort of figures that looked good in the papers. For the underbosses, one million dollars was the price of freedom; the family leaders had to shell out up to two million each. Big Paul got the max. He had now plunked four million dollars into the kitty that guaranteed his appearances in court. It was a figure calculated to reinforce the man's sense of honor about facing the music.

CHAPTER 73

Tommy, where ya parked?"

"What's it to you, O'Brien?"

"Tommy, listen. Just this once, don't be an asshole. Where ya parked?"

Bilotti crossed his arms and looked up at the agent from under the fringes of his wig. They were standing in the packed courthouse corridor. The hearing had just ended; most of the Commission members were at that moment leaving the building, along with their lawyers and their bodyguards. The Godfather had lingered at the back of the hearing room, visiting with his children.

Outside, all hell was breaking loose. An infantry charge of reporters was surging up the courthouse steps. Police barricades were toppled, and city cops were carried along in the tide they were powerless to stem. Yellow jolts from flashbulbs cut through the icy blue of arc lamps in the early-winter dusk.

"I'm parked right in front," said Bilotti, grudgingly. "But on the other side of the divider. Why?"

"How long would it take you to reach the car?"

Castellano's darling looked through a narrow window onto the crush below. "If I push?" he asked. The prospect seemed to cheer him up. "Forty-five seconds."

"Good," said Joe O'Brien. "Here's what I want you to do."

He was nearly finished with his instructions, when Andy Kurins appeared at his elbow.

"Don't turn around," he said, "but there's a guy behind you pretending to talk on the phone. He's not. And he looks familiar."

Very casually, O'Brien swiveled to see a handsome young man, immaculately groomed, with a neat Afro and a television-blue shirt. The agent recognized him as John Miller, then a reporter for NBC News. He had the phone receiver cradled on his shoulder; on the shelf below the phone was a walkie-talkie through which he could contact his camera crew.

"Shit," said O'Brien. "Well, it's still worth a shot. Andy, get Paul. Tommy, you got three minutes from right now."

Bilotti bolted.

In a few seconds, Kurins returned with the Godfather. Big Paul had no overcoat, but around his neck a maroon muffler had been added; apparently Nina had brought it for him. The three men slipped out of the stream of people headed toward the front entrance and walked, instead, toward the elevators.

Fortunately, a car was waiting, and only a single passenger preceded them into it. Kurins held the doors as Castellano and O'Brien entered; O'Brien punched the button for the fifth floor. Then, just as the doors were starting to close, John Miller slipped in, his walkie-talkie now out of sight. Andy Kurins hit the button for the fourth floor.

The elevator stopped, and the two agents stepped out, the Godfather between them. The television reporter followed. Then Kurins stopped and bent down to tie his shoe. So as not to be too obvious, John Miller kept walking. The FBI men and Big Paul jumped back into the elevator. Kurins just had time to note how beautifully the reporter's nails were cut and buffed as he gently but firmly pried the grasping fingers away from the closing doors.

At the fifth floor, they got out and walked briskly down a long and empty corridor. In the silence, all that could be heard were the clicks of their hurried steps and the steady wheeze of the Godfather's breathing. His face reddened as the pace increased; his nostrils flared and his forehead glistened slightly with sweat. He set his shoulders forward, like a man walking against a stiff wind.

The hallway ended at a locked door marked No Unauthorized Entrance. Only as they reached it did Kurins and O'Brien realize that the other passenger from the elevator was trailing them. And only then did they notice that his shirt was also television blue. "Sorry, friend," said Joe O'Brien as he punched in the combination on the cipher lock. "This is the end of the line for you."

The fellow reached into his jacket pocket and pulled out a press credential that said CBS News.

"That's nice," said O'Brien. "Goodbye."

"Where are you taking him?" the CBS man demanded. The agents didn't know then who he was, and don't know now.

O'Brien regarded him wiltingly. "Don't you know it's rude to call someone *him* if he's standing right in front of you?"

They went through the door, and the CBS fellow ran back down the hallway. At least two networks were now aware that Paul Castellano, the Godfather, was being spirited away.

"We've got to haul ass, Paul," said Andy Kurins. "Are you okay?"

Castellano nodded resolutely, though his color was not good. The flush had left his face and he was greenish. Almost instantly his eyes had grown bloodshot, and his knees seemed to be somewhat unsteady under him.

But his pace did not flag as the three men jogged through the pedestrian bridge connecting the courthouse with the office building that contained the chambers of the U.S. Attorney. This bridge—one of those ancient connections sheathed in copper that had long since taken on a marbly-green patina—crossed over a dead-end alley called Cardinal Hayes Place. It was here that Tommy Bilotti had been instructed to meet his Boss. He was supposed to drive in, turn the car around, and be ready to nose out the instant Big Paul arrived. But he was not there yet, and if he didn't get there within another forty-five seconds or so, the whole caper would be for naught.

In the office building now, Kurins, O'Brien, and Castellano dashed down yet another stone-floored, fluorescently lit corridor toward yet another bank of elevators. The agents were wet under their suits. Big Paul's mouth was hanging open as he gasped for air. Through an open office door, a cluster of prosecutors could be seen drinking champagne.

The three men took the elevator to the basement level. They clambered through a storage room and a reeking passageway lined with small trash bins. Then there was a tunnel, badly lit with bare bulbs in metal cages, its moist walls furry with mold. The tunnel led to a half-flight of concrete steps, and the Godfather didn't so much climb them as pull himself up the banister. Finally there was a door that said Emergency Exit Only.

Joe O'Brien pushed it open, and an impossibly loud fire bell began to clang. The sound bounced crazily between the buildings, making the very bricks vibrate. Ten yards away, Tommy Bilotti was standing alongside the idling Cadillac limousine, holding the door for his master.

Fifty yards from the car, a horde of journalists was rounding the corner into the alley. The determined John Miller was leading the charge; behind him came beefy technicians hauling videocams and photojournalists absurdly dressed in camouflage vests.

"You'll make it if you run," O'Brien screamed above the infernal clanging.

"I'm sorry," the Godfather screamed back. "I don't do that."

Like a consummate actor, he took just a moment to put himself in character. He straightened his tie. He pushed back his hair. He wiped his sweaty face on his handkerchief and put on an expression of imperial calm. Then, as if he had all the time in the world, he extended a huge, meaty hand toward the two agents.

"I want you to know," he said, "that I appreciate the way you've treated me."

Kurins and O'Brien could find no words to reply, and the Godfather broke into one of his rare, crooked smiles. "So how many do I owe you now?"

At last, with a regal gait and not the slightest sign of hurry, he strolled to the car.

Tommy Bilotti closed the door behind him just as the forwardmost reporters were coming within camera range; he used the mere threat of his elbows to clear himself a path to the driver's door.

Paul Castellano looked through the side window at the agents. He nodded at them, and offered a gesture that was midway between a wave and a salute. Then, in an instant of slapstick, Tommy Bilotti floored the Caddy, and the Godfather's face, contorted like that of an astronaut, disappeared as he was thrown backward against the seat.

And that was the last that Joe O'Brien and Andy Kurins saw the man alive.

CHAPTER 74

JUSTICE, THEY SAY, is swift, but the law is slow, and it would be more than a year and a half before either the Commission case or the Castaway case—the prosecution centrally based on the Todt Hill mansion surveillance tapes, and focusing specifically on the Gambino family—would be ready for trial.

In the meantime, the work that Joe O'Brien and Andy Kurins had done in pursuit of Paul Castellano was essentially over, and they were pulled toward new aspects of the investigation. True, there always seemed to be one more bit of refining of the transcripts, and of course, the agents needed to stay in touch with prosecutors who would turn to them both as witnesses and as background sources. But Paul Castellano, the Godfather, the man, became less and less a part of their daily routine.

He remained in their thoughts, however. Their time with him lived in memory with the vividness of a child's glimpse of a head of state in a Main Street motorcade. The man was a leader, he was in some strange way marked, and it was part of his stature to cut a deeper impression than that left by ordinary people. You didn't forget those shadowed eyes, patient, knowing, and ruthless behind the aviator glasses. You didn't forget the small gestures—the silent pomp with which he straightened his tie, the kingly fastidiousness with which he smoothed the crease of his trousers. Even his follies, God knows, were writ large, but there was something majestic in his indulgence of them, his refusal to hide them or play them down. His errors didn't diminish him, because he utterly declined to acknowledge that they might.

So yes, Big Paul stayed with them. And in late September 1985, on the eve of the Godfather's first trial—in the questionable case having to do with the Roy DeMeo stolen-car and murder ring—Joe O'Brien found himself driving around Staten Island. He could not have said exactly why he was there. With Castellano due in court, the mansion and the man himself were off-limits to law enforcement. Still, the agent was somehow drawn to the neighborhood. He cruised Richmond Road. He drank coffee at the Country Club Diner. He weaved in and out through the privileged precincts of Todt Hill.

Then he spotted Tommy Bilotti, apparently coming from the White House, driving a new dark blue Buick.

O'Brien followed at a discreet distance, and Tommy did not seem to pick him up. Perhaps his vigilance had grown slack during the months that the Bureau had turned its attention away from Castellano; perhaps he was just preoccupied at that moment. In any case, O'Brien tailed him all the way to Hylan Boulevard, where he pulled into a car wash. Loyal Tommy. Thoughtful Tommy. He did not want his master's glory to be tarnished by arriving in court in anything short of a spanking clean vehicle.

The car wash was of the old-fashioned kind, where cars are pulled through by a chain. O'Brien waited until Bilotti was hooked up to the conveyor, then parked his own car and walked into the garage. He badged the attendant and told him to throw the main switch when the blue Buick had come through the soap-up cycle. Then he positioned himself behind a gigantic brush.

When the machinery went dead, Bilotti's car was totally engulfed in suds. O'Brien stepped forward and scrawled the letters I8H across the windshield. Tommy rolled down his window and propped his massive arm on the frame.

"Christ, O'Brien, what is it *now?*" He said it like a man whose conversation has been suspended for thirty seconds, not seven months, but he didn't quite seem able to muster the old pure, steely hatred for the agent.

"Hi, Tommy."

"Hi, Tommy, what?"

"I want you to give Paul a message for me. Will you do that?"

Bilotti drummed his fingers on the roof of the wet and sudsy Buick. "Sure. What the hell."

"Just tell him I said good luck."

And in fact, as far as the cars-and-killings case was concerned, Big Paul's luck could hardly have been better. The trial turned out to be a comedy of errors. One prosecution witness, Vito J. Arena, seemed to view his court appearance as a moment of grisly stardom, and described in almost clinically graphic detail three murders pulled off by the DeMeo crew; having set the stage for a damning revelation, however, he then acknowledged that he had never in his life met Paul Castellano and had only hearsay knowledge of the Godfather's involvement. Then a government informant, asked to identify the man who had told him of an impending hit on a rival car thief, pointed to the wrong fellow; the *New York Times* reported that prosecutors were "visibly rattled" by this gaffe. They were rattled, too, by Judge Kevin Thomas Duffy's public assertion that they had come in "unprepared" for trial. While the eventual outcome will never be known, it seemed that Big Paul was headed for acquittal.

Not that it would have mattered. On December 2, Aniello Dellacroce, after a long illness, finally died, and the fragile truce between the opposing factions of the Gambino family died with him. Dellacroce and Castellano—the balance between the two men was crucial, yet the nature of their relationship remains elusive. They were neither friends nor enemies. They were not allies exactly, nor were they competitors. They needed each other badly, yet that need seemed devoid of all personal connection, seemed to hinge on an inevitability as empty of emotion as a chemical reaction.

With Dellacroce alive, none of his lieutenants would have dared to move against Castellano. The old pug peacemaker would have forbidden it, and besides, Dellacroce himself, crotchety, infirm, but inviolable, was glutting up the line of succession. With Mr. Neil gone, the road to power seemed suddenly wide open—and it may be that Dellacroce's death rattle and the pronouncement of Big Paul's fate were one.

It is also true, however, that Castellano responded to Dellacroce's passing with a pair of misjudgments so egregious, so inexplicable, as to raise the possibility that they were in some way suicidal.

The Godfather did not attend Dellacroce's wake, and in a milieu that places such a huge importance on ceremony, ritual, and tokens of respect, this was a tremendous and seemingly gratuitous insult. Why didn't he go? No one knows. He had troubles of his own, of course. His trial was in progress; his own health was problematical. But still—not to take an hour to visit the corpse of the man who had been his underboss for nine years? This was hard to understand, and it gave rise to the conjecture that Paul was losing sight of his priorities, abdicating the obligations of his office. It was known that Castellano's trial would be recessed for the Christmas holidays; it was known that the Godfather had received permission to travel to Florida. Was it conceivable that the man was so tied up making plans to frolic with his maid at Pompano Beach that he could not show a final regard for Aniello Dellacroce?

Big Paul's second monstrous error was more strictly professional in nature. He unilaterally decided that the new underboss of the Gambino family would be Tommy Bilotti.

Tommy Bilotti? No, this was unthinkable. First of all, it showed reckless disregard of the precedent that had shared family leadership between the two factions; it certainly blew any chance of using Dellacroce's death as an opportunity to reconcile the factions. But beyond that, there was Tommy himself—spluttering, violent, tongue-tied Tommy. Even in an organization as ragtag and beaten down as the New York Mafia had become, this was not leadership material, and everybody knew it. Okay, Big Paul rewarded loyalty with loyalty; that was right behavior. But could anyone imagine that the Gambino family would be best served by having Tommy Bilotti as its next Boss?

There was no way, and it is probably the case that in promoting his true-blue driver, Big Paul also signed Bilotti's death warrant. Chances are, Tommy would have been rubbed out anyway, to forestall his pit bull's vengeance for the slaying of his master. Now that he was underboss, however, there was no question that he would have to be clipped. This was the advantage of being a top executive.

* * *

On December 16, 1985, G. Robert Blakey—the Cornell professor who had largely conceived and drafted the RICO statute—came to New York University to present a seminar on the effective application of the vastly complicated law. At a preseminar cocktail reception in Blakey's honor, FBI men, city detectives, and prosecutors sipped drinks from plastic cups, smoked cigars, and swapped stories.

Then, just before six P.M., beepers started going off all over the room. Dozens and dozens of them, hooting from belt loops, trilling in jacket pockets, screeching, chirping, playing little tunes. A surge of adrenaline coursed through the throng of cops, a rush of excitement tinged with dread. People ran to the phones—of which there were exactly two—and the news fanned out through the crowd like an outbreak of a new virus. Details got garbled along the way. The hit had taken place on Forty-second Street. It had taken place inside of Sparks. There were four gunmen. There were two. There was an exchange of fire. There was no exchange.

About the central fact, however, there was no confusion. Big Paul Castellano, along with his driver and perhaps the only friend he had left, had just been whacked. Gangland style. Neat.

Joe O'Brien found he had to sit down in one of the aluminum folding chairs at the periphery of the reception room. He had a milky feeling in his stomach; he felt electricity around his knees. He had spent half a decade of his life trying to bring Paul Castellano to justice; through Paul, strangely, he had come to know ever more clearly that justice has to do not primarily with punishment, still less with righteous posturing, but with the clean satisfaction of getting to the bottom of something, getting some questions answered, the value of some rules affirmed. They would never get to the bottom of anything now. The shooters had seen to that. When Paul and Tommy went down, they took five years' work along with them.

Andy Kurins sat down next to his partner. He took a puff of his cigar and a pull of his beer. "Their way sure is faster," he said.

"Our way's better," said O'Brien, though he admitted to himself that there were moments when it was hard to believe it.

T HE AUTHORS have taken pains not to preach, but simply to tell a true story and let the facts speak for themselves. It is perhaps worthwhile to note, however, that the overwhelming majority of characters in this book are either in jail or dead.

All defendants in the Commission case were convicted; not one is on the street. Anthony "Fat Tony" Salerno, seventy-five years old when he came to trial, was sentenced to one hundred years, as were Anthony "Tony Ducks" Corallo, Salvatore "Tom Mix" Santoro, Gennaro "Gerry Lang" Langella, and Ralph Scopo. Carmine "the Snake" Persico, who provided moments of comic relief by acting as his own attorney, was also sentenced to a century of incarceration.

Prosecutor Rudolph Giuliani became something of a celebrity for his vigorous and well-publicized efforts against organized crime. In the later 1980s he turned his attention to then-more-fashionable Wall Street cases, in which he compiled a mixed record. In 1989, he put his fame to political use by running for mayor of New York. He lost.

The Castaway case, directed specifically against the Gambino family, came to trial in 1986, by which time several defendants in addition to Castellano and Bilotti were deceased. Augustus "Big Gus" Sclafani disappeared on March 1, 1986, and is believed to have been murdered by colleagues; according to one FBI informant, the mountainous soldier was "split like a tree." As Big Gus committed so many blunders, it is hard to know for which one he was eradicated. Robert "D.B." Di Bernardo, the pornography specialist, has not been seen since June 5, 1986, and is presumed dead. Frankie De Cicco, believed to have been the set-up man for Big

Paul's assassination, was killed by a car bomb on April 13 of that same year.

Mildred Russo, Gambino associate and deputy clerk in the United States District Court, was found guilty of passing sealed indictments to Mob members, for which she received a sentence of one year's house arrest, during which time she was allowed to leave her Mulberry Street apartment only for grocery shopping, doctor's appointments, and religious observances. She also lost her job, but not her pension.

Joseph "Joe Butch" Corrao, the handsome restaurateur and loan shark, was convicted of obstruction of justice in 1989; the conviction was subsequently overturned.

Julie Miron, frustrated architect and consummate doodler, received a five-year sentence for his part in handling Gambino family payoffs and kickbacks on Staten Island construction jobs.

Alphonse "Funzie" Mosca, emissary between Paul Castellano and Fat Tony Salerno on bid-rigging matters, was jailed in 1986 for contempt of the grand jury, after refusing to furnish a voice exemplar that would confirm his participation in conversations intercepted on the Castellano bug. His health deteriorated badly in prison, and after nine months he was granted a release on humanitarian grounds. He died of natural causes on July 26, 1987.

Tommy Agro was tried in Florida on charges of loansharking, extortion, and attempted murder. Convicted largely on the testimony of his former friend and beating victim Joseph "Joe Dogs" Iannuzzi, he was sentenced to fifteen years; he, too, was allowed to go home to die, which he did on June 27, 1987, of lung cancer.

As for Joseph N. Gallo, the white-haired *consigliere,* his decline into bitterness and impotent old man's rage seemed to accelerate after the death of Big Paul Castellano. When it was time for Gallo's arrest, Andy Kurins, heeding the man's threat that he would drop dead on the spot, did in fact arrange for an ambulance to be present. Far from keeling over, though, Gallo exploded into a fit of obscenity and vituperation against the FBI—an outburst that attracted a large and partisan crowd on Crescent Street in Astoria.

For the Gambino counselor, this tantrum was the last hurrah. By the time of his trial, he was utterly spent. Seventy-four years old, he often dozed during testimony and had to be nudged awake. He was convicted on December 22, 1987, and sentenced to ten years.

As Joe Gallo continued to fade, so Joseph "Piney" Armone grew in stature during this time of adversity. He accepted his arrest with dignity and comported himself as a gentleman during his trial. His finest hour, however, came later, after he had been convicted of racketeering and was facing a sentence of fifteen years.

Armone's lawyers argued that the death of Paul Castellano and the change of regime in the Gambino family had effectively ended Armone's career. He was an old man and not in any way a threat to society, they claimed; he should be immediately released on bail. Rather to the surprise of prosecutors, Judge Jack Weinstein agreed to hold a hearing on this matter.

Even more to the government side's surprise, Armone's lawyers called Andy Kurins as a character witness for Piney. An FBI agent called to stand up for a known Mafioso? It was a strange tactic, but effective. Asked under oath if, based upon his knowledge of Armone's past behavior, he believed that the courtly old mobster would abide by the terms of his release, Kurins answered that if Armone himself made the pledge, he, Kurins, would believe him.

For this bit of candor, Kurins received only angry stares and pointed silence from his allies on the prosecution side.

But the final beau geste in this dance of honor was to be Armone's. On the day before Christmas, 1987, Judge Weinstein made Piney an offer. If he would publicly renounce his association with the Gambino crime family and resign any office he may have held in that or any other criminal organization, he could go free. All he had to do was say the words.

He refused, of course. To renounce La Cosa Nostra was to concede the existence of La Cosa Nostra, and this Armone would not do. It would be a violation of *omertà;* it would rend the fabric of the morality he had lived by all his life. He uttered the single word "No," and was remanded to custody.

351

*　　*　　*

Less than an hour after her father's murder, Connie Castellano presented Gloria Olarte with a sealed envelope containing eighteen thousand dollars in cash. "My father wanted you to have this," she said. "Now get out."

The maid left immediately, deeply shaken by her benefactor's death. She is now a travel agent in Bogotá, Colombia, and has lost most of the weight she put on during happier times.

Nina Castellano has moved back into the Todt Hill mansion, and one can only guess at the mix of emotions she must have felt at reclaiming those premises and unseating her briefly successful rival. Presumably to lighten the burden of memories, she almost immediately undertook a major redecoration effort. The chrome gooseneck lamp that contained the FBI microphone was thrown out in the trash. Only Big Paul's upstairs bedroom was exempted from the rearranging and the sprucing up; it has been kept as a kind of family shrine, in precisely the condition it was in on December 16, 1985.

At this writing, Nina still lives in the mansion, along with Connie and Joe Catalonotti and their child.

In December 1987, Special Agent Joseph F. O'Brien was summoned to Washington to receive the Attorney General's Distinguished Service Award as the outstanding law enforcement officer of the year. While the Joint Armed Forces Color Guard marched up the center aisle of the Great Hall at the Department of Justice, O'Brien sat, proud but nervous, between his wife and his mother, surrounded by relatives, friends, and colleagues. In what would surely be the crowning moment of any agent's professional life, he received the coveted plaque from Attorney General Edwin Meese III and FBI Director William S. Sessions.

O'Brien's acceptance speech was extremely brief, consisting only of expressions of gratitude for the support and forbearance of his family, for the vision and energy of Bruce Mouw and his teammates on the Gambino squad, and for the friendship and professionalism of his partner, Andris Kurins.

On the way back to New York, however, O'Brien realized that he had made a serious omission in his acknowledgments of the people who had made possible his moment of triumph at the Great Hall. He realized, and Andy Kurins realized, that they had a pair of graves to visit.

The Moravian Cemetery is just off Todt Hill, on high and well-drained ground. On that December day in 1987, the last of the season's fallen leaves crackled underfoot as Kurins and O'Brien searched out the final resting places of their fallen adversaries. Tommy Bilotti's grave was easy to find, marked by a headstone with a curious and incongruous bit of sweetness to it: It featured two carved, overlapping hearts. In one of the hearts was inscribed "Thomas 1940–1985." The other heart was vacant, patiently waiting for the passing of Bilotti's second wife, Donna. A bouquet of faded flowers lay atop the grave.

"Can you imagine Tommy dead?" Kurins asked O'Brien.

"I can imagine him murdered," was the answer. "But then I see him getting up again, to fight some more. He didn't know when to quit. It's Tommy resting that I can't see."

The agents now looked for Paul Castellano's grave, but could not find it. They read the names on the grand mausoleums, the inscriptions on the expensive marble crypts. Finally, as the shadows were lengthening and the air growing chillier, they sought out an old caretaker with a white-stubble beard and black stumps for teeth.

"Where is Paul Castellano buried, please?" O'Brien asked.

"He ain't," replied the caretaker.

O'Brien regarded the old man skeptically. "I know he's in this cemetery."

"Didn't say he wasn't," said the caretaker, fingering a hole between his teeth. "I said he wasn't buried. He's above ground."

"Where?"

"I ain't supposed to tell ya."

Joe O'Brien shuffled his cold feet and reflected on the vagaries of life. One minute you're shaking hands with the Attorney General, next minute you're arguing with a gravedigger. "Look, we'd really like to pay our respects. We knew him."

Now it was the caretaker's turn to look skeptical. "Sure," he said. "If you were such good friends, you'da been at the funeral."

"We're FBI agents," said Andy Kurins.

They showed their credentials, and suddenly the caretaker was eager to chat as he led the way. "Cardinal wouldn't allow a public Mass, you know, on accounta he was a gangster. Me, I don't think that's right. First off, who's to judge? Second, who needs a Mass more? Plus, Castellano was good to the Church. Coupla years ago, he gave enough money so the old nuns from St. Anne's could get a new elevator and wouldn't have to climb those stone steps. The money's good enough but the man's soul ain't? Me, I don't buy that."

His breath labored as he climbed the slope, the caretaker pointed out a monolith of pink marble crypts not more than fifty yards from the Bilotti grave. "He's in there. I'll show you the slot, though it ain't marked. The family didn't want people coming to gawk. Mafia nuts, you know? Maybe they'll put the name on when the old lady dies." He pointed out a blank square of stone on the second tier of slabs, then left the agents to their contemplation.

But what does one see, or imagine one sees, when one contemplates a grave? Here there was not even a name, no image or symbol for memory to latch onto, no hook on which to hang a reputation. Private in life, the Boss of Bosses is even more so in death. Alone in life, separated from others by the monstrously neutral sort of greatness he was called to, he is more alone now. No mate shares his rest; there is no twinned heart binding his remains to someone still alive. His life's work has been virtually undone by the law and by his successor. His loved ones' recollections of him have been tarnished by the follies of his final years.

What remains of Paul Castellano? There is a big house, on the highest hill in the city of New York, looking down at the Verrazano Bridge. There is a vast archive now occupying some twenty-five file drawers among the records of the FBI. And, in the minds of some at least, there is a lingering presence, redolent of cigar smoke and after-shave, fueled by roast beef and candy bars, capable of murder and of romance, gruffly arguing certain unallowable but stirring convictions as to how a man should live.

354